BUILD YOUR BRAND, GROW YOUR BUSINESS

A COMPLETE GUIDE TO BRANDING
FOR ENTREPRENEURS
AND SMALL BUSINESSES

DUSTIN SARTORIS

ISBNs:
eBook: 978-1-968936-00-6
Paperback: 978-1-968936-01-3
Hardcover: 978-1-968936-02-0
Audio Book: 978-1-968936-03-7

Disclaimer:
This book is provided for informational purposes only. The author has made every effort to ensure the information provided is accurate and helpful, but it should not be considered legal, financial, or professional advice. Readers should consult qualified professionals for specific advice tailored to their individual circumstances. The author and publisher disclaim responsibility for any liability or loss arising from using this information.

TABLE OF CONTENTS

Part IV - Connect and Grow

Conclusion

WELCOME: WHY BRAND BUILDING MATTERS

Feeling Stuck or Overwhelmed? You're Not Alone

If branding or marketing your business feels confusing, you're in the right place. Whether you're just starting out or trying to grow, this book is your friendly guide. Forget jargon or complicated strategies. Here, you'll find real steps you can use, no matter your experience level.

A Roadmap to Build Your Brand

This book will walk you through practical, timeless steps to create a brand that truly stands out. It's not about being loud or flashy. It's about being authentic and smart in how you present yourself. We'll start with the basics, like identifying what makes your business unique, and work up to more complex challenges, such as building a loyal customer base. Along the way, you'll learn that a brand is much more than just a logo or a tagline. It's your core promise to customers and the personality you project in everything you do. Branding well isn't about spending a ton of money. It's about communicating the right message clearly and consistently, so the right people find you and love what you do. When you master these fundamentals, you connect with the right customers, inspire their loyalty, and leave your competition in the dust.

What You'll Learn

In the chapters ahead, we'll break down the branding process into simple, doable pieces. Here's a glimpse of what you'll learn to do:

- **Define your brand's purpose and personality.** You'll pinpoint what your business stands for, how you want people to feel when they interact with you, and build a strong foundation for everything else.

- **Connect with your ideal customers.** Figure out who your "fans" are and how to speak their language, so you can genuinely reach the people who matter most

- **Create an eye-catching identity.** No art skills required. You'll shape your brand's look and voice so it stands out and feels uniquely "you" (from name and logo to your tone on social media).

- **Build a loyal community around your brand.** Over time, you won't just have customers, you'll have fans who support you, recommend you, and stick around for the long haul.

Each chapter focuses on one step at a time, with examples and exercises to keep things practical. You can read through at your own pace and even revisit sections later when you need a refresher.

"Fans," "Brand Blueprint," and Your Why

To make this journey fun and easy to follow, we'll use a few recurring terms and metaphors throughout the book:

- **Fans:**
  This is our friendly way of talking about your brand's community. Your fans are the people who love what you do, come back for more, and spread the word to others. As you build your brand, you'll also be building a base of fans, a supportive group that feels like an extended family for your business.

- **Brand Blueprint:**
  Think of this as the game plan for your brand. Just like an architect uses a blueprint to build a house, we'll use a Brand Blueprint to build or renovate your brand step by step. It outlines all the key components (your story, visuals, and customer experience) that we'll be putting together in this book. Whenever things feel overwhelming, we'll go back to the blueprint and see what the next simple step is.

- **Your Why:**
  This is your guiding purpose. The big goal or core reason behind your business. Whenever you're in doubt or have to make a big decision, your why reminds you of what matters most for your brand.

Don't worry if these terms sound new now. We'll explain each concept clearly when it comes up, and by the end of the book, you'll be using them like second nature.

No Experience? No Jargon? No Problem!

You don't need any advanced business knowledge or marketing experience to get value from this book. We promise to keep things jargon-free and straightforward. If we mention any marketing concept, it will be in plain English. And if there's ever a buzzword, we'll break it down with an example so it actually makes sense. Our goal is that anyone can pick this up and follow along, whether you're a first-time entrepreneur, a local shop owner, or just someone with a passion project on the side.

We've also filled the chapters with relatable examples and stories. You'll meet fictional business owners (and a few real ones) facing the same questions you have, so you can see how the principles apply in real life. Think of it like having a friendly mentor walking you through each step. By the time you finish a chapter, you'll understand why that step matters and how to put it into action for your own brand.

Most importantly, you can take things at your own pace. Feel free to pause and think about the questions we pose, jot down ideas, or even reread parts that resonate with you. This isn't a race or a test. It's a personal journey for you to gain clarity and confidence in your brand.

By the Final Chapter... (Your Sneak Peek of Success)

So what's waiting for you at the finish line? By the final chapter of this book, you'll have a brand-new sense of confidence about your business. You'll have a clear brand story that you're proud to share, an eye-catching identity that truly represents you, and a growing base of loyal fans excited about what you offer. You'll know how to make your business stand out in the best way and keep people coming back.

Imagine looking back and realizing that the thing that once felt so overwhelming (branding your business) is now one of your biggest strengths. You'll have the tools to continue growing your brand with purpose, the knowledge to make smart marketing choices, and the confidence to face the competition knowing exactly what makes you unique. Those wins and breakthroughs that seemed out of reach before will be within your grasp.

Ready to Get Started?

Turn the page, and let's build a brand that shines and grows, one easy step at a time. Your journey from feeling stuck to feeling in charge of your brand begins right here. Let's do this together.

PART I - GETTING READY

CHAPTER 1: FIND YOUR SPARK

Welcome to the beginning of your branding journey! In this opening chapter, we're diving into how to find your spark, that business idea or vision that truly lights you up. Think of your spark as the intersection of what you care about, what excites you, and what you can see yourself pursuing for the long haul. Finding this personal spark is crucial because building a business (and a brand) is a marathon, not a sprint. It will challenge you, consume your time, and test your commitment. That's why it's so important to choose an idea that genuinely resonates with you. If you're not fired up about it, it's hard to muster the motivation to go the distance.

But passion alone isn't the whole story. This chapter will help you think about aligning a business idea with your interests, values, and deeper motivations, the ingredients of a spark that's worth building a brand around. By the end of this chapter, you'll have clearer insight into the kind of business you truly want to create. Let's get started!

Why Your Spark Matters

You've probably heard advice like "follow your passion" or "start with why." It might sound cliché, but there's truth in it. Your spark, built from your passions, values, and purpose, is the foundation of a meaningful business. Your values are your non-negotiables, passion is what excites and motivates you, and purpose is your deeper reason for doing what you do. When you bring those things together, you have a powerful sense of direction for your business idea.

This matters because when you're clear on why you're building your business and you genuinely care about it, that enthusiasm shines through and keeps you going. Passion is the fuel that helps you weather obstacles and setbacks. If you deeply believe in what you're creating, you'll find it easier to push through long nights, solve tough problems, and stay committed when things get challenging. On the other hand, if you choose an idea solely because it might make money, but you have zero personal interest in it, keeping up the momentum will be an uphill battle. Your business will likely take up a big chunk of your time, so make sure it's something you care about, not just a project that seems lucrative. Don't chase a trend that doesn't spark your enthusiasm. Your time and energy are too valuable for that.

Building a brand around something that matters to you helps your business feel authentic and real. When your idea aligns with who you are, you naturally create a sense of purpose and authenticity. That's not just a feel-good bonus. It's a real advantage. If your core values are at the heart of your business, your brand will stand for something people can trust, and you'll attract fans who share those values. For example, if you value sustainability and your business reflects that, you'll resonate with eco-conscious customers and feel proud of what you're building. Bottom line: finding your spark sets you up to build a business that means something to you and your future fans.

Aligning Ideas With Your Interests and Values

How do you actually spot a business idea that lines up with your interests and values? Start by looking inward. Grab a notebook or just take a minute to reflect on the things that genuinely excite you and the principles you stand for. Think about:

- **Hobbies, skills, and topics you love:** What could you spend hours doing or learning about without getting bored? These passions are big clues to your spark. Maybe you're into coding, gardening, fitness, art, or baking. Any interest can be the seed of a business idea.

- **Problems or needs that bother you personally:** Have you ever thought, "I wish there was a better way to do this," or "Someone should create X"? If a problem affects you or people around you, it probably affects others too. Solving a problem you care about can be incredibly motivating.

- **Core values that guide you:** Consider what truly matters to you. Is it creativity, freedom, helping others, honesty, sustainability, community? When your idea reflects your values, you're more likely to stay committed and attract people who feel the same.

As you brainstorm, look for the sweet spot where these areas overlap. The key is to find an idea that sits at the intersection of what you love and what could provide value to others. For example, maybe you're passionate about cooking and care about health and wellness. That could spark an idea for a healthy meal prep service or a cooking blog with nutritious recipes. Or perhaps you're a tech-savvy person who cares about education. That might inspire an ed-tech app for students. Be open-minded and list as many ideas as you can that align with who you are. Don't censor yourself too early.

There are no wrong answers at this stage! The goal is to surface possible sparks first.

Once you have a few glimmers of ideas, test them against your heart and gut: Does this idea excite me? Can I see myself working on this day in, day out? You don't need the whole business plan right now, just a sense of genuine interest. The best business ideas often emerge where your interests intersect with a real need in the world. If an idea checks both boxes (it fascinates you and solves a problem or fulfills a desire for others), you may have struck gold.

It's important to remember that alignment with your interests and values doesn't mean you ignore practicality. Passion is essential, but you also want an idea that can realistically work in the world. It's always smart to do a quick reality check, but for now, focus on ideas that bring both passion and purpose to the table.

Follow Your Curiosity

Curiosity is your secret superpower when searching for that perfect idea. When you're curious, you naturally explore more, ask questions, and spot opportunities that others might miss. Curiosity helps you question the status quo and look for new ways to do things. By staying curious about the world, you notice things that could turn into a business.

So, how do you harness curiosity? Start by observing your daily life and the lives of people around you. Pay attention to little frustrations, unmet needs, or trends you find interesting. Ask "why" and "what if" often. Why does this process take so long? What if there was a simpler way? Many great businesses begin when someone is curious enough to solve a problem they keep running into. Maybe you notice your neighborhood lacks a good coffee shop. What if you started a cozy café? Or your friends keep talking about how hard it is to find affordable childcare. Maybe you have a solution. Every complaint or wish can be a clue if you look at it with curiosity.

Being curious also means being open to learning. Dive into subjects that interest you, even if they're outside your comfort zone. Read articles, listen to podcasts, watch videos, or talk to people who know more than you. You never know. A random story or bit of information could ignite a business idea you never considered. Try talking to people and hearing their stories. You might spot patterns, pain points, or passions that spark a new idea.

A helpful habit is to keep an idea journal. It can be a note on your phone or a small notebook you carry. Jot down any interesting thought, problem, or solution that crosses your mind. Most ideas won't turn into a business, and that's fine. The point is to train your brain to notice opportunities. Curiosity is like a muscle. The more you use it, the stronger it gets.

Curiosity also makes this whole process more enjoyable. Instead of feeling pressured to "find the next big thing," treat it like a treasure hunt or creative adventure. When you follow your curiosity, idea-finding becomes a fun journey. Often, curiosity leads you directly to an idea that truly resonates with you because it grows out of genuine interest and engagement with the world.

Thinking Long-Term: Purpose and Commitment

Let's fast-forward for a minute. Imagine the business idea you're considering becomes a reality. Could you still see yourself being excited about it in five years? Ten? Building a brand is a long-term play. The most successful and enduring brands are built on a sense of purpose: a clear answer to why the business exists beyond just making money. Right from the start, it's worth thinking about your "why." Ask yourself: Why do I want to build this business? What change or value do I hope to create? The answer will guide you.

Knowing your why gives you a solid foundation. If your idea lines up with a purpose you care about, you'll stay motivated and resilient. For example, if your why is to help people live healthier lives, and your idea is a fitness app, that purpose can inspire you and your fans every day. Purpose also helps you when you have to make tough choices: you can ask, "Which option stays true to my mission?" It becomes your compass for decision-making.

Your purpose doesn't have to be grand or world-changing. It could be about spreading joy, making life easier for families, or honoring a family tradition. The only thing that matters is that it feels meaningful to you. Your idea should be something you're excited to stick with. Motivation fades if it's just surface-level. But when your idea connects to a vision you believe in, it creates a deep well of energy to keep you going.

Purpose-driven sparks also attract others who share your values. When you communicate the why behind your brand, you'll connect with customers and partners who share your vision and believe in what you're building. People are drawn to brands with heart and honesty. If your business is driven by a purpose, like supporting fair trade or helping people save time, your fans will rally around you. Their enthusiasm reinforces your own, and that cycle keeps you going.

Be honest about your willingness to commit as well. Ask yourself: Am I willing to stick with this idea when things get tough? Every business faces rough patches. The spark isn't always a raging fire; some days it will be a slow burn, and that's normal. The reason we focus on finding a spark that matches your interests, values, and purpose is so you have something real to draw from on tough days. Passion makes you resilient. When you care, you'll want to solve problems and keep going, instead of feeling like you have to. So think long-term. Don't choose an idea just because it's hot right now. Choose it because, deep down, it feels worth it. Worth the effort, worth your creativity, worth building a brand around.

Spotting Your Spark in Everyday Life

You might be thinking, "This all sounds great, but how do I actually find my spark?" The good news is, sparks are often hiding in plain sight. You usually don't have to look far. Your everyday experiences are the best place to start. Here are some practical ways to spot promising business ideas:

- **Pay attention to pain points:** Every time you or someone else says, "This is such a hassle," or "I wish there was a better way," take note. Is there a recurring frustration at work or home? Great businesses often start by fixing everyday problems. If you face an issue, chances are others do, too.

- **Notice what people ask of you:** Do friends always ask you for advice on a particular topic? Do colleagues admire your knack for organizing, or do neighbors ask for your baked goodies? These can hint at things you're good at and enjoy, which are excellent grounds for a business idea.

- **Explore communities and trends:** Look at groups you're part of, online or offline. What are people excited about lately? What needs or gaps are they talking about? Being part of a community can help you spot a spark that's both personal and relevant.

- **Recall your "aha!" moments:** Maybe you've had a lightbulb moment in the past, an idea that made you think, "Someone should make this!" Revisit those thoughts. If they still interest you, there might be something there.

As you gather observations, remember to filter them through your own perspective. Two people can see the same problem and create completely different solutions based on what they care about. Your unique lens (your interests and values) will shape how you might solve a problem or fill a need. For example, if both a designer and an engineer notice that remote workers feel isolated, the designer's spark might be a social app, while the engineer's might be a new virtual office tool. There's no one right idea. There's only the idea that's right for you.

Give yourself permission to be playful in this process. Spotting ideas is as much about creativity as it is about analysis. Daydream a little. If an idea sounds exciting, but wild, don't dismiss it. Write it down and mull it over. Sometimes the craziest ideas contain a bit of genius once you refine them. The difference between a daydream and a business is often just execution. For now, we're not building yet, just looking for your spark. Enjoy the freedom to imagine.

Finally, trust your gut. When you come across an idea that could be "the one," you'll often feel a burst of energy or a sense of "Yes, I want to do this." It might even scare you a bit, in a good way. That's a sign you've hit on something meaningful. Finding your spark is partly about logic (interests, needs), but it's also very personal and emotional. When both your head and your heart light up about an idea, you've likely found your spark.

Embrace the Journey Ahead

Finding your spark is a personal journey of discovery. It's about understanding yourself just as much as understanding the market. As we wrap up this chapter, take a moment to reflect on what excites you and why you're drawn to starting a business. Don't worry if you don't have a perfectly formed idea yet. That comes with time, exploration, and refinement. What matters now is that you know what to look for: an idea that aligns with your passions, reflects your values, and motivates you from within.

When you build a business around your genuine interests and purpose, you set yourself up for both fulfillment and success. You'll wake up eager to work on it, persist through challenges, and talk about it to others with real enthusiasm. People notice authenticity. It's inspiring and contagious. In the chapters ahead, we'll dig into how to shape and validate your idea, but none of that will matter if you haven't chosen an idea that truly sparks something in you.

Keep your eyes open and your mind curious. Your spark might be something you've known all along, a lifelong passion ready to be unleashed, or it could be something you discover tomorrow in a conversation or "aha" moment. Curiosity and passion together are a powerful force. As you move forward, nurture both within yourself.

To sum it up: Find a business idea that you care about deeply. Make sure it aligns with what matters to you, fires up your curiosity, and feels worthwhile for the long run. That's your spark. Once you've found it, you've got the foundation upon which great brands are built. And when you do find it, you'll know. Your instincts will say, "This is it."

Are you excited? Good! This is just the beginning. In the next chapter, we'll take that spark and start fanning it into a flame: one that can light up your business and attract your first real fans. For now, spend a little time with your thoughts, dreams, and ideas. Your spark is out there, and it's going to set your entrepreneurial journey aglow.

Get ready to ignite.

CHAPTER 2: PICK A PROBLEM WORTH SOLVING

The Seed of Every Great Brand

Every powerful brand begins as the answer to a problem. Think of a moment when something in your day didn't work right. Maybe you spilled coffee on your shirt during your commute or struggled to find a taxi on a rainy night. In those moments of frustration, there's a spark: *"There has to be a better way!"* That spark is the seed of innovation. Many successful entrepreneurs have stood right where you are, facing an everyday annoyance or a big-world challenge, and decided to create a solution. This chapter is about finding **your** spark (identifying a real-world problem, frustration, gap, or even a missed joy) and turning it into the foundation of a meaningful business idea.

Notice we're talking about a problem worth solving. Not every irritation in life needs a business built around it. A problem *worth* solving is one that real people (including you) genuinely care about. It's an issue that causes real pain or holds real opportunity for joy. Solving it would make life easier, better, or happier for a group of people. Big or small, if addressing that problem creates true value for others, it can become the beating heart of your brand. The goal here is to help you recognize those meaningful problems and select one to build your brand around. By the end of this chapter, you should feel confident in pinpointing a need that excites you and is worth your effort. Let's dive in!

Noticing Everyday Frustrations

One of the easiest places to start looking for a problem worth solving is your own daily frustrations. Day-to-day life is full of minor annoyances and inefficiencies. Pay attention to them. The next time you catch yourself thinking, *"Ugh, this is so inconvenient,"* pause and take note! Is your phone charger cable always tangling? Do you hate how long it takes to cook a healthy dinner after work? Maybe you've wished for a faster way to get through your morning emails. These everyday gripes are golden opportunities in disguise. Each frustration is a clue pointing toward an unmet need.

Consider this scenario: You're waiting in a long line at the coffee shop, running late and feeling your patience wear thin. *"If only I could order ahead and skip this line,"* you grumble. That thought could be the spark of a business idea (in fact, apps that let you pre-order coffee were born from precisely this kind of frustration!). Or perhaps every time you ride your bike, you end up with a soaked backpack when it rains, prompting you to imagine a better waterproof bag or a new kind of bike accessory. The key is to be curious about your own complaints. Instead of just shrugging them off, ask *"What would fix this problem for me?"* If you need it, chances are others do too.

Now, don't stop at your own frustrations. Look at the people around you. What are your friends, family, or coworkers complaining about? Maybe your roommate keeps talking about how difficult it is to find healthy snacks at the office. Your colleague might joke every week about how there's no good tool to organize their tasks. Listen closely. Every complaint is a hint. Sometimes the best ideas come from solving someone else's pain point. If a problem keeps coming up in conversation or you see a bunch of people improvising clumsy fixes, you've likely spotted a gap waiting for a great solution.

How to Spot Frustration-Fueled Opportunities

- **Keep a Problem Journal:** Dedicate a small notebook or a notes app to jot down any annoyance or problem you notice, no matter how small. After a couple of weeks, review your notes and look for patterns or particularly challenging problems that repeat frequently.

- **Ask and Observe:** Talk to friends, family, or potential customers about their daily challenges. Ask questions like, "What's the most tedious part of your day?" or "If you could fix one everyday problem, what would it be?" Often, people have pet peeves ready to share. Also, observe how people use products and services. Where do they get stuck or frustrated?

- **Follow the Frustration:** When you identify a specific frustration, dig deeper. Why does it happen? How are people currently coping with it? Understanding the root cause can inspire an innovative fix. For example, if commuters are frustrated by long coffee lines, the root issue might be time scarcity in the morning, leading to solutions like pre-order apps or ready-to-brew coffee kits.

By actively seeking out frustrations, you train yourself to view problems as opportunities. Instead of thinking *"Someone should really fix this,"* you start to think *"Maybe I could be the one to fix this!"* That mindset shift is powerful. It turns you from a passive consumer into a problem-solving entrepreneur.

Finding Inspiration in Joy and Passion

Not every great business idea comes from a complaint or pain point. Some come from joy, passion, or curiosity. Perhaps you have something in your life that you absolutely love (a hobby, a special skill, or a product you can't live without) and you notice others haven't experienced that joy yet, or it's not widely available. In this case, the "problem" is that people are missing out on something wonderful! Solving it means spreading joy or fulfilling a desire that's gone unmet.

Imagine you're a food lover who discovered a delicious gluten-free bread recipe after much trial and error. You're over the moon because it tastes like the real thing, and it brings you joy every morning. The gap here is that most gluten-intolerant folks still suffer through mediocre options. You've identified a missing delight in their lives. By turning your recipe into a business (say, a bakery or a mix sold online) you're solving a problem and sharing a joy: providing tasty bread to people who thought that experience was lost to them.

Passions can highlight opportunities, too. Ask yourself: *"What's something I enjoy or care about deeply, and how could it be even better or more accessible?"* Maybe you love gardening, but in your city, apartments have no yards. There's an opportunity to create indoor gardening kits or a community garden service. Or you're an avid gamer who notices your friends struggle to find family-friendly games. Perhaps you design a game platform that fills that gap. When you build a business around something that lights you up, two extraordinary things happen: you stay motivated (because you care about it), and your enthusiasm becomes contagious to customers. They'll feel that genuine passion behind your brand.

Also, consider positive experiences that could be amplified. For example, the joy of a perfectly organized closet. How many people have never felt that because they lack the tools or know-how? A professional organizer saw that gap and started a business teaching people how to declutter and organize, bringing a sense of calm and joy into their lives. In this way, *spreading joy can be as powerful as eliminating frustration.* Whether it's frustration or excitement that drives you, the common thread is recognizing an unmet need, be it relief from pain or an increase in happiness, and envisioning a way to fulfill it.

Why Solving a Real Need Builds a Strong Brand

Solving a real need isn't just about coming up with a product or service. It's about establishing the core purpose of your brand. When your business idea is rooted in meeting a genuine need, your brand automatically gains a strong foundation. Here's why that matters:

- **Built-In Purpose:** A brand is more than a logo or a name; it's a promise of value. If you start with a clear problem to solve, you start with a clear *purpose*. For instance, if your problem is "busy parents don't have healthy dinner options," your brand's purpose might be to provide quick, nutritious meals for families. That purpose will guide everything you do. It gives your work meaning beyond making money, and customers can sense that. People are drawn to brands that stand for something and make a positive impact on their lives.

- **Emotional Connection:** When you solve a problem that really matters to people, you're not just selling a product. You're selling relief, hope, or joy. Think about the relief a person feels when they finally find a solution to a persistent hassle (like a stain remover that actually works, or a budgeting app that finally makes saving easy). That relief creates gratitude and loyalty. Customers remember that your brand helped them out of a tough spot. Likewise, if you introduce them to a new joy (say, a toy that keeps their dog happily entertained for hours), they'll love you for it. Solving real needs builds trust and emotional loyalty, the kind of connection that keeps people coming back and telling their friends.

- **Differentiation:** In a crowded marketplace, a strong problem-solution focus sets you apart from the competition. So many businesses falter because they offer a "nice-to-have" or a copycat product without a clear reason for being. But if your brand is the *only one that truly solves X problem*, you have a built-in differentiation. Your marketing practically writes itself: "We are the company that fixes ___." That's a powerful statement. It cuts through the noise and tells customers exactly why they should care. Moreover, when new competitors emerge, your deep understanding of the problem will help you continue innovating and staying ahead. You'll always be attuned to what the customer needs next, because solving that need is your brand's DNA.

- **Authentic Storytelling:** Every great brand has a story, and at the heart of the best brand stories is a problem-solution journey. When someone asks, "What inspired you to start this business?", you won't have to scramble for a clever marketing line. You can tell the honest story: *"I noticed this problem, and I set out to solve it."* Authentic stories resonate. They humanize your brand. Whether your story is about the time you couldn't find a taxi or how you hated that traditional paint cans always made a mess, sharing how you encountered the problem and built a solution makes your brand relatable and memorable. People love to cheer on problem-solvers and be a part of that journey.

In short, focusing on a real need infuses your brand with purpose, passion, and direction. It ensures that from day one, your brand is about something that matters to people. This clarity will help you make decisions as you grow (because you can always ask, "Does this serve the mission of solving our customers' problem?"). It will also attract supporters (customers, partners, even investors) who believe in what you're trying to do. A brand built on solving a worthwhile problem has an anchor; no matter how stormy the business seas get, you can always return to that anchor and realign with your mission.

Big Problems vs. Small Problems: All Are Welcome

When we talk about a "problem worth solving," you might immediately think of grand, world-changing issues: curing diseases, ending hunger, reversing climate change. Yes, those are certainly worth solving. However, a problem doesn't have to make headlines to be the foundation of a powerful brand. Minor, everyday problems count too, often more than we realize. People spend money and love brands that make the little things in life better, just as much as the big things.

Let's differentiate: Big problems tend to affect large swaths of society or touch on deep human needs. Solving them can lead to a huge impact (and potentially huge businesses). If a big mission drives you (say, providing clean drinking water in developing communities or revolutionizing how people use renewable energy) that can become a phenomenal brand with a world-changing purpose. It might also require more resources and persistence, but if that's where your passion lies, don't shy away. Big problems often inspire big innovations. Just remember that even huge problems are tackled step by step. Great brands with global impact (like those bringing electricity or internet access to remote areas) started by solving the problem for *one community at a time.*

On the other hand, small problems may seem trivial at first, but solving a common small problem can improve daily life for millions of people. Think about a simple invention like the Post-it Note. The "problem" was just that people needed a convenient way to leave short notes or reminders that could stick and move without damage. Not exactly curing cancer, but solving that small problem made life easier for office workers, students, and families everywhere, and it spawned a hugely successful product and brand. The same goes for the app that lets you split a restaurant bill effortlessly, or the company that delivers razors to your door so you never run out. These started as solutions to small annoyances or gaps, and they grew into beloved brands.

The lesson here is: Don't dismiss a problem just because it seems small or niche. If *you* find it annoying or *you* care about it, chances are others do too. A small problem that affects a lot of people is a fantastic opportunity. So is a niche problem that affects a passionate group who are willing to pay to have it solved (for example, a specialized tool for hobbyist woodworkers who struggle with a particular task). What matters is not the size of the problem in the abstract; it's how much it matters to the people who have it.

If you're solving a huge problem, you'll likely need to narrow your focus to a specific aspect that you can realistically tackle first (no single startup can solve *all* of climate change at once, for instance, but you might focus on a better solar panel for home users as a start). If you're solving a small problem, you might need to highlight the impact it has ("This gadget saves you 10 minutes every morning" or "prevents you from losing your keys, which saves you stress and money"). Either way, big or small, the principle is the same: identify a genuine need and fulfill it. Both paths can lead to a strong brand because both are rooted in making someone's life better.

Is It Worth Solving? Ask These Questions

Not every problem you notice will be the right one for you to tackle. Before you pour your time and energy into a particular idea, it's wise to evaluate it carefully. This isn't about being negative or poking holes in your dream. It's about making sure you choose a problem that has the best chance of leading to a thriving and fulfilling business. A problem worth solving will meet certain criteria. Try asking yourself the following questions about the idea or problem you have in mind:

1. **"Does this problem really bother people (or really inspire them)?"**
   Think about how painful or pressing the problem is. Is it a minor inconvenience or a major headache? The more it genuinely affects people, the more they'll value a solution. If it's a "nice to have" improvement, that's okay, but you'll need to educate customers on why it's worth paying attention to. If it's something that causes daily frustration or lost time/money, you've got a strong motivator right there.

2. **"How many people have this problem?"**
   Is it a widespread issue or a niche one? Both can be fine, but the approach differs. A widespread problem (like, say, "wet shoes on rainy days") means a huge potential market. A niche problem (such as a specialized software need in a certain industry) can still be great if those who have it are willing to pay for a solution. What you want to avoid is solving something *so* obscure that hardly anyone cares. You don't need millions of people to start a business, but you do need a *critical mass* of customers who want what you're offering.

3. **"Are there existing solutions, and if so, why aren't they fixing it?"**
   It's rare to find a problem no one has ever tried to solve. Usually, there's *something* out there, even if it's clumsy or incomplete. Study what's available. If competitors or old workarounds exist, what are their shortcomings? Perhaps current solutions are too expensive, too complicated, or simply inaccessible to those who need them. If you can pinpoint what's lacking in existing options, you'll understand how your brand can stand out from the crowd. On the other hand, if a problem is already solved *well* by others, you may need to either choose a different angle or a different problem. Your goal is to either be the first with a solution or be *better or unique* in a clear way.

4. **"Why am I the right person (or team) to solve this?"**
   This is a bit personal, but important. You don't need to be a world-renowned expert (you can always learn or partner with others), but having some connection to the problem gives you an edge. Perhaps you have firsthand experience with it, a background that enables you to understand it deeply, or simply a ton of passion for fixing it. If the problem resonates with you strongly, that's a good sign. It will keep you motivated when things get tough. If you realize you're chasing something just because it sounds lucrative, but you don't

actually care about it, consider revisiting your choice. The journey of building a brand is much more rewarding (and likely more successful) if you care deeply about the mission.

5. **"Will solving this problem make life significantly better for someone?"**
Envision the end result. Picture a person who has this problem using your product or service. What changes for them? Do they save time, save money, reduce stress, gain joy, improve their health, feel more connected, or otherwise experience a meaningful improvement? A litmus test for a strong idea is seeing a clear, positive *impact*. If you can't articulate exactly how your solution will improve someone's life, even in a small way, the idea might need refining. The best brand foundations come from delivering real improvement that customers can feel. When you *do* see that your idea could, say, *"save a busy parent an hour every day,"* or *"help a student learn a tough subject more easily,"* or *"give an amateur photographer a professional result without the hassle,"* then you've got something worth pursuing.

As you reflect on these questions, be honest with yourself. It's okay if an idea doesn't pass every test with flying colors; the goal is to be aware of potential challenges and significance. Perhaps you realize the problem you've chosen is real, but not very frequent. You might adapt your concept to address a more frequent need or find an angle that encourages more frequent use of your solution. Alternatively, you might find that a problem is important but currently being addressed by a giant company. That doesn't necessarily mean you give up, but you might niche down or innovate further to differentiate your brand.

The outcome of this self-questioning isn't typically a simple yes/no answer. It's a deeper understanding of the problem and confidence that it's the right one. When you can confidently say, *"Yes, this is a real issue, I know who struggles with it, current options aren't good enough, and I'm excited to fix it,"* then you're well on your way. That clarity will fuel your progress and also help when you eventually pitch your idea to customers or partners. They'll sense that you truly grasp the problem and are committed to solving it.

From Problem to Brand Story

Identifying a problem worth solving is a huge milestone. Now let's talk about how that problem can shape your brand story. Your brand story is the narrative that ties together who you are, what you do, and *why* you do it.

And the "why" almost always comes from the problem you set out to solve. In this chapter's context, your story might go something like, *"I started [Your Brand] because I saw [this problem] and I wanted to [your solution]."* This simple formula is incredibly effective for communicating your brand's purpose.

Think of some of your favorite brands or even classic entrepreneur stories: often, there's a founder who faced a challenge or noticed an issue and decided to make something to fix it. For example, a founder might say, "I was tired of misplacing my keys and wasting time every morning, so I invented a smart keychain that beeps when you whistle. Now, our company helps thousands of people find their lost keys quickly every day." See how the problem (losing keys) and solution (smart keychain) combine into a neat little tale? It's relatable and clear. When you share a story like that about your own brand, it draws people in. They see the human driving force behind the business.

Your journey of solving the problem is part of the story, too. Don't be afraid to let customers peek behind the curtain. If you struggled with the problem yourself, talk about that experience. If you spent nights tinkering with a prototype or interviewed dozens of people who had the problem, that shows your dedication. It also subtly highlights how *real* the problem is. For instance, saying "After talking to 50 parents of toddlers about their bedtime challenges, I realized most bedtime storybooks were too short to help kids wind down. So, I created a longer-form bedtime story series that keeps little ones engaged just long enough to fall asleep." In that one anecdote, you've shown that you did your homework, you understand your customers (because their problem was your problem), and you delivered a thoughtful solution.

Another advantage of having a clear problem-solution story is consistency. As you build your brand (through your website, packaging, social media, etc.), you can keep coming back to that core narrative. It ensures all your messaging is aligned. Your tagline, for example, could reflect the problem and solution: "Never Lose Your Keys Again" or "Healthy Dinners in 10 Minutes." Your blog posts can discuss various aspects of the problem and tips to solve it (with your product being one great way). Your customer testimonials will naturally mention the problem ("I used to struggle with ___, but thanks to [Brand], not anymore!"). In short, the problem you solve becomes entwined with the brand's identity.

Remember, *people don't buy what you do, they buy why you do it*. Solving a worthwhile problem gives you a very compelling "why." It transforms your brand from just another business into a mission-driven endeavor. Customers love to support missions they believe in. If someone believes "Yes, losing keys is super frustrating and I love that this company is finally fixing it," they feel connected to your mission. They're not just buying a gadget. They're buying into the idea that life can be a little easier, thanks to you.

As you pick the problem you want to solve, start imagining how you'll tell the world about it. How will you explain the spark that led you to create your solution? What anecdotes can you share about discovering or understanding the problem? Even if you're at the very beginning, it's okay to speak from the heart: "I've always felt ___ was harder than it should be, and I'm on a mission to change that." By framing your brand as the hero on a quest to solve X problem, you set up a story that customers can follow and root for. It's inspiring, approachable, and it gives your brand a soul from day one.

Your Action Plan: Finding and Embracing Your Problem

Now it's time to turn this insight into action. Talking about problems is useful, but taking steps to identify and choose your problem is where the magic begins for your brand journey. Here's a straightforward action plan to help you zero in on a problem worth solving and get ready to build a brand around it:

1. **Brainstorm Problems (Big and Small):** Set aside some quiet time and list out every problem, annoyance, gap, or unmet need you can think of. Don't censor yourself here. Write down everything that comes to mind, from "there's no good late-night food delivery in my town" to "elderly people in my community feel isolated" to "I always lose socks in the laundry." Include personal frustrations, things you've heard others complain about, and issues you've read or thought about in areas that interest you. Aim for at least 20-30 items on this list. Remember, you're not committing to all these. You're just getting them out of your head and onto paper.

2. **Highlight What Excites You:** Go through your brainstorm list and mark the problems that light a fire in you. Which ones make you nod vigorously and say, "Yes, this needs fixing!"? Which could you see yourself being passionate about in the long run? Perhaps you feel strongly about environmental issues, making the composting idea particularly appealing, or you're a tech enthusiast, and the

pesky software glitch you noted intrigues you to solve. Trust your gut feelings here. The best idea for you is one that *energizes* you, because you'll be spending a lot of time with it.

3. **Research the Top Contenders:** Take your top 2-3 problem ideas and do a bit of research on each. This can be as simple as a quick internet search, asking people who might have the problem how they currently deal with it, or seeing if there are existing businesses addressing it. The goal is to gather insight. Are people talking about this problem online? (If you search for "solution for ___" or look at forums, what do you find?) What do potential customers say about it? This research will help you gauge interest and see opportunities. Maybe you discover that one of your ideas already has several solutions. That doesn't automatically kill the idea, but you might refine it to be different or better, or you might find that nobody is tackling one aspect of the problem, an excellent opening for you!

4. **Refine the Problem Statement:** For the most promising problem, craft a concise and clear problem statement. One formula you can use is: *"[Target people] struggle with [describe the problem] whenever [context]. The current solutions out there are [inadequate/missing] because ___. Solving this would [benefit] by ___."* For example: "Busy working parents struggle with finding time to cook healthy dinners on weeknights. The current solutions (fast food or meal kits) are either unhealthy or too expensive, leaving them feeling guilty or strained. Solving this would give them healthier meals with less stress, improving family well-being." When you articulate the problem this way, it clarifies exactly what you aim to solve and why it's worth solving. This statement becomes a guiding light for your brand concept.

5. **Imagine the Solution (Just Broad Strokes):** You don't need a full business plan yet, but take a moment to imagine what solving the problem might look like. This is a creative exercise to ensure you feel enthusiastic about the direction. Jot down a few possible ways one might solve it. Could it be an app? A physical product? A service or community effort? There might be multiple ways, and that's fine. The point is to connect the problem with a vision of a solution. If thinking about it gets you excited, like you start visualizing people using your solution and loving it, that's a great sign. If you feel stuck here, you might need to learn more about the problem or consider

partnering with someone who has the expertise. Usually, if the problem is one you relate to, you'll have some intuitive ideas for solutions already.

6. **Commit to the Problem:** Finally, make the decision. Pick the problem that you feel is truly worth your effort. It's normal to have some doubts, but once you've done the above steps, trust yourself. Write down on paper or say out loud: *"The problem I'm going to solve is ___."* Congratulations! That's a huge step in building your brand! By committing to a problem, you've essentially defined your mission. Everything from here on (developing a product, creating your brand identity, marketing, etc.) will center around this mission of solving your chosen problem. It's both focusing and freeing to have that decision made.

As you work through this action plan, remember that no choice is absolutely permanent. Many brands evolve and sometimes even pivot to new problems as they learn more. However, you have to start somewhere, and focusing on one primary problem now will give you direction. You'll learn a lot by taking action on one idea versus endlessly pondering many ideas.

Embrace the problem you've chosen. Get to know the people who have it, immerse yourself in understanding every nuance of why it exists, and how your future brand can help. This deep dive and commitment sets the stage for the next chapters of your journey: developing solutions, crafting your brand identity, and delivering value to your audience.

Conclusion: Your Problem, Your Purpose

You've now explored how to recognize problems worth solving, from everyday frustrations to gaps that keep people from joy, and seen how such a problem can ignite a business idea and ground a brand in purpose. This chapter's title, "Pick a Problem Worth Solving," is truly a rallying cry. It's an invitation to step into the shoes of a problem-solver and a difference-maker. When you choose a problem and dedicate yourself to solving it, you're not just launching a business venture. You're embracing a purpose. That purpose will guide you, motivate you, and connect you with others who share the same concern.

Take a moment to reflect on what you've picked (or are close to picking). Feel good about it! You're setting out to alleviate a pain or deliver joy for people out there. That's a noble thing, whether it's saving someone a few minutes in their day or addressing a major life challenge. No matter the scale, making life better for someone is meaningful. That meaning is the soul of your brand.

Keep this in mind as you move forward: whenever you face uncertainty or decisions, you can ask, *"Does this action help me solve the problem I set out to solve?"* If yes, it's likely on the right track. If not, it might be a distraction. In this way, your chosen problem becomes a compass for your brand-building journey. It keeps you aligned with your mission.

Finally, remember to stay flexible and keep listening. Solving a problem is rarely a straight line. You may discover new aspects of the problem or receive unexpected feedback from those you're trying to help. That's all part of the process. Your commitment is not to a rigid idea, but to the *essence* of the problem and the people it affects. If you stay tuned to that, your brand will evolve in the right direction.

You have the passion, you have the problem, and that means you have a purpose. That's an incredibly strong foundation for building a brand that matters. In the next chapter, we'll build on this foundation by exploring how to develop a solution or refine your business idea around this problem, and how to ensure it truly resonates with your target audience. For now, give yourself a pat on the back. You're doing what many people overlook: starting with *why*, beginning with a real need. That choice alone sets you on the path to creating a brand that not only succeeds but also stands for something meaningful.

Go forth and embrace the problem you've chosen. It's time to make a real difference, one solution at a time!

CHAPTER 3: GET INTO A BRAND BUILDER MINDSET

Building a brand isn't just about logos, marketing plans, or products. It's also about you, the person driving the brand. In the previous chapters, we laid the groundwork for your brand's vision and strategy. Now it's time to focus on the internal foundation: your mindset. The journey of brand-building can be challenging and unpredictable, but embracing the right mindset will carry you through. A brand builder mindset means thinking like a resilient entrepreneur: being confident, adaptable, customer-focused, and unafraid of setbacks. You might imagine that successful brand builders are born with these traits, but the truth is that none of them are "required" from day one. Many celebrated entrepreneurs began their journeys full of doubts and fears. Fortunately, qualities like confidence and resilience are not inborn talents at all. They are skills you can learn and strengthen with practice. In this chapter, we'll explore how to cultivate the mindset of a brand builder and tackle common mental hurdles along the way. By the end, you'll feel empowered to step forward with confidence, knowing you can develop any trait you need to succeed.

Cultivate Confidence

Confidence is the quiet inner voice saying, *"I can do this."* As a brand builder, you need to believe in yourself and the value of what you're creating. This doesn't mean you'll never have self-doubts. Even the most accomplished entrepreneurs question themselves at times. The good news is that confidence isn't some innate personality trait reserved for a lucky few. You don't have to be born confident to build a great brand. Confidence is something you develop over time through experience and effort. In other words, confidence is like a muscle, one you strengthen with each small win, new skill learned, and challenge overcome.

Building confidence starts with acknowledging your achievements and capabilities. Take stock of your strengths (maybe you have a knack for storytelling or you're great at connecting with people) and remind yourself of them often. Celebrate the little victories, whether it's positive feedback from a customer or hitting a minor milestone. Each success, no matter how small, reinforces that you are capable. On tough days when doubt creeps in, reflect on how far you've already come. Remember that every expert was once a beginner, and every strong brand started as an idea in someone's mind. The more you focus on your progress and personal growth, the more your confidence will bloom.

Another key to confidence is reframing how you think about setbacks. Instead of seeing a failure or misstep as proof that you're "not good enough," try to view it as part of the process. Every entrepreneur faces obstacles: a campaign that flops, a deal that falls through, or a product that doesn't resonate. These moments do not define you. What matters is that you show up again the next day, a little wiser and more determined. Tell yourself the same thing successful brand builders tell themselves: *"I am learning, adjusting, and giving my best each day."* This kind of positive self-talk isn't just fluff. It keeps you focused on moving forward rather than being perfect. When you believe that you can grow and improve (sometimes referred to as a growth mindset), you give yourself permission to try new things and trust your ability to figure them out. Bit by bit, that outlook creates genuine confidence.

Finally, remember that confidence doesn't mean never feeling afraid. It means not letting fear hold you back. You might feel nervous before a big pitch or uncertain about a decision, but confidence helps you act anyway. One practical tip: when self-doubt or impostor feelings strike, shift your attention outward. Focus on the value you're providing rather than your inner critic. By concentrating on how your brand helps customers or brings something positive to the world, you naturally start worrying less about your own limitations. This outward focus can build confidence and quiet those nagging voices of doubt. You have something unique to offer. Trust that, and step forward boldly.

Build Resilience

Every brand building journey has its bumps in the road. You might launch a campaign that doesn't perform well, get negative feedback, or face an unexpected crisis. This is where resilience comes in. Resilience is your ability to bounce back from setbacks, learn from them, and keep going. It's often said that resilience, even more than raw talent or resources, is what separates those who succeed from those who give up. Challenges and failures are inevitable in business. Knowing this, resilient brand builders treat setbacks not as the end of the road, but as opportunities for learning. It's the ability to get back up after a fall that differentiates a thriving entrepreneur from one who falters.

How can you cultivate resilience? First, accept that setbacks are a normal part of life. It's not a sign that you're incapable or that your brand is doomed. It's simply part of doing something new and ambitious. When a problem arises, take a deep breath and remind yourself that you're in good company. Every successful brand has weathered its share of storms. Instead of asking "Why me?" ask "What can I learn from this?". Resilient people have a habit of extracting lessons from each challenge. For example, if a product launch falls flat, a resilient mindset might find insight in the failure. Maybe the marketing message missed the mark, or perhaps it's an opportunity to refine the product based on feedback. Viewing challenges as chances to grow is a hallmark of resilience. By regularly reflecting on what went wrong and how you can adjust, you turn setbacks into springboards for improvement. This practice not only makes you stronger but also encourages adaptability (another key trait we'll discuss shortly).

Another aspect of resilience is maintaining a sense of purpose and optimism. When you have a clear *why* behind your brand (a mission or set of values that inspire you), it's easier to stay motivated during tough times. Let that bigger vision pull you forward when the day-to-day gets hard. And don't forget to acknowledge progress, no matter how incremental. Give yourself credit for every step forward, including completed tasks, solved problems, and small wins. Celebrating small victories keeps you motivated and builds the mental toughness to persevere. Each time you overcome a hurdle, you prove to yourself that you can handle whatever comes next. This creates a positive feedback loop: resilience leads to wins, which in turn lead to greater confidence, which fuels even more resilience.

Finally, resilience doesn't mean going at it alone or toughing everything out by yourself. Part of being resilient is knowing when to seek support. Every entrepreneur faces moments of doubt or exhaustion. Talking to a mentor, coach, or fellow brand builder can provide comfort, new perspectives, and practical advice. There is real strength in saying, *"I could use some help"* or *"What would you do in my situation?"* Lean on others when you need to. It's not a weakness, it's a smart strategy. By building resilience (through learning from setbacks, keeping your purpose in mind, celebrating progress, and getting help when needed), you'll develop the grit to handle the ups and downs of brand building. Every challenge overcome is proof that you're growing tougher and wiser.

Focus on Your Customers

Successful brand builders share a crucial mindset: they are relentlessly customer-focused. This means always keeping the customer's needs, feelings, and desires at the forefront of your decisions. It's easy to get wrapped up in your own vision for your brand or the excitement of your product features. However, remember that your brand ultimately resides in the hearts and minds of your customers. When you put customers first, you create a brand that truly resonates and builds loyalty over time.

Being customer-focused starts with empathy: seeing things from your customer's perspective. Ask yourself, *"How does this decision benefit our customers? Does it solve their problem or improve their life in some way?"* Brand builders with a customer mindset invest time in understanding their audience deeply. They listen to feedback, engage with their community, and even invite customers to participate in the creation process. By doing so, they ensure their brand isn't operating in a vacuum. This focus on delivering real value pays off. Companies that prioritize their customers tend to experience higher revenue and increased loyalty from their clients. Most people will stick with brands that make them feel heard and cared for. The takeaway is simple. Caring about your customers is not just the right thing to do; it's smart business. When people feel heard and cared for, they stick around and share their experiences with others.

To adopt a customer-focused mindset, make "What's best for our customers?" a guiding question in everything you do. This might mean adjusting a policy that isn't user-friendly, improving your product based on user feedback, or providing extra-mile customer service. Great brands are built on relationships, not one-off transactions. Think of your customers as long-term partners in your brand's journey. Nurture trust with honesty and consistency. Deliver on your promises and fix mistakes when they happen. Over time, this approach turns customers into true fans who support your brand through thick and thin.

Staying customer-centric also helps when your motivation dips or self-doubt looms. How so? It shifts your focus outward, away from anxieties and toward a purpose. If you ever feel stuck or question why you're doing this, reconnect with your customers' stories. Remember that you're building this brand to serve them. For instance, maybe your product empowers a customer to solve a problem, or your service brightened someone's day. Let those impacts inspire you. Some entrepreneurs even keep a "happy folder" of positive reviews or thank-you notes to read on hard days, a tangible reminder of why their work matters. By anchoring yourself in the people you serve, you'll find renewed energy and drive to keep improving. As a bonus, focusing on others can quiet imposter syndrome. When you channel energy into delivering value, there's less room for doubting yourself. In short, making your customers the heroes of your brand story creates a win-win: they feel valued, and you build a brand that's beloved and resilient.

Embrace Adaptability

If there's one guarantee in the brand-building journey, it's that things will change. Markets shift, customer preferences evolve, new competitors emerge, and unexpected challenges pop up. That's why adaptability is such a critical mindset for a brand builder. Being adaptable means staying flexible and open-minded in the face of change by adjusting your strategies as needed and continuously learning so your brand can thrive no matter what. Brand builders who embrace adaptability see change not as a threat, but as an opportunity to improve and innovate.

Think of adaptability as the art of the pivot. When something isn't working as well as you hoped, an adaptable mindset asks, *"What can we try next?"* instead of clinging to the original plan. This doesn't mean abandoning your core vision or values. It means being willing to change how you get there. For example, imagine you launch a product feature that customers aren't using much. Rather than forcing it, an adaptable approach would be to seek feedback, find out what customers truly want, and refine the feature (or develop a new one) to better meet those needs. Adaptable leaders excel at listening and iterating. They stay curious and keep experimenting until they find the right fit. This agility is a huge advantage. It allows your brand to stay relevant and valuable as the world around it evolves.

Adaptability also involves continuously updating your skills and knowledge. The most effective brand builders see themselves as lifelong learners. They read about industry trends, pay attention to emerging technologies or cultural shifts, and are willing to admit when they need to learn something new. This humility and curiosity go hand in hand with adaptability. If you adopt the mindset that there's always something new to learn, you'll be better prepared to handle whatever changes come your way. For instance, when social media algorithms change, the adaptable marketer learns the new rules and pivots strategy accordingly. Or when a new consumer behavior trend arises, the adaptable brand adjusts its offerings to align with what people want now. By staying open to change, you ensure that your brand continues to grow instead of getting left behind.

Crucially, adaptability is not about perfection or never making mistakes. It's about responding to mistakes and surprises with creativity and calm. Give yourself permission to change course when needed. Some of the most iconic brands succeeded because they started doing one thing and then discovered through trial and error that their true strength lay elsewhere, and they had the courage to pivot. If something isn't working, it's okay to say, "Let's try a different approach." In fact, being too rigid can be dangerous in business. Clinging to "the way we've always done it" can cause a brand to stagnate. Meanwhile, those who stay agile can turn challenges into breakthroughs. A mindset that embraces adaptability will have you constantly asking, *"What can I improve? What does the market need now? How else could we achieve this goal?"*

Finally, don't fear change. Prepare for it. Change can be intimidating, but it's also where growth happens. Remind yourself that every change your brand navigates (even the unwelcome ones) is making you stronger and more experienced. When you cultivate adaptability, you build a brand that is resilient, valuable, and scalable, regardless of what the future holds. You become like a surfer who can ride any wave, adjusting your balance as needed. Trust that you have the ingenuity to figure things out. If something completely new comes up and you don't have the skill for it yet, you can learn it, just like you've learned everything else up to now. With an adaptable mindset, you won't only survive changes; you'll use them to your advantage.

Overcoming Common Mindset Challenges

Even with the best intentions, mindset hurdles will arise. You're human, after all! Let's address a few common challenges that brand builders often face in their mental journey, and discuss how to overcome them. Remember, feeling these things is completely normal, and overcoming them will make you even stronger.

- **Fear of Failure:** Starting or growing a brand can be scary, and many of us carry a deep fear of falling short. You might worry, "What if I put myself out there and it doesn't work? I'll disappoint everyone." Here's the truth: even wildly successful people feel this fear. They aren't magically fearless. They've learned to accept and manage fear of failure so it doesn't paralyze them. Failure will happen in some form, but it's not fatal. It's often the price of progress. Try reframing failure as feedback: each "failure" is teaching you something invaluable for your next attempt. If you never risk failure, you also risk never growing. When fear of failure looms, ground yourself in reality. Ask, *"What's the worst that could happen if this fails, and could I handle that?"* You'll usually find the worst-case scenario, while not fun, is survivable and often far less dire than our imaginations suggest. Take that first step despite the fear, because the journey of a thousand miles begins with one step. *Prompt: Imagine the worst case isn't as bad as you think. What might you learn if things don't go as planned?*

- **Imposter Syndrome:** This is that nagging feeling that you're not as good as people think. That you're "faking it" and might be exposed as a fraud. If you've ever thought, "Who am I to do this? Others know more than me," you're not alone. Imposter syndrome affects even the most accomplished entrepreneurs, causing them to doubt their abilities and success. Remind yourself that feeling like an impostor doesn't mean you are one. Often, it means you're pushing yourself into new territory, which is a good thing! To combat impostor feelings, start by acknowledging them ("Okay, I'm having those doubts again") and then counter them with facts. Make a list of your wins, skills, and positive feedback you've received. It's not bragging. It's evidence. Look at that list whenever self-doubt creeps in, as proof that you are capable and making progress. Also, focus on the value you provide rather than on perfection. When you shift your mindset to "How can I help my customers?", imposter syndrome tends to fade, because your attention is on serving others, not scrutinizing yourself. Finally, remember that real impostors rarely worry about impostor syndrome. The very fact that you care about doing well is a sign that you're genuine and on the right track. *Prompt: Write down three things you've accomplished (big or small) in your brand journey so far. Keep this list handy for a confidence boost when self-doubt hits.*

- **Perfectionism:** Many brand builders are passionate and have high standards, which is great! But this can tip into perfectionism, where nothing ever feels "good enough" to launch or share. The result? You get stuck polishing and tweaking endlessly, or you delay putting your work out into the world. Perfectionism is often driven by fear (fear of failure or judgment), and it can stop you from moving forward at all. The antidote is embracing progress over perfection. Realize that no brand is flawless, and that's okay. Your goal is to continually improve, not to be perfect on the first try (or ever). In fact, trying to be perfect can hold you back from learning. Sometimes you need to release version 1.0, get feedback, and iterate. The key is finding a balance between completion and perfection. Done is better than perfect, because done means you're in the game and learning. To break free from perfectionism, set realistic goals and deadlines that are achievable. Give yourself permission to be "good enough for now" and evolve over time. Also, pay attention to your self-talk. If you catch yourself thinking in all-or-nothing terms ("If this isn't the best ever, it's a failure"), gently reframe it. Think in terms of experiments and drafts. Each project, campaign, or piece of content is a step in the journey, not the final destination. Remember, your brand is a living, breathing work in progress. Prioritize continuous improvement and let go of the pressure to be perfect. You'll move faster and feel happier doing it. *Prompt: What's one task you've been putting off or over-polishing? Commit to finishing it in a timely way and releasing it, even if it's not 100% perfect. You can always refine it later!*

Stay Motivated and Keep Growing

Embracing the brand builder mindset is a continuous journey. You won't suddenly wake up one day with 100% confidence, unshakable resilience, perfect customer focus, and seamless adaptability, and that's okay! The goal is progress, not perfection (yes, that mantra again). With each day that you intentionally work on your mindset, you'll find that it gets a bit easier to think like a successful brand builder. You'll catch negative thoughts sooner and replace them with positive ones, bounce back from setbacks a little faster, and center your decisions more consistently around your customers and long-term vision. All of these traits are like muscles. They strengthen with use. None of them are fixed qualities. You can improve every one of them with practice and patience.

On days when motivation runs low, revisit this chapter. It might also be helpful to use light prompts or affirmations. For example, start your morning by reminding yourself, *"I am adaptable and open to whatever today brings,"* or *"I focus on serving my customers and learning as I go."* Such statements can set a powerful tone for your day. If you encounter a setback, pause and say, *"This is tough, but I will learn something from it and come back stronger."* These little mindset shifts, practiced regularly, add up to a big change in how you approach your brand and its challenges. Over time, you'll notice that what used to feel overwhelming now feels manageable, maybe even exciting.

That difficult client call or unexpected market change becomes less a crisis and more an interesting puzzle to solve. That's the brand builder mindset taking root!

Finally, remember to be kind to yourself throughout this process. Building a brand (and growing yourself) is a courageous endeavor. You're stepping out of your comfort zone and striving for something great. Not everyone has the bravery to do that. Celebrate yourself for every effort. When things go well, take a moment to appreciate it. When things go poorly, refuse to beat yourself up. Instead, treat yourself with the same encouragement you'd give a good friend. Keep in mind that every expert was once a beginner, and every success story has chapters of failure and doubt. You are never alone in what you feel. Countless others have walked this path and emerged victorious by refusing to give up. Successful people aren't free of fear or doubt. They've simply learned to befriend those feelings and move forward regardless. You can do the same.

As you continue to develop your brand builder mindset, you'll find that confidence, resilience, customer focus, and adaptability start to become second nature. These qualities will guide you in making wise decisions and staying motivated through any challenge. And the best part? None of these traits were prerequisites for starting. You've been developing them along the way. Give yourself credit for the growth you've achieved so far. You're well on your way to thinking (and thriving) like a true brand builder. Now, with this empowering mindset, you're ready to take the next steps in building your brand with renewed energy and enthusiasm. You've got this, and your future fans are waiting to be amazed by what you'll create. Go get it!

CHAPTER 4: DEFINE YOUR CORE BELIEFS

Why Your Brand's Beliefs Matter

What does your brand stand for? Why did you start this journey in the first place? These questions get to the heart of your brand's core beliefs. Your core beliefs are the foundation of your brand's identity. They include your values, your origin story, and your core purpose (your "why"). Defining these beliefs clearly will give your brand a soul and a direction. When you know what you stand for, every decision becomes easier and more authentic. It's not just about selling a product or service anymore; it's about standing up for an idea and inviting others to join you.

In today's world, people connect with authenticity and meaning. Think about brands you personally love. Chances are, you resonate with what they believe in or the story behind them. When your audience understands and shares your brand's beliefs, they feel a deeper loyalty. Core beliefs set you apart from competitors because while anyone can copy a product, no one can duplicate *why* you do what you do or *how* your story shaped you. By defining your core beliefs, you give customers a reason to care beyond price or features. You're saying, "This is who we are and what we believe," which draws in those who believe the same.

Your core beliefs also act as a compass for your business. As you grow, you will face tough choices, including new opportunities, challenges, and changes in the market. If you have a clear set of values and a clear purpose, you can use them to guide these choices. They help ensure you stay true to yourself. For example, if one of your core values is quality, that value will remind you *never* to cut corners just to save a buck. If your core purpose is to help people lead healthier lives, that purpose will inspire you to develop products and services aligned with wellbeing. In short, knowing your brand's beliefs keeps you grounded and consistent. Consistency builds trust. When customers see you living up to your promises and principles over time, they know you're the real deal.

Uncovering Your Origin Story

Every brand has a beginning. Your origin story is the tale of why and how your brand came to life. This isn't just a history lesson. It's a chance to reveal the passion and purpose behind your business. By sharing the spark that ignited your brand, you give it human depth and emotional resonance. Why is this important? Because people don't just buy *what* you sell; they often buy *why* you started in the first place. Your origin story can inspire others to join your mission or at least understand the heart behind your enterprise.

Start by reflecting on the moment (or series of moments) that led you to create your brand. Was there a personal experience that pushed you to solve a problem? Maybe you noticed something missing in the market, or you were frustrated by the way things were done and knew there had to be a better way. Perhaps your journey began with a small incident years ago that planted a seed of an idea. Dig into those memories. Who were you trying to help, or what were you trying to change? How did you feel at the time? Within those answers lie the key themes of your origin story, and often, clues to your values and purpose.

When crafting your origin story, focus on the *motivation and values* that drove you, not just the facts and dates. For instance, instead of simply saying "I started a bakery in 2019," talk about *why* you started that bakery. Maybe you grew up baking with your grandmother and believed in the power of homemade food to bring people together. That belief, bringing people together with warmth and tradition, is a core value that shines through your story. The details (like the year or the city) matter less than the meaning behind them. An authentic origin story doesn't need to be grand or dramatic; it just needs to be genuine and heartfelt. Share the challenges you faced or the passion that kept you going, because these elements reveal what truly matters to you.

Reflection Prompt: *Take a moment to write down your brand's origin story in a few sentences. Why did you start, and what problem or need lit the fire in you? Don't worry about making it perfect. Focus on the feelings and beliefs that guided you. For example, "I started [Your Brand] because I saw... and I believed that...."*

By articulating your origin story, you lay bare the *why* behind your brand's birth. This story will become a powerful tool in branding. You can share it with customers to help them connect with you on a human level. More importantly, it reminds **you** of the purpose that started it all. Whenever you feel lost or disconnected, revisiting your own story can reignite your passion and realign you with your core beliefs.

Identifying Your Core Values

If your origin story is the why of your beginning, your core values are the principles that guide you every day. Core values are the handful of beliefs and standards that your brand stands for no matter what. Think of them as your non-negotiables, meaning the values you will uphold in good times and bad because they define what your brand is all about. When you clearly identify these values, you set the tone for your company culture, customer experience, and even the kind of future you want to build.

Start by thinking about what truly matters to you in running your business. What qualities or ideals do you never want to compromise? Perhaps it's integrity: being honest and transparent with your customers, innovation: always looking for creative ways to improve, customer care, sustainability, inclusivity, quality, or community. To figure out your core values, consider these angles:

- **Proud Moments:** Recall a moment when your brand did something that made you especially proud. What value was shining through? (e.g., You went above and beyond to help a customer. That shows a value of service or care.)

- **Big Decisions:** Think about a tough decision you had to make in your business. What principle helped you choose? (Maybe you turned down a partnership because it clashed with your ethical standards, highlighting integrity.)

- **Daily Culture:** Consider the work environment and culture you want to create for yourself and your team members. What values do you want everyone to embody? (For example, respect, creativity, or teamwork.)

- **Customer Praise:** What do your customers or clients appreciate about you? If they often say you're reliable or personable, those could be core values you hold.

As you brainstorm, list any words that resonate with how you want your brand to be known. Then narrow that list down to the 3-5 core values that feel most essential. Having too many can dilute your focus, so pick the ones that truly capture your brand's spirit. Each value you choose should be authentic. It should reflect who you are and how you actually operate, not just what sounds good in marketing. If you claim a value like "innovation," make sure you are actively embracing new ideas and not clinging to old ways. Your values must align with your actions, or they'll ring hollow.

Reflection Prompt: *Write down three core values that define how you want to do business. For each value, add a short note about what it means to you in practice. For example: "Quality – we take pride in crafting our products carefully even if it takes more time," or "Community – we welcome customer feedback and support local projects."*

Identifying your core values is empowering. These values will guide how you hire employees, how you interact with customers, and how you make both big and small decisions. When a dilemma comes up, you can ask, "Which choice aligns with our values?" This makes your brand consistent and principled. Customers notice this consistency. They see when a brand stands firm on its values and delivers on its promises. Over time, this builds a strong reputation. People will start to describe your brand using the very values you've chosen. "They're so trustworthy," "That company truly cares about community," and so on. That is the sign of a well-defined, values-driven brand.

Discovering Your "Why" (Core Purpose)

Your origin story and values build up to perhaps the most important belief of all: your core purpose, or your "why." This is the deep reason your brand exists beyond making a profit. It's the impact you aim to have and the change you want to see in the world or your customers' lives. Defining your core purpose gives you a guiding star, a constant reminder of what all your efforts are for. It's what will keep you motivated on tough days and inspire others to believe in your brand.

To discover your "why," think about the ultimate goal or belief driving your work. Ask yourself: *"Why do I do what I do? What would be missing if my brand didn't exist? What do I want to achieve for others through this brand?"* The answer shouldn't be "to make money". Profit is important for any business, but your core purpose goes deeper. It could be something like, "to help people feel confident in their own skin," "to bring joy to families through delicious food," or "to make sustainable living easy for everyone." It might help to finish the sentence, "I started this brand because I believe...". Fill in the blank with your heartfelt belief about what you're trying to change or contribute.

Sometimes your core purpose is very closely tied to your own story or values. For example, if you started a tutoring business because you struggled in school and believe every child deserves patient guidance, your core purpose might be "to empower students to discover their own potential." If you run an eco-friendly product company and you value sustainability, your "why" could be "to reduce waste and protect the planet for future generations." Notice how these purposes are broad, inspiring, and focused on making a difference. They're not about being the #1 market leader or having the highest revenue. Those are results. The core purpose is about impact and meaning.

Reflection Prompt: Try writing a single sentence that captures your brand's core purpose. Start with phrases like "We exist to...", "Our mission is to...", or "We believe...". Don't worry about perfect wording; just aim to express the change you want to make or the value you want to create. For now, write it for yourself. You can always refine the wording later.

When you clarify your "why," it will resonate not only with you but with everyone who encounters your brand. A clear purpose is magnetic. It attracts employees who are excited to contribute to that mission and draws in customers who share the same beliefs or aspirations. Remember, people often support brands that stand for something that matters to them. If your why is genuine and meaningful, it will set you apart from competitors in a way that goes far beyond pricing or features. It becomes the heartbeat of your brand, the thing that stays constant, even as you grow, develop new products, or adapt to change.

Bringing Your Beliefs to Life

Defining your values, origin story, and purpose is a big accomplishment. Now it's time to live those beliefs out loud. Your core beliefs shouldn't just live in a document or on your "About Us" page. They should influence every aspect of your brand as it moves forward. When you infuse your daily operations and future plans with your core beliefs, you ensure that your brand grows with integrity and clear direction.

Start by integrating your beliefs into your brand story and messaging. Share snippets of your origin story on your website or social media, highlighting the passion and purpose that started it all. Let your values shine through in how you interact with customers. If one of your values is friendliness, make sure every customer interaction is warm and respectful. If another value is innovation, regularly communicate the new ideas or improvements you're pursuing. Your core purpose should be evident in your marketing. For example, if your purpose is to help people live healthier lives, your content might include educational tips or inspirational customer success stories that align with that purpose. In short, ensure that what you say as a brand consistently reflects your values and beliefs.

Living your beliefs also means weaving them into the experience of your brand. Consider how your products or services can embody your values. For instance, a company that values sustainability can utilize eco-friendly packaging and ethical sourcing to demonstrate its commitment to these values. A brand that values community might host local events or support causes that matter to their audience. These actions speak louder than words and prove that your core beliefs are not just marketing fluff, but real principles that guide you. Internally, if you have a team, encourage and reward behaviors that align with your values. Celebrate the employee who went the extra mile to uphold quality or the one who showed great compassion to a client. These reinforcements foster a culture that aligns with your core beliefs.

As you plan the future of your business, use your core beliefs as a filter for opportunities. Not every trend or idea will be right for you. Some opportunities might look lucrative but could conflict with your values or dilute your purpose. By checking each major decision against your brand's beliefs, you'll make choices that feel right and maintain your authenticity. This might mean sometimes saying "no" to things that aren't a good fit, and that's okay. In the long run, staying true to your core beliefs will strengthen your brand's reputation and loyalty.

Reflection Prompt: Envision your brand five years from now, thriving because you stayed true to your core beliefs. What does that look like? Imagine a future where your values are evident in every product, every customer review, and every employee's smile. How have your core beliefs guided your success and growth? Jot down a few thoughts about what staying true will mean for your brand's future.

Finally, remember that defining your core beliefs is not a one-time task, but a lifelong commitment for your brand. Over time, your business might evolve, and you might refine the wording of your values or purpose, but the essence should remain. Keep your origin story alive by retelling it to new team members or new customers, reminding everyone why you began this journey. Revisit your values periodically with your team to ensure everyone interprets them in the same way and remains aligned. Keep your purpose front and center when setting new goals or launching new initiatives. When you lead with your beliefs, you create a brand that's consistent, trustworthy, and inspirational.

By living your core beliefs, you transform your brand from just another business into a beacon for something bigger. You give people a reason to take part, whether by buying from you, working for you, or simply cheering you on. In the next chapters, you'll continue to build on this strong foundation, but everything you do will trace back to the values, story, and purpose you have defined here. Your core beliefs are the heart of your brand's identity. Nurture that heart, and it will guide you to a brand future you (and your customers) can genuinely believe in.

PART II - BUILD YOUR FOUNDATION

CHAPTER 5: NAME AND FRAME YOUR BRAND

Naming and framing your brand is one of the most exciting steps in building your business. By this point, you've likely honed your brand identity. You know what your business stands for, who your customers are, and the message you want to send. Now it's time to express that identity through a clear and memorable brand name, a compelling tagline, and a trustworthy brand promise. These elements will become the words people associate with your business. They should instantly communicate what you're about and stick in your audience's mind. In this chapter, we'll guide you through choosing a name, crafting a tagline, and defining your brand promise, all in a way that aligns with your unique identity and vision.

The Power of a Name

Your business name is often the very first thing people learn about your brand. It's your first chance to make a positive impression and introduce your business's personality. A great name helps customers remember you and understand something essential about your business right away. On the other hand, a confusing or forgettable name can make your branding journey harder than it needs to be.

Why Your Name Matters: Think of your favorite brands. Their names probably feel like they *belong* to what they offer. That's no accident. The right name can convey meaning, emotion, or imagery that represents your product or service. It also differentiates you from competitors. A strong name can become a valuable asset, helping your business stand out in conversation and search results. Most importantly, your name should resonate with **your** story and values. When you say it out loud or see it on a sign, it should feel authentic to what you're building.

What Makes a Name Great?

While there's no formula for the perfect name, great brand names tend to share some common traits. Here are a few qualities to aim for when brainstorming your business name:

- **Clarity:** It should be easy to understand and pronounce. Avoid overly complex words or acronyms that confuse people. A clear name gives customers instant insight into your brand, or at least doesn't leave them guessing.

- **Memorability:** The best names stick in our minds. Short or punchy names are often easier to remember. You might use alliteration (for example, Coca-Cola for a catchy "C" sound) or a rhythmic cadence, but simplicity is usually key. Ask yourself, will someone recall this name after hearing it just once?

- **Alignment with Identity:** Your name should hint at your industry, values, or unique personality. A name can be descriptive (e.g., *Friendly Paws Dog Grooming*), suggestive (*Silver Horizon Tech*), or abstract (*Zeniko*), but whatever style you choose, it must fit your brand's character. If you run a fun, creative enterprise, a playful name could work well. For a professional service firm, you might choose a name that sounds trustworthy and established.

- **Distinctiveness:** Ensure your name sets you apart. It should be unique in your market so customers don't confuse you with someone else. Research other businesses in your space to avoid names that are too similar. Distinctiveness also helps with online search and securing a website domain.

- **Emotional Impact:** A great name can make people *feel* something. Consider the mood or feeling you want to evoke. It might be excitement, calm, luxury, or reliability, so see if your name can echo that. A name like *Bright Beginnings* (for a coaching service) feels uplifting and positive. Whatever feeling you want your brand to convey, ensure the name reflects that vibe.

- **Scalability:** Imagine where your business might be in five or ten years. Will the name still fit if you expand your offerings or enter new markets? Try not to choose something so narrow that it limits you. For instance, a bakery named "Cupcake Corner" might start selling more than just cupcakes one day, and a too-specific name could become limiting.

- **Legal Availability:** Before you fall in love with a name, thoroughly check that it isn't already trademarked or in use by another business in a similar field. Failing to do so could force you to change your entire business name after investing significant time and money, a potentially devastating and costly mistake. Also, ensure the corresponding website domain and social media handles are available for a strong online presence. A truly unique name offers not only easier protection but also helps you build a distinct and enduring brand.

Brainstorming Your Name

Coming up with the right name can be a time-consuming and creative process. Don't worry if the perfect idea doesn't strike immediately. It's normal to go through many ideas before finding the one that feels just right. Here are some steps to help you generate and choose a strong name:

1. **Start with Your Brand Basics:** Jot down keywords that relate to your business's core identity (your product, mission, values, and personality). Think about what makes you special. For example, if your company offers eco-friendly home goods, words like "green," "pure," "haven," or "earth" might come to mind.

2. **Brainstorm Freely:** Let your imagination loose. Write down all name ideas that pop up, even the silly or obvious ones. Sometimes, you need to look beyond the straightforward ideas to find something truly unique. Mix and match words, try translations from other languages, or combine words into new forms. At this stage, no idea is a bad idea.

3. **Consider Different Name Styles:** There are many approaches to naming. You could use:

   o *Descriptive names*: clearly stating what you do (e.g., Speedy Clean Car Wash).

   o *Evocative names*: hinting at an experience or benefit (e.g., Silver Lining Consulting, suggesting hope and positivity).

   o *Invented names*: completely new words or mash-ups (e.g., Zeniko or Floravista).

   o *Personal or founder names*: if it suits your story (e.g., Lucas & Lane Bakery).

   o *Geographical or cultural references*: if tied to your identity (e.g., Oak & Olive for a business rooted in a town with those trees).

Think about which style aligns with the image you want to project.

4. **Prioritize Simplicity:** From your brainstorm list, highlight the names that are simplest and clearest. If a name is hard to pronounce or spell, it might frustrate potential customers. Try saying the names out loud. Do they roll off the tongue? Would someone hearing it know how to spell it? Simplicity will usually win out.

5. **Gather Feedback:** Share your top name ideas with trusted friends, family, or potential customers and ask for their impressions. Do they understand what your business might do from the name alone? How does the name make them feel? Sometimes, an outside perspective will catch an association (good or bad) that you overlooked.

6. **Imagine the Name in Use:** Picture your favorite options on a business card, a storefront sign, or at the top of a website. Does it look appealing? Does it fit visually and sound good in a sentence like "We are [Name]"? This mental test can help you sense which names have the right *feel* for your brand.

7. **Check Uniqueness:** Before you make a final decision, do a quick online search for each name. Is anyone else using it or something similar, especially in your industry? You want to avoid confusion or legal issues down the line. If everything looks clear, also check if you can reserve a web domain (ideally a .com) and social media profiles with that name.

8. **Trust Your Instincts:** In the end, you, as the founder, need to love the name. It should feel good to say and share. If a name meets all the practical criteria but doesn't *excite* you, it might not be the one. The right name often gives you a gut feeling of "Yes, this is us."

Reflection Prompt: Take a moment to write down three to five words that capture the essence of your brand (for example: bold, caring, innovative, family, adventure). How can these ideas be reflected in your name? Do any of these words spark name ideas? Jot down a few possibilities and imagine how they'd introduce your business to a newcomer.

Crafting a Tagline that Captures Your Brand

Once you have a name (or even while you're deciding on one), the next step is to create a tagline. A tagline is a short, catchy phrase that often accompanies your brand name in marketing. Think of it as the finishing touch that frames your brand's message in a few memorable words. If your name is the title of your story, the tagline is like the subtitle. It provides a little more context or emotion.

A well-crafted tagline can quickly communicate what's special about your business or the core benefit you offer. It helps people understand why they should care about your brand, often evoking a feeling or inspiring curiosity. A strong tagline can also stick in someone's mind, increasing the chances they'll remember your brand later.

Qualities of an Effective Tagline

Creating a great tagline is both an art and a science. Here are key qualities to keep in mind as you develop yours:

- **Clear and Concise:** Aim for a short phrase (usually just a few words, often no more than a single sentence). Every word should count. A clear tagline gets the message across instantly. Avoid jargon or complicated language. Anyone who sees or hears it should "get it" right away.

- **Memorable:** The tagline should be easy to recall. This often means using simple, vivid words or a snappy rhythm. Rhyme, alliteration, or a clever turn of phrase can help a tagline lodge in the memory, but don't force it. Sometimes the most straightforward statement is the most memorable (for example, *"Always fresh"* for a food brand).

- **Reflective of Your Identity:** Your tagline must align with your brand's identity and values. It should sound like *you*. If your brand is playful, the tagline can be humorous or quirky. If your brand is about trust and care, the tagline might be warm and reassuring. Make sure the tone of the tagline matches the tone you want in all your communications.

- **Benefit-Oriented or Evocative:** A good tagline often highlights a key benefit or positive outcome for the customer. Think about what your audience gains from your product or service. Do you save them time, make them happier, improve their life in some way? If so, hint at that. Alternatively, you can evoke an emotion or a vision that your brand aspires to. An aspirational tagline can inspire people, inviting them to join a mindset or lifestyle your brand promotes.

- **Unique to You:** Just as with your name, your tagline should set you apart. It shouldn't be something any other company could easily say. Try to capture what only your brand can promise or the vibe only you provide. Steer clear of buzzwords or clichés that are overused in your industry. You want a line that people recognize as uniquely yours, not a generic slogan.

- **Timeless:** Ideally, your tagline will serve you for years to come. Be cautious about using trendy slang or overly specific claims that may become outdated. You want a line that can grow with your brand and still ring true as you evolve.

How to Write Your Tagline

Developing a tagline may take several drafts. Here's a process you can follow to come up with a line that clicks:

1. **Revisit Your Mission and Promise:** Reflect on your brand's mission statement or the core promise you make to customers (we'll delve more into brand promise in the next section). Often, the heart of a good tagline lies in the intersection between what you offer and why it matters to your audience. Write down a one-sentence answer to: "What does my brand really do for people?" or "Why does this business exist beyond making money?" This can give you raw material for your tagline.

2. **Brainstorm Freely (Again):** Just like with naming, start jotting down any short phrases or words that come to mind when you think about your business. Don't worry about making it perfect at first. List as many ideas as possible. You could try finishing prompts like:

   o "We help people ___."

   o "We believe ___."

   o "Our product/service is ___."

   Look at the keywords you wrote and see if any combinations form a compelling phrase. Sometimes a tagline might come directly from how you naturally describe your business to a friend (for example, if you often say, "It's like a personal trainer for your finances," that could spark a tagline like *"Your money's personal trainer."*).

3. **Keep It Simple and Genuine:** Once you have a list of rough ideas, start refining them. Edit out extra words. See how each option sounds out loud. Your tagline should feel natural to say and not overly grandiose (unless a bold tone fits your brand). It's okay if it's simple. Clarity is more important than sounding fancy.

4. **Inject Personality:** Is there a way to add a little personality to the phrase? This could be through a playful twist, a rhyme, or a powerful action verb. For instance, a travel agency's tagline could be *"Adventure awaits,"* which is short and evokes excitement. If your brand were a person, what catchphrase might it have? Ensure the personality aligns with what your customers find appealing and is consistent with your brand image.

5. **Test It Out:** Just like with your name, get some feedback on your top tagline options. Do people understand what you mean? Do they get a positive feeling from it? You can also ask yourself whether the tagline complements your name when used together. Say your brand name followed by the tagline. Do they flow well together as a single idea? They should feel connected, like two pieces of the same puzzle.

6. **Ensure Originality:** Run a quick check online to make sure your tagline isn't identical to an existing one in your field. It's possible to accidentally come up with a phrase that another company already uses. While a common phrase might not be legally protected, using a tagline that's famously associated with someone else can confuse your audience. Aim for something that clearly points to you.

Illustrative Example: Imagine a local café called Morning Bloom. The owner's mission is to brighten customers' days with friendly service and great coffee. A simple, yet uplifting tagline might be *"Fresh coffee, brighter days."* In just four words, it tells you what they provide (coffee that's fresh) and hints at a positive outcome (making your day better). It's clear, true to the café's identity, and speaks to the customer benefit.

Self-Reflection Prompt: Try writing three potential taglines for your brand. Don't overthink it. Just draft a few ideas that feel right to you. Say them aloud after your brand name, like "YourBrandName: ___." How do they make you feel? Do they get you excited about what you offer? Share them with a friend and see which one sticks in their mind.

Defining Your Brand Promise

Beyond your name and tagline, there's a deeper message you need to clarify: your brand promise. This is the core commitment or assurance that you, as a brand, make to your customers. It's what you promise to deliver consistently, every time someone interacts with your business. Your brand promise isn't usually a marketing slogan (though sometimes a tagline can reflect it); rather, it's a guiding idea that influences everything you do, from product quality and customer service to marketing and company culture.

Think of your brand promise as an internal compass. It keeps you and your team aligned with the experience you strive to create for your customers. When clearly defined, a brand promise helps you build trust and loyalty because customers learn over time that you *mean* what you say. It sets an expectation in their minds. Meeting or exceeding that expectation is how strong brands are built.

What a Brand Promise Looks Like

A brand promise can take a few forms. Sometimes it's a straightforward, explicit statement you share publicly (for example, a delivery company might state, "Your package on your doorstep in 24 hours, guaranteed"). At other times, it's more of an internal mantra that employees rally behind, which is indirectly reflected in marketing messages. Whether publicly stated or not, a brand promise has a few key characteristics:

- **Authentic and Rooted in Your Values:** Your promise must come from what truly matters to your company. It should tie directly to your core values or mission. If innovation is one of your core values, your brand promise may involve consistently delivering cutting-edge solutions to customers. If your focus is on customer care, your promise might center on providing friendly and attentive service. Make sure it accurately reflects your identity.

- **Relevant to Your Audience:** The promise should speak to a key desire or concern of your target customers. Think about what your audience really wants from you (reliable service, transparency, creativity, safety, etc.). Your brand promise is essentially telling them, "We know what you need, and we commit to providing that."

- **Clear and Consistent:** Like other brand messages, clarity is crucial. Your promise should be stated in simple terms, even if it's just something you articulate internally. Once defined, it should stay consistent. Your whole team should understand it the same way and be able to express it. Consistency also means you strive to uphold that promise in every product release, every customer interaction, and every piece of content.

- **Ambitious but Achievable:** A brand promise can be aspirational, but it shouldn't be unrealistic. You don't want to promise something you can't deliver reliably. For instance, promising "perfection every time" is very risky. Nobody is perfect every single time. It's better to promise something like, "If we ever fall short, we make it right," which shows commitment to high standards and honesty. Set a promise that inspires your team to excel and your customers to trust you, but make sure it's within your power to fulfill.

- **Measurable (to You):** While you don't always share metrics with customers, internally, you should be able to tell if you're keeping your promise. If your promise is fast service, define what "fast" means (e.g., responding to all inquiries within one hour, or shipping orders within one business day). This way, you can hold yourself accountable and maintain credibility.

Crafting Your Brand Promise

Creating a brand promise begins with introspection and a deep understanding of your customers. Here's how you can define your promise:

1. **Identify Your Customer's Key Expectation:** Consider what your ideal customer expects or needs most from a business like yours. If you run a daycare, parents likely expect safety and nurturing care above all else. If you have a tech gadget brand, maybe customers expect cutting-edge innovation and reliability. List the top one or two things that people absolutely count on you for.

2. **Look at Your Core Values and Mission:** Recall the fundamental principles that guide your business (perhaps you outlined these in an earlier chapter). Which of those values translates directly into something you can promise your customer? For example, if one of your core values is *community*, your promise might be to treat every

customer like family and to be actively involved in the local community.

3. **Formulate a Short Statement:** Write a simple sentence (or even a phrase) that encapsulates that commitment. It might be something like, "We promise to ___." Fill in the blank with your distinguishing commitment. For instance, "We promise to make luxury affordable," or "We promise to bring you [specific benefit] every time." Don't worry about making it fancy; the goal is to clearly capture the essence of what you will deliver consistently.

4. **Ensure It's True and Inspiring:** Examine your draft promise critically. Is this something you can really do every day? Would it excite your customers and your team? A good brand promise often has a bit of inspiration in it. It should remind everyone why your brand matters. If it sounds too bland or too lofty, tweak the language. Make it concrete and meaningful.

5. **Share and Internalize It:** Communicate your brand promise to your team (even if that's just you and a partner at first). Discuss what it means in practical terms. How will you uphold this promise in various situations? By talking it through, you'll reinforce its importance and ensure it's understood uniformly. The brand promise isn't meant to live only in a document. It should guide decisions daily.

6. **Infuse It Into Your Story:** While you might not plaster your brand promise on your homepage like a tagline, you should weave it into your brand story and messaging. For example, if your promise is "innovation in every experience," your advertisements, social media posts, and customer communications should consistently highlight new and creative aspects of what you do. Over time, customers will subconsciously recognize what your promise is because you'll demonstrate it consistently.

Remember: A brand promise is a two-way street. You're setting an expectation, and customers will give you their trust (and business) in return for you keeping that promise. If circumstances change or you find the promise isn't quite right, you can refine it, but do so carefully. Changing a brand promise too often can confuse your audience. It's better to commit thoughtfully from the start, knowing this is a long-term pledge.

Reflection Prompt: Ask yourself, "What is the one thing I want every customer to say about our business after they've interacted with us?" Is it that you were the fastest, the friendliest, the most reliable, the most creative? That one thing is a key indicator of your brand promise. Write it down in a sentence or two. Does it excite you and align with your vision? If yes, you've likely found a strong basis for your brand promise. If not, keep refining until it clicks.

Aligning Name, Tagline, and Promise with Your Identity

By now, you have the three key pieces of your brand's verbal identity: a name that captures attention, a tagline that adds meaning, and a promise that guides your every action. The final step is to ensure that all these pieces work together in harmony and truly reflect your brand identity.

Think of your name, tagline, and brand promise as a trio that should sing the same tune. When they align well, they reinforce each other and create a clear, cohesive picture of who you are.

- **Consistency is Key:** Review each element side by side. Do they all convey a similar tone and attitude? For example, if your brand identity is all about youthful energy, a lively name paired with an inspiring tagline and a promise centered on excitement will feel consistent. However, if you have a playful name but a very formal tagline, it might seem mismatched. Strive for consistency in style and tone so that nothing feels out of place.

- **Unified Story:** Your name might spark curiosity, your tagline might explain a key benefit, and your promise underpins the value. Together, they should tell a mini-story of your brand. There shouldn't be any contradiction among them. If your name is abstract, perhaps your tagline provides clarity. If your tagline is emotive, your brand promise should reinforce that emotion with real action. Check that when someone hears your name and tagline, or reads about your brand, the overall message matches the experience you intend to deliver.

- **Aligned with Your Audience:** Consider your target audience one more time. Are these elements effectively speaking to that audience? If you're targeting busy young professionals, is your name or tagline appealing and relevant to them? If you're targeting families, do your choices feel welcoming and trustworthy? Consider getting feedback from a few people in your target audience on your name and tagline combination. Their reactions will tell you if you're hitting the right note.

- **Flexibility for Growth:** Ensure that, as a set, your name, tagline, and promise don't unintentionally limit you. For instance, you wouldn't want a tagline that's so specific it boxes you into one product if you plan to expand. Likewise, your brand promise should be broad enough to guide the brand even as you add new services, yet specific enough to mean something real. It's a balance. Keep your core message broad in scope but strong in impact.

Illustrative Example: Suppose your brand identity is all about simplicity and peace of mind in financial planning. You might choose the name "ClearPath Finance." A complementary tagline could be *"Guiding you to financial peace."* Your brand promise might be, "We promise to make managing your finances simple and stress-free." Notice how each element supports the others. The name *ClearPath* suggests transparency and direction, the tagline speaks directly to the benefit (peace of mind), and the promise commits to an experience (simplicity and no stress). Together, they present a cohesive identity centered on clarity and calm confidence.

When you achieve this kind of alignment, your branding becomes much stronger. Customers will hear your name, see your tagline, experience your service, and it will all feel connected. That consistency builds trust. People love it when a brand delivers on exactly what it says it will.

Bringing It All Together

Choosing your business name, tagline, and brand promise is a milestone in your brand building journey. It's the moment your brand's identity takes a more concrete form in the minds of your audience. Take pride in the creativity and thought you've put into this process. By selecting a clear and memorable name, crafting a tagline that resonates, and committing to a genuine brand promise, you have built a strong foundation for how your brand will be perceived.

As you move forward:

- **Use Them Everywhere:** Start incorporating your name and tagline across your website, social media profiles, business cards, packaging, and any marketing materials. Repetition will make them stick in people's minds. Ensure your brand promise, while not always explicitly stated, is evident in how you run your business and communicate with customers.

- **Deliver on Your Promise:** Every day, let your brand promise guide your actions. It should be the standard you hold yourself to. Over time, as customers see you living up to your word, your brand's reputation will grow in a positive way.

- **Stay Open to Refinement:** While you want to remain consistent, it's okay to refine your tagline or adjust messaging as you learn what resonates most with your audience. Some brands even tweak their names early on if they find something isn't clicking. If you do make changes, ensure they still align with your core identity. Any adjustments should strengthen, not dilute, your brand message.

- **Stay Motivated:** Remember why you chose this name and what your tagline and promise represent. They're born from your passion and vision. If you ever feel stuck or face challenges, come back to these core brand elements. They can re-inspire you and keep you focused on the big picture.

Building a brand is a blend of heart and strategy. You've got the heart (your identity and values) and the strategy (your name, tagline, and promise). Now, carry them forward with confidence. Every time someone hears your brand name or reads your tagline, they'll get a sense of who you are and what you stand for. Make it count, and enjoy the process of watching your brand come to life!

CHAPTER 6: GIVE YOUR BRAND A LOOK

Why Your Brand's Look Matters

Your brand's visual identity is how people recognize you at a glance. Even before someone reads your tagline or visits your website, your look (a combination of logo, color palette, and style) sends a powerful first signal. It's a shortcut for what you stand for and how you want customers to feel. A great visual identity can make you seem more trustworthy, established, or approachable, even if you're just starting out.

You don't have to be a designer to make strong choices. You do, however, need to be intentional and consistent. A homemade logo is fine at the start, but what matters most is that your colors, fonts, and overall style align with your personality and the feeling you want your business to give. The good news? Anyone can start this process with a little bit of creativity, a willingness to learn, and an understanding that it's okay to evolve and upgrade your look later.

The Essentials of Logo Design

A logo is the face of your brand. It's the visual symbol that customers will connect with your business. Think of famous logos: the apple with a bite, the golden arches, the simple swoosh. You don't need to copy them, but you can learn from what makes them work.

What Makes a Logo Work

- **Simplicity:** The best logos are simple and easy to understand at a glance. This means clean shapes, limited detail, and just one or two main ideas. A logo should be recognizable, whether it's tiny on a business card or large on a banner.

- **Memorability:** Your logo should be easy to remember. Unique symbols, clever uses of space, or even an interesting font can help you stand out. A great logo is something people could draw from memory.

- **Relevance:** The style and imagery in your logo should fit your business. For example, a children's party planner might use bright colors and playful shapes. An accounting firm might choose a solid, trustworthy font and a simple monogram. Let the design "feel" like your brand.

- **Versatility:** A strong logo works well in both color and black and white, and looks great on social media, packaging, invoices, or even a t-shirt. It should be clear in all sizes. Ask yourself: if my logo were printed as a tiny icon, would it still be recognizable?

- **Originality:** Try to avoid logos that look like everyone else in your industry. Browse local competitors or businesses online and make sure you're not too similar. Being different (even in a small way) helps you get remembered.

DIY or Designer?

If you're on a budget, it's okay to use online tools like Canva, Looka, or Wix Logo Maker to create a simple logo. You can choose shapes, fonts, and colors to get something that works. But remember: most DIY logos tend to look generic or "template-y," and might not be unique enough for long-term success.

Here's the bottom line: a DIY logo is a short-term solution. It's great for getting started and feeling official. However, as soon as your business grows or you have the resources, invest in a professional designer. A pro will create something unique to you, provide the right file formats, and help you build a truly memorable look. Plus, a professional can help you avoid legal headaches, ensure your logo is original, and future-proof your brand for expansion or trademarking.

Don't let the fear of not having a perfect logo stop you from launching your business. You can always improve your design later, but it's better to get out there and start connecting with customers. Please note that if you change your look down the road, you'll need to update all your materials, and it might take time for customers to adjust. That's normal and happens to brands of all sizes. Focus on consistency and clarity first. Perfection can come with growth.

Choosing Your Brand Colors

Color is a shortcut to emotion. Before a customer reads a word of your website, they'll feel something based on your color palette. That's why picking the right colors is more than an aesthetic choice. It's a branding decision.

The Psychology of Color

- **Red:** Excitement, energy, urgency. Red is bold and grabs attention, often used for sales, food, or entertainment.

- **Blue:** Trust, calm, professionalism. Blue is popular in finance, technology, and healthcare.

- **Green:** Growth, health, nature, eco-friendliness. Green works well for wellness, sustainability, and food brands.

- **Yellow:** Cheerfulness, optimism, warmth. Yellow feels friendly and approachable. It's great for brands that want to seem positive or fun.

- **Purple:** Creativity, luxury, wisdom. Purple is often used for beauty or premium brands.

- **Black/Gray:** Sophistication, authority, simplicity. These are used in luxury or serious brands, or to create a clean, minimal look.

- **Orange:** Adventure, energy, friendliness. Orange can feel youthful and dynamic.

Building Your Color Palette

- **Pick a primary color:** This is the main color associated with your brand.

- **Choose 1–2 secondary colors:** These can complement the primary color or add energy to the design.

- **Add a neutral:** White, black, or gray to balance the palette and help text stand out.

For example, a natural skincare brand might choose soft green as its primary color, warm beige as a secondary, and white as a neutral. A tech startup might use bright blue as the primary color, silver-gray as the secondary color, and black for contrast.

Pro Tip: You don't need to use a rainbow. Most iconic brands use just two or three colors. Too many can make your brand feel scattered and unprofessional.

Consistency Is Key

Once you've chosen your colors, use them consistently throughout your website, logo, packaging, signage, and even social media posts. This helps customers instantly recognize your business across all platforms.

Fonts, Icons, and the Rest of Your Visual Toolkit

Fonts: The style of your text says a lot about your brand. A modern sans-serif font (e.g., Arial, Helvetica, or Montserrat) feels clean and professional. Serif fonts (e.g., Times New Roman, Georgia, or Playfair Display) can appear classic, elegant, or trustworthy. A hand-drawn or script font might give a creative or playful vibe. Limit yourself to one or two fonts for your brand to maintain consistency and readability. Ensure your main font remains clear, even at small sizes.

Icons & Imagery: Think about other visual elements you might use, including patterns, graphic shapes, or simple icons. For example, a gardening business might use leaf icons, or a bakery might use a whisk or cupcake silhouette. These little touches help reinforce your brand's personality. Avoid generic clipart if possible. Unique touches are more memorable.

Photo Style: If you use photographs in your branding, decide on a style. Are your photos bright and candid, or moody and artistic? Are people front and center, or do you focus on products? Try to maintain a consistent style, even when taking photos with your phone.

DIY vs. Professional Design – Pros, Cons, and When to Level Up

DIY Design
Pros:

- Affordable or free (just your time and maybe a small fee for a tool).

- Fast. You can get started today and feel official.

- Gives you complete control if you already have a clear vision.

Cons:

- Likely to look generic or similar to others using the same templates.

- Might not have the right file types or scalability for future needs.

- May not fully reflect your unique brand personality.

Professional Design

Pros:

- Custom, original artwork that sets you apart.

- You get the right file formats for all uses (web, print, signage, etc.).

- Professional insight into color, type, and how everything fits together.

- Makes it easier to trademark and protect your brand.

Cons:

- Higher up-front cost (anywhere from a few hundred to several thousand dollars).

- May take longer, as designers need time to understand your brand and present concepts.

- You'll need to communicate your vision clearly to get the best result.

Many successful brands started with something simple, then later upgraded. You are *not* behind if you use a DIY logo to launch. Focus first on building a business customers love and as you grow, plan for a visual refresh. Just keep in mind that when you update your design, it can cause some confusion (such as with old materials, an updated website, or customer recognition), but it's a normal part of building a real brand.

Example Visual Journeys

- **A local coffee shop:** Starts with a simple brown coffee cup logo created with an online tool, using warm brown and cream as the brand colors. After two years and lots of regulars, they hire a designer who creates a hand-drawn cup with steam that forms a heart, modernizes the color scheme, and refreshes the font. The new look feels much more personal and unique, but regulars still recognize it as the same friendly place.

- **A tech startup:** Launches with a blue-and-gray wordmark (just the business name in a bold, clean font) created on Canva. A year later, as funding allows, they work with a pro designer to create an abstract symbol that represents "connection" and update the color palette for digital accessibility. The old blue lives on as an accent; everything else is now crisper and more recognizable.

- **A handmade jewelry brand:** Begins with a pink script logo designed by a friend. Over time, as their audience grows, they invest in a designer who refines the logo to make it readable at small sizes and expands the palette to include soft gold and white, echoing the materials used in the jewelry.

Reflection Prompts and Checklist

Prompts:

- What 2–3 words describe the feeling you want your brand visuals to give? (Friendly, modern, natural, bold, etc.)

- What colors, shapes, or images come to mind when you picture your brand?

- Does your logo idea look clear and readable in black and white, as well as in color?

- If you could only use two colors to represent your business, what would they be and why?

- How do your chosen fonts and icons make you feel? Do they fit your brand's personality?

Checklist:

- ☐ I have chosen a primary color and 1–2 secondary or neutral colors.

- ☐ My logo is simple, clear, and works in different sizes.

- ☐ I have selected 1–2 main fonts that match my brand's vibe.

- ☐ My visual style is consistent across my website, business cards, and social media.

- ☐ I am currently using a DIY logo or design, but I plan to upgrade to professional help when I can.

- ☐ I understand that updating my design later may require changes everywhere, but that's part of growing a real brand.

- ☐ I've asked a friend or potential customer for their honest impression of my brand's look.

Your Visual Brand is a Work in Progress

No brand look is "final" on day one. The most important thing is to start with visuals that feel authentic to you and consistently reflect your brand's personality across every touchpoint. Your logo and colors are the uniform your brand wears to the world. As your business grows, so will your resources and your understanding of what visuals truly fit you. Give yourself permission to start simple and level up when you're able.

Remember: it's more important to be clear and consistent now than to have a perfect logo. The right look will evolve as you do. Focus on building your brand's foundation, knowing you can constantly refine your design as your business and your budget grow. Your visuals are just one way your brand tells its story. Make them count, and don't let perfectionism keep you from sharing your business with the world.

CHAPTER 7: FIND YOUR VOICE

What It Means to "Find Your Voice"

Have you ever read something you wrote and thought, *"Does this even sound like me?"* Perhaps you've drafted a work email or given a presentation and felt like you were putting on an act. If so, you're not alone. Many people struggle with using a voice in communication that doesn't truly reflect who they are.

Finding your voice means identifying and embracing the unique style, tone, and personality that are authentically yours in every form of communication. In essence, your *voice* is the "you" behind your words, the distinctive way you express your thoughts and values. It's not just about using correct grammar or a certain level of formality. It's about letting your genuine self shine through, whether you're writing an email, posting on social media, or speaking to an audience. When your communication has the same heart and character as you do in person, you've found your authentic voice.

Why do so many of us lose our voice when we communicate? Often, it's because we believe we have to sound a certain way to be taken seriously. We might slip into overly formal language, corporate jargon, or someone else's style, thinking it makes us appear more professional or intelligent. The result? Our messages end up sounding stiff, generic, or insincere. The disconnect between our true selves and our communication can leave both us and our audience feeling that something is off.

Why Sounding Like "You" Matters

Speaking and writing in your authentic voice isn't just about feeling good. It has real benefits for your relationships and effectiveness. When you sound like *you* in every message, people can sense your sincerity, and that builds trust. Colleagues, clients, and friends are more likely to connect with and believe someone who communicates in a genuine way, rather than someone who sounds like they're reading from a script or hiding behind big words.

Consistency is another key advantage. In today's world, we interact through many channels: face-to-face conversations, video calls, emails, texts, and more. If each of those interactions feels like it's coming from a different person, it creates confusion. However, if your tone and character remain consistent (if an email from you carries the same warmth or humor as when you speak), people perceive you as a coherent and trustworthy individual.

Consistency in voice strengthens your personal brand and helps others know what to expect from you, whether they're reading your report or listening to you in a meeting.

Sounding like yourself also helps you stand out. In environments where everyone is using the same dull clichés or "corporate speak," an authentic voice is refreshing. It cuts through the noise. Your unique perspective and way of expressing ideas become an asset, making your messages more memorable. Instead of blending in with cookie-cutter communications, you highlight what makes you (or your organization) different.

There's an internal benefit too. Using your real voice is empowering. It takes effort to constantly filter and alter your natural way of communicating. When you drop the act and speak from the heart, you feel more confident and comfortable. You don't have to worry about "slipping up" and revealing your true self. You're already using it! This confidence allows you to focus on *what* you're saying, not just *how* you're saying it. In turn, that confidence makes your delivery more convincing and enjoyable for both you and your audience.

In short, sounding like "you" in every message makes you more credible, more relatable, and more effective. It creates a genuine connection with your audience and saves you from the burnout of maintaining a façade. Now, let's explore how to ensure your authentic voice comes through clearly in both written and spoken communication.

Sounding Like You in Writing

Written communication often poses a challenge: without the benefit of tone of voice or body language, our words carry all the weight. Many people default to a stiffer or overly formal style in writing, which can strip away their personality. The goal is to make your reader *hear* you through the text. Here are some strategies to ensure your writing sounds authentic to you:

- **Write like you talk:** Imagine you're explaining something to a friend or colleague in person, and write *that* way. Use natural language and phrases you would actually say. This doesn't mean abandoning professionalism; it means conveying information in a conversational, human tone. If you tend to use a touch of humor or warmth when speaking, it's okay to let that show in your writing (when appropriate to the context).

- **Avoid overly formal language and jargon:** Let go of the idea that every email or document needs to sound like a legal brief. Using unnecessarily complex words or buzzwords can make your writing sound not like you, and sometimes not even understandable. For example, instead of "Utilizing the aforementioned resources will optimize our outcomes," you might say, "Using these resources will help us get better results." It's still professional, but far more *you* (and also clearer!).

- **Use personal pronouns and warmth:** Don't be afraid to say "I" and "you" in your messages when it's appropriate. Addressing your reader directly creates a connection and makes your writing feel like a dialogue rather than a lecture. Similarly, using a friendly tone, like saying "Hi everyone," instead of diving straight into a dry update, can make your written voice more genuine and approachable.

- **Read it aloud to test it:** One of the best ways to check if your writing sounds like you is to literally read it out loud. As you listen, ask yourself, "Would I actually say it that way?" If you stumble over a sentence or cringe at a pretentious phrase, that's a clue it might be too stiff or unnatural. Reading your words aloud helps you catch awkward wording and adjust the tone. You might find yourself naturally rephrasing something as you speak. Go ahead and edit your text to match that more comfortable phrasing.

- **Maintain a consistent tone (with context in mind):** Strive for a tone in writing that reflects your personality. If you're usually upbeat and positive, let that friendliness shine through. If you're more straightforward and no-nonsense, embrace that. At the same time, adapt to the context without becoming a whole different person. A serious project update or a note to a client might be a bit more formal than a text to a close teammate, but in both cases, you can still be *you*. Consistency doesn't mean using the exact same words in every situation; it means the overall feel of *you* is present in every message. People should be able to recognize "your touch" in what you write.

Sounding Like You When Speaking

Speaking in front of others, whether in meetings, presentations, or even on the phone, can be intimidating. It's easy to slip into a "performance" mode that doesn't feel genuine (like using a stiff, rehearsed tone or mimicking a speaker you admire). The key to spoken communication is to present the best version of yourself, not an imitation of someone else. Here are ways to keep your voice authentic when you talk:

- **Make it a conversation, not a recital:** If you have a script or prepared text, avoid reading it word-for-word unless absolutely necessary. Reading directly often makes you sound robotic or disconnected. Instead, aim to speak *to* your audience, not *at* them. Picture that you're simply talking with your listeners. This mindset enables you to adopt a more natural tone and pace, as if you were engaging in a one-on-one conversation rather than delivering a formal monologue.

- **Practice until you're comfortable:** Preparation gives you the confidence to be yourself. If you're giving a presentation or speech, know your material well enough that you don't have to cling to your notes. Practice out loud multiple times. When you are familiar with what you want to say, you can focus on connecting with the audience rather than scrambling for words. This kind of preparation *frees* you to ad-lib a little or adapt to the moment, which makes your speaking style more relaxed and authentic.

- **Be yourself, even "on stage":** In live situations, let your personality come through. Speak in your natural tone of voice. Don't force an imitation of someone else's style. If you're energetic and enthusiastic by nature, allow that energy to show in your voice and gestures. If you're more calm and thoughtful, embrace that. You can be quietly compelling without pretending to be outgoing if that's not you. Authenticity doesn't mean being loud or flashy; it means being *aligned* with who you are. Audiences appreciate speakers who are genuine and comfortable in their own skin.

- **Use breathing to stay grounded:** Nervousness can make anyone's voice shaky or cause you to race through your words. To sound like yourself, you need to manage those nerves. A simple but powerful tool is mindful breathing. Take a deep breath before you begin talking, and remember to breathe during pauses. Proper breathing not only calms your mind and body, but it also gives your voice strength and clarity. When you breathe fully, you support your voice (no more trailing off or running out of air) and you slow down just enough to choose words naturally. This leads to a steadier, more confident sound, the sound of *you* at your best, rather than you under stress.

- **Embrace imperfection and connection:** Remember, you don't have to be a "perfect" speaker to be an effective one. If you stumble on a word or lose your train of thought for a moment, it's okay. Instead of panicking, take a brief pause and a breath, then continue. You can even acknowledge a slip with a quick, lighthearted comment if it feels right. It humanizes you. Audiences usually won't mind a small mistake; in fact, they often find it relatable. What people remember is how you made them feel and whether they felt connected to you and your message. When you're not obsessing over every detail, you can focus on genuinely engaging with your audience. Authentic engagement matters far more than delivering a perfect, yet sterile, performance.

Discovering and Developing Your Voice

Your authentic voice is already within you. However, incorporating it into all your communications requires a conscious effort. Here are some steps to help you discover and refine your voice:

1. **Know yourself and your values:** Take a moment to consider what you stand for and how you want to come across. Think of a few adjectives that describe your personality or style (perhaps *friendly*, *direct*, *humorous*, or *empathetic*, whatever feels true to you). These qualities are the core of your voice. When you know who you are and what traits you want to convey, it's easier to let that guide your tone and word choice.

2. **Listen to your natural speech:** Pay attention to how you sound in unguarded moments. You might even record yourself in a casual conversation (with permission, if others are involved) or record a voice note while discussing an idea you're passionate about. When you play it back, note the phrases, pace, and energy in your voice. What words do you use? Do you inject humor, ask questions, speak energetically, or calmly? This exercise can reveal the *unfiltered* you. Those elements you notice (your genuine humor, warmth, clarity, etc.) are things to consciously infuse into your more structured communications.

3. **Align your writing with your speaking:** Try a simple experiment. Pick an idea and *say* it out loud first, as if explaining to someone, then write down what you just said. Notice how the spoken version might differ from how you'd usually write it. Alternatively, take something you've written (like a paragraph from a report or an email) and read it aloud. Does it sound like something you'd say? If not, tweak the wording until it feels more natural. Practicing this back-and-forth approach (writing as you speak and speaking as you write) will help you unify your voice across various media.

4. **Practice in low-stakes situations:** Strengthen your authentic voice in everyday communication. For instance, try incorporating a bit of your natural humor or warmth into a team email where it's appropriate, or be more candid (yet polite) when sharing your opinion in a casual meeting. Pay attention to the response. You'll likely find that people respond well to authenticity. These smaller, low-pressure situations are perfect for building confidence. Over time, you can extend the same authenticity to higher-stakes communications because you'll have proof that *being you* works.

5. **Learn from voices you admire (but don't copy):** Think of a speaker or writer whose style you enjoy. What about their voice appeals to you? Perhaps it's their clarity, storytelling, or approachable tone. Identify those aspects and see how you might incorporate similar principles into your own communication. For example, if you love how a certain leader uses personal stories in their speeches to make points, you could try adding a relevant anecdote when you present data to your team. The idea isn't to mimic someone else's personality. It's to expand your toolkit by learning from effective communicators. You're still *you*, just a continually improving version.

6. **Be patient and stay authentic:** Finding and refining your voice is a journey. You may find that as you gain experience, your voice evolves. That's natural. The key is to ensure it's evolving in a way that still feels true to you, not turning into someone else's voice. Periodically take stock. Do you feel genuine in your recent communications? If you find yourself slipping into a false persona (perhaps due to a new job or outside influence), revisit these steps. And remember, every time you choose to communicate authentically, you reinforce a habit. Over time, using your authentic voice will become second nature.

By taking these steps, you'll gradually develop a voice that is confident, consistent, and unmistakably yours. The better you understand who you are and how you express yourself, the more powerful your communication will be. People will come to recognize and trust the *real* you, and that is a tremendous asset in both personal and professional life.

Reflection Prompts

- **Message Makeover:** Think of a recent work email or message you sent that felt *off* or overly stiff for your style. Now, rewrite it as if you were saying it to the person face-to-face, using a more natural tone. What differences do you notice between the original version and your rewrite?

- **Define Your Voice:** List three words that describe how you ideally want to sound (for example, *warm, confident, clear*). Now consider: does the way you currently write and speak show those qualities? Note one change you could make to bring your communication closer to your ideal voice (if you want to be "warm," maybe add a friendly greeting or a personal touch in your emails).

- **Get Outside Feedback:** Ask a trusted friend or colleague to describe the tone or style of your emails and conversations. Do they use words that match the voice you *want* to project? If not, discuss with them one or two things you might do differently so that your intended voice comes across.

- **Plan and Reflect:** Think about a communication you have coming up soon (perhaps a meeting, presentation, or important email). Plan two specific ways to infuse it with your authentic voice. For example, include a brief personal story in that presentation, or read your email draft aloud to check that it sounds like you. After it's over, reflect on how it went. Did you feel more "yourself" while communicating, and how did others respond?

Take a moment to reflect on these points. They will help you become more aware of your communication habits and give you practice in aligning *what you say* with *who you truly are*. With each conversation you have and each message you send in your authentic voice, you reinforce the habit of genuine communication. Over time, you'll find that sounding like **you** isn't something you have to try to do. It's just what happens naturally when you speak or write, and that is exactly how it should be.

CHAPTER 8: MAKE IT OFFICIAL

Starting a business involves more than a great idea and a catchy name. It requires making things official. In this chapter, we'll cover how to establish your business's professional presence and legal foundation. From securing your domain name and setting up a professional email address, to choosing the proper business structure, obtaining necessary tax IDs, and opening a business bank account, these steps will legitimize your venture and protect you in the long run. Taking the time to get these basics right will build credibility with customers and partners and set you up for future growth.

Securing Your Domain Name

Securing a domain name ensures you stake your claim to your business's address on the web. Your domain name (e.g., yourbusiness.com) is the online identity of your company. It's the address customers will type in to reach your website, and it will likely appear in your email address as well. An essential early step is to register a domain name that matches your business name or brand so that your website and email clearly identify your business. This consistency helps customers easily find you and recognize your brand online.

Choosing a good domain: Ideally, pick a domain that is simple, memorable, and related to your business name. Most businesses opt for a ".com" domain if available, as it's widely recognized. However, many other top-level domains (TLDs), such as ".net" and ".org", or country-specific TLDs (like ".co.uk" for the UK), are also viable options. If your first choice is taken, consider slight variations, but avoid confusing or very long names. It's also wise to check that the domain (or something very similar) isn't trademarked by someone else to avoid legal issues down the line.

Registering your domain: Domains are obtained through domain registrars, which are services that let you search for available names and purchase them. You usually pay an annual fee to keep the domain registered in your name. There are many reputable registrars. Each registrar offers similar core services, so you can compare prices and features (like email, security, or privacy options) before choosing. The registration process is straightforward: you search for your desired name, add it to the cart, and provide your contact and payment information.

Provide accurate information (and protect it): When registering a domain, you are required to provide accurate contact details (name, address, email, and phone number) to the registrar. This information is passed to ICANN (the global domain authority) and often published in the public WHOIS database. That means if you use your personal home address or phone number, it could become publicly visible as the domain registrant. Fortunately, most registrars offer WHOIS privacy protection, either included or for a small fee, which replaces your info with a proxy contact to shield your personal details. It's highly recommended to use a privacy service or a business address when registering to keep your sensitive information off the public record.

If you've already set up a formal business entity (like an LLC or company), you can even register the domain under the business's name. Listing your LLC or company as the domain owner is both legal and smart. It keeps the domain as a business asset and maintains a clear separation between personal and professional assets. In other words, the domain becomes part of your company. This can offer you additional privacy (your personal name isn't front-and-center in a WHOIS lookup) and reinforces that the website and email belong to the business rather than you individually.

Where to buy your domain: To keep things unbiased, here's a quick list of a few well-known domain registrars (not an endorsement, just examples): Namecheap, GoDaddy, 101domain, IONOS (1&1), Squarespace Domains, Dynadot, Porkbun, Name.com, Network Solutions, SiteGround, Bluehost, and DreamHost. Some providers offer a free domain when you purchase website hosting with them. When you register, you'll typically be offered additional add-ons, such as an SSL certificate or email service. You can choose what you need, and many of these can also be added later. The key outcome here is that you own your domain name and have official control of that piece of online real estate.

Setting Up a Professional Email Address

In today's world, email is a primary communication channel for businesses, so it's essential to have a professional-looking email address. This usually means using your new domain name in your email (for example, info@yourcompany.com) instead of a generic address, such as Gmail or Yahoo. A custom business email isn't just about appearances. It's a simple but powerful way to build trust with customers and partners. It shows that you've invested in your business identity, instantly signaling that you mean business and aren't just running a hobby or scam. In fact, sending business emails from a personal address can send the wrong message; it might appear that you haven't fully "set up shop" or aren't serious enough to establish proper communications.

Why not just use my personal email? Consider how an email looks to a customer: an invoice coming from coolgirl88@gmail.com or billing@yourbusiness.com. Which one seems more legitimate? Using a personal email for business can undermine confidence. Here are some key reasons to avoid using personal email and get a professional address:

- **Professionalism & Trust:** Customers may doubt the legitimacy of an email that isn't from an official business domain. Using a personal @gmail.com or @yahoo.com email address can look unprofessional. It might even lead people to suspect your business is not established or worry that it's a scam. Moreover, marketing or mass emails sent from personal accounts are often filtered into spam folders, so your message may not even reach the recipient's inbox. A company-branded email shows you take your business seriously.

- **Security:** Business email services typically provide stronger security measures than a free personal email. They offer features such as two-factor authentication, advanced encryption, and administrative tools to enforce strong passwords. Personal email accounts are more vulnerable. For example, they often have simple security questions that hackers can guess. When you're dealing with client data or confidential info, you want the extra security layers. A secure business email helps protect sensitive information about your customers, vendors, and operations.

- **Control & Ownership:** If you ever grow to have employees or partners, using personal emails can create messy situations. You have no control over a personal account if an employee (or co-founder) leaves the company. They could walk away with business contacts and emails, or even continue representing themselves as your company without authorization. With official business email accounts (under your domain), the company owns the addresses. You can create accounts for new team members and shut them down when someone leaves, ensuring all communications stay within your control. Consistent "info@yourcompany.com" style addresses also reinforce your brand identity with every message sent.

- **Compliance Requirements:** In certain industries, using proper business email isn't just good practice. It might be legally required. For instance, companies handling health information (subject to HIPAA in the U.S.) must take precautions with email, and it's nearly impossible to meet those security and archiving standards on a personal account. Even outside of healthcare, many businesses need to retain communication records (e.g., HR communications, financial advisors, legal services). Business email solutions often provide archiving and compliance features to meet these requirements. In short, if you're dealing with any regulated information, a secure business email is a must.

How to get a professional email: The good news is that setting up a custom domain email is straightforward once you have your domain. Essentially, you have two main routes:

1. **Use an Email Hosting Service:** Services like Google Workspace (Gmail for business) or Microsoft 365 (Outlook for business) are popular, offering robust email hosting on your domain along with additional tools (calendars, cloud storage, etc.). You sign up with the provider, verify you own the domain, and then you can create addresses like info@yourcompany.com. These services are paid (usually on a per-user-per-month basis), but they are reliable and come with numerous features and support. There are also others to consider: Zoho Mail, for example, offers a free plan for up to five users on your own domain, which is a great entry point for small teams or solo entrepreneurs. Proton Mail has business plans that emphasize security and encryption. Shop around for the service that fits your budget and needs. Many have free trials, and all major providers support custom domains.

2. **Use Your Web Hosting or Registrar's Email Feature:** If you've purchased web hosting for your site, your hosting provider often includes a number of custom email accounts as part of the package. Similarly, some domain registrars offer basic email forwarding or mailboxes. For example, IONOS includes a free email account for the first year with the purchase of a domain. These can be cost-effective, especially in the early stages. The trade-off is that the interfaces and features may be more basic compared to those of Gmail or Outlook, and you'll need to configure email clients or webmail. Still, for a small startup budget, it's perfectly fine to start

here. You can always migrate to a more advanced service later as your needs grow.

Whichever route you choose, you'll typically need to tweak your domain's DNS settings (adding MX records, which any good provider will guide you through) to direct email for your domain to the correct service. Once set up, you can send and receive messages from your professional address, and even configure it on your phone or email apps.

Pro Tip: Set up your business email early, ideally before you start corresponding with customers. That way, you won't have to transition people from an old personal address to a new one. Even if you're not fully operational, you can begin using your professional email for all business communications (and it will be ready to put on your business cards, website, and social media profiles). This provides a consistent, professional image for all interactions from day one.

Establishing Your Business Structure and Legal Basics

With your online identity secured, it's time to formalize your business structure, which is essentially choosing how your business will be legally organized. The structure you choose will influence many aspects of your operations: how you pay taxes, how much personal risk you face, how easy it is to raise money, and what paperwork or compliance requirements you'll deal with. Getting this right is essential for protecting yourself legally and financially. In this section, we'll discuss common business structures, obtaining tax IDs like an Employer Identification Number (EIN), and why separating your business finances (e.g., a dedicated bank account) is crucial.

Common business structures: Every country has its own laws and terminology, but most share similar basic types of business entities. Below are a few of the most common structures, with a U.S. perspective (note that other countries have equivalents; examples will be provided). It's a good idea to research the structures available in your country and their respective requirements, or consult a legal professional if you're unsure.

- **Sole Proprietorship:** This is the simplest form of business. If you start doing business on your own under your own name (and don't formally register as any other entity), you're by default a sole proprietor. There's minimal paperwork to start and often no special registration at the federal level, though you may need a local business license. However, a sole proprietorship is not a separate legal entity from you. This means all business assets and liabilities are merged with your personal assets and liabilities. You receive all the profits, but you are also personally responsible for any debts or legal actions against the business. For example, if the business can't pay a bill or loses a lawsuit, your personal funds and property can be used to settle it. This unlimited personal liability is the biggest downside. Sole proprietorships can work well for low-risk, one-person businesses or for testing an idea, but as you grow, you might consider forming a more formal entity for protection. (Outside the US, similar concepts exist: e.g., in the UK this is called a sole trader, and it functions very similarly in terms of liability and tax.) If you do use a name other than your own (e.g., "Sunshine Designs" instead of "Alice Smith"), most places require you to file a DBA (Doing Business As) or trade name registration so the owners of the business name are on record.

- **Partnership:** If you're starting a business with one or more partners (co-owners), a partnership is the basic form of a joint business. In a general partnership, all partners typically share in managing the company and are personally liable for business debts (again, not a separate entity from the owners by default). There are also variants, such as Limited Partnership (LP) and Limited Liability Partnership (LLP), that tweak this formula. In an LP, there is at least one general partner with unlimited liability and active management, and other limited partners who invest money but have limited liability (and typically less control). In an LLP, often used by certain professionals (lawyers, accountants), every partner has limited liability, protecting each partner from debts or legal issues caused by the other partners. Partnerships require trust and clear agreements. It's wise to have a written partnership agreement that covers how decisions are made and how profits and losses are split. Many small multi-founder businesses start as partnerships (or LLCs with a partnership tax classification) before perhaps evolving into a corporation.

- **Limited Liability Company (LLC):** An LLC is a very popular structure for small businesses in the US, because it offers a middle ground between a corporation and a sole proprietorship/partnership. The key advantage of an LLC is right in the name: limited liability. The LLC is a separate legal entity from its owners (who are called members). This means that, in most cases, if the business incurs debts or is sued, the owners' personal assets (such as their house, car, and personal savings) are protected. Creditors can only go after what the LLC owns, not the owners' personal belongings. (There are exceptions if an owner personally guarantees a loan, or in cases of fraud or not following legal formalities, but generally, the "corporate veil" protects you.) In essence, an LLC separates your personal life from your business life. LLCs also offer flexibility: they are easier to set up and run than a full corporation (less paperwork and formality, no need for a board of directors or shareholder meetings), and you can choose how you want to be taxed (many LLCs default to "pass-through" taxation, meaning the business profits are reported on the owners' personal tax returns, avoiding the double-taxation issue of C-Corps). Single-member LLCs and multi-member LLCs are possible. In short, an LLC can give you the liability protection of a corporation with the simplicity and tax advantages of a partnership. It's an excellent choice for many small businesses in the U.S. For example, if you run an online store or a freelance consultancy, forming an LLC can protect your personal assets in the event of a business-related issue. Internationally, the concept of an LLC (an entity that provides owners with limited liability without a full corporate structure) exists under different names. In the UK, an LTD (private limited company) is the closest equivalent and is indeed the most common small business structure there. It similarly protects owners' personal assets up to the value of their investment in the company. Many other countries have their own versions of limited companies or partnerships. Make sure to research the options in your jurisdiction.

- **Corporation (Inc./Ltd.):** A corporation is the most formal (and usually complex) type of business entity. It is a completely independent legal entity owned by shareholders. A corporation can enter into contracts, own assets, incur debt, sue, and be sued, all of which are separate from its owners. As a result, it provides the strongest personal liability protection to its owners (shareholders). Generally, they can't be held personally responsible for corporate debts or lawsuits beyond their stock investment. That benefit comes at a cost: corporations are more expensive and complicated to establish and operate. They require adhering to more regulations and formalities (like creating bylaws, issuing stock, holding regular board meetings, keeping minutes, filing annual reports, etc.). Corporations are also subject to separate business taxes. In the US, a standard "C Corp" pays corporate income tax on its profits. If those profits are distributed to owners as dividends, the owners pay tax again on their personal returns. This double taxation is a drawback (though there is an "S Corp" status for smaller corporations that can avoid double taxation for U.S. companies). On the positive side, corporations can be ideal for businesses that intend to raise significant capital (by selling shares to investors) or plan to scale up and possibly go public in the future. Investors are often more comfortable with the corporate structure. If you're aiming for a startup that will seek venture capital, for example, you might start (or eventually convert into) a corporation. For many small businesses, an LLC offers sufficient protection without the red tape of a corporation; however, it's beneficial to understand both options. (Note: outside the US, the term "Limited Company (Ltd)" usually refers to what is essentially a corporation by another name. For instance, a private limited company in the UK or an incorporated company in Canada. The exact laws and tax treatment vary, but they all create a separate legal entity with limited liability for owners.)

Choosing the right structure: Your choice depends on your specific situation. Consider factors like how much risk is involved in your business, whether you have co-founders, how you plan to handle taxes, and future goals for growth. If you're unsure, consulting with a business attorney or an accountant who specializes in small business law can be very helpful. They can advise you on the best fit. Remember, it's possible to change your structure later (e.g., from sole proprietorship to LLC, or LLC to corporation) as your business evolves, but doing so can involve additional paperwork, costs, and potential tax implications. It's worth putting thought into it at the start to save headaches down the road.

Registering your business: Once you've decided on a structure, you'll typically need to register your business with the appropriate government authority. This step establishes your business as a formal, legal entity. The process varies by location and structure:

- In the United States, corporations and LLCs are registered at the state level (usually with the Secretary of State's office). You'll file articles of incorporation (for a corporation) or articles of organization (for an LLC) and pay a filing fee to create your entity. Partnerships might not require a formal state filing (unless you choose to register an LLP, which some states allow). Sole proprietorships generally don't require state registration as a business entity, though you may still need local permits or a DBA filing if using a trade name. After state registration, many businesses then register with the IRS and state tax agencies.

- In other countries, the process will be different. For example, in the UK, you register a company (Ltd) with Companies House and receive a Company Number. In Canada, corporations can be incorporated federally or provincially (e.g., via Corporations Canada or provincial registrars), and you receive a corporation number and a Business Number for tax purposes. The specific steps and agencies differ, but the concept of officially registering the business is universal.

After registration, you'll receive proof, such as a certificate or incorporation documents, which you should keep safely. Many jurisdictions have online databases, where you can often look up your business name later to retrieve these documents if needed. However, it's best to keep your own copies.

Get your tax ID numbers: Most businesses will need to obtain a tax identification number for tax filings, banking, and other purposes. In the U.S., this is typically the Employer Identification Number (EIN) issued by the IRS. Despite the name, you don't actually need to have employees to obtain an EIN. It's used by LLCs, corporations, partnerships, and even some sole proprietors as a unique identifier for the business. An EIN is a unique nine-digit number that essentially acts like a Social Security Number for your company in the federal tax system. You can apply for an EIN online on the IRS website (it's free). Having an EIN is useful even for sole proprietors because it lets you open business bank accounts and file certain forms without using your personal SSN, thus adding a layer of privacy and professionalism.

For readers outside the U.S., note that the EIN is a U.S.-specific term. Other countries have their own equivalents:

- **Canada:** uses a Business Number (BN), which is a 9-digit number issued by the Canada Revenue Agency for companies and sole proprietors, used for tax filings, payroll, etc. The BN plays a similar role in identifying businesses for government purposes.

- **UK:** companies are issued a Company Tax Ref (Unique Taxpayer Reference) by HMRC for corporation tax, and if you hire employees you'd get a PAYE reference, etc. Sole traders use their personal

UTR. While there isn't a direct EIN equivalent, the Company Number and VAT number (if registered for VAT) serve identification roles in different contexts.

- **European Union countries:** usually have a business registration number and a VAT ID if applicable.

- **Australia:** uses an Australian Business Number (ABN) and possibly a Company Number (ACN) for companies.

The bottom line is to ensure that you obtain the necessary tax IDs or business numbers required in your jurisdiction. This will be important for tasks such as opening bank accounts, paying taxes, invoicing clients (who may request your business number on invoices), and hiring employees. If you're unsure what's required, your local government's small business portal or tax authority website should provide guidance.

Licenses and permits: In addition to registration, consider whether your business requires any special licenses or permits to operate legally. This depends on your industry and location. For instance, running a restaurant typically requires a health department permit, a construction contractor may need a state license, and even home-based businesses may require a local permit. Since this chapter focuses on general business setup, we won't delve into specific licenses or permits; however, please make sure you research this further. It's part of "legal basics" to ensure you have all necessary approvals to operate. Most businesses will need to obtain licenses and permits relevant to their specific field. Check your city, county, and country requirements early to ensure you don't operate without proper licensing.

Opening a Business Bank Account (and Why It Matters)

One final "make it official" step is setting up a business bank account solely for your business finances. This might seem like a chore, especially if you're a one-person business, but it is extremely important to keep your business's money separate from your personal money. Even if legally, you could use your personal account (for example, a sole proprietor can use their personal account since the business isn't a separate entity), it's not advisable to mix funds. Here's why a dedicated business bank account is a must-have:

- **Protecting Your Liability Shield:** If you've formed an LLC or corporation, one of the most significant benefits is the limited liability protection. Your personal assets are protected only as long as you clearly separate business from personal finances. If you pay personal bills out of the business account or deposit business checks into your personal account, you risk commingling funds. Courts can decide that your company is just an alter ego, and remove the liability protection, a concept known as "piercing the corporate veil". To preserve that legal separation, you must maintain separate accounts and records. Commingling funds is one of the fastest ways to lose LLC or corporate protection! By consistently using a business account for business transactions, you establish a clear legal boundary between your personal and business affairs. Even as a sole proprietor, keeping separate accounts can shield you in practical ways. For example, if someone sues the business, it's clearer what is business property versus your personal property if they've never been mixed.

- **Simplified Accounting & Tax Filing:** Come tax time, having all your business income and expenses flow through one dedicated account is a lifesaver. If you mix personal and business transactions in one account, you (or your accountant) will have to painstakingly sort out which is which (a recipe for errors and frustration). With a separate business checking account, you can easily see what the business earns and spends. It's much easier to track deductible expenses, calculate profit, and prepare financial statements. Moreover, a separate account creates a clear audit trail for the tax authorities. If you are ever audited by the IRS (or your local tax agency), having separate bank records for the business greatly helps substantiate your figures. In contrast, if your personal and business finances are tangled together, an audit can become invasive (since your personal finances get scrutinized), and you might miss deductions or make mistakes. Using one account per purpose is just good bookkeeping hygiene.

- **Professionalism & Credibility:** Paying suppliers or receiving customer payments from a bank account under your business's name (e.g., CoffeeCat LLC) looks far more professional than using a personal account (e.g., Jane Doe). When clients see that you can accept checks or payments to a business name, it reinforces that you are a legitimate, established business. Some vendors or customers might even be uncomfortable writing checks to an individual for a business service. Using a business account instills confidence. It shows you've "set up shop" properly. Additionally, when you write checks or swipe a debit card, your business name on those instruments helps build your brand presence. This credibility can subtly influence purchasing decisions in your favor. Many small business owners also find that having a business account makes them feel more committed and serious about their venture, which is a nice psychological bonus.

- **Access to Business Banking Services:** Business bank accounts often come with features tailored for businesses that personal accounts don't offer. For example, you may gain the ability to accept credit card payments or utilize merchant services linked to the account, which is essential if you plan to process customer payments beyond cash or checks. You can also establish a line of credit or obtain a business credit card to help manage your cash flow. Banks typically require a business account and financial history to extend those to you. Over time, building a relationship with a bank through your business account can help if you ever need a loan to expand. Additionally, having a separate account with an associated debit card enables you to entrust an employee or bookkeeper to handle banking on your behalf without exposing your personal finances. In short, a business bank account is the gateway to financial tools that can help your business grow.

Opening the account: To open a business bank account, you'll usually need certain documents depending on your structure, e.g., your business registration documents (articles of organization/incorporation), your EIN (or equivalent tax ID), and identification for yourself. Banks have different fee structures; some offer free business checking for small balances, while others charge a monthly fee if minimum balance requirements aren't met. It's worth shopping around for a bank (or credit union, or online fintech) that suits your needs. Many online banks now offer convenient business accounts with low fees, whereas traditional banks might offer local branch access if you need in-person services. Choose what's best for you, but do make this a priority. Even in a single-owner business, discipline yourself to deposit all business income into the business account and pay all business expenses from it (or transfer money to yourself for salary/draw and then spend, rather than spending directly out of business funds for personal needs).

Finally, once you have that account, maintain the separation. Never dip into business funds for personal expenses directly, and vice versa. Pay yourself formally (as an owner's draw or salary) and then use those funds for personal expenses. This habit will pay off in terms of legal protection and financial clarity. Maintaining separate bank accounts and never mixing personal and business expenses are critical practices to maximize the protection offered by your business structure.

With your domain, email, legal structure, tax IDs, and bank account in place, your business is truly official! You've built a strong foundation for your enterprise. These steps might not be the most glamorous parts of entrepreneurship, but they enable you to operate professionally and avoid many pitfalls down the road. You can now confidently present your business to the world, knowing that you have the proper infrastructure supporting it.

Reflection and Action Items

Now that you've learned the essentials of making your business official, take a moment to reflect and plan your next steps. Here are some prompts and action items to consider:

- **Domain Name:** Have you decided on a domain name that best represents your business? If it's available, register it now before someone else does. If not, what alternative domain could work for your brand?

- **Professional Email:** What will your business email address look like (e.g., info@yourcompany.com)? Set up a professional email service or check if your domain provider offers email. Make sure you've switched any business communications away from personal email accounts.

- **Business Structure:** Which business structure seems most appropriate for you (sole proprietor, partnership, LLC, corporation, etc.), given your situation and goals? List one or two reasons for your choice. If you're unsure, consider consulting a business advisor or mentor for guidance.

- **Legal Registration:** What steps do you need to take to register your business in your country or region? Research the specific requirements (e.g., filing documents with the government, registering a trade name, etc.) and make a to-do list with deadlines.

- **Tax IDs:** Do you need an EIN or local tax ID for your business? If you're in the US and haven't done so, visit the IRS website to apply for your EIN (it's quick and free). If you're outside the US, determine what tax identification number or business number is required and how to obtain it.

- **Licenses & Permits:** Consider if your business requires any special licenses or permits (industry-specific or local). Make a note of any you need to apply for, or confirm that none are needed in your case.

- **Business Bank Account:** If you haven't opened a separate business bank account yet, set a target date to do so (the sooner, the better). Research a few banking options. What features or fee structures are important to you? Once open, outline how you will transition any existing transactions to this account and keep it strictly business-only.

- **Financial Separation:** Think through your plan to keep personal and business finances separate. For example, how will you pay yourself from the business (draw or salary), and how will you document transfers? Implement a simple record-keeping practice for yourself (even a spreadsheet or using accounting software) to track income and expenses from that business account.

By taking action on each of these items, you'll reinforce the legitimacy and health of your business. As you proceed, remember that making it official is not a one-time task, but an ongoing commitment. Keep your registrations up to date, renew your domain each year, maintain accurate records, and continue to present your business professionally to the world. You've got this!

PART III - CREATE YOUR PRESENCE

CHAPTER 9: BUILD A HOME ONLINE

Having an online presence is no longer optional in today's digital age. It's a must. In this chapter, we'll cover how to create your business brand's own "home" on the internet with a business website and how to set up your brand's social media profiles to complement that website. Don't worry if you're new to this. Modern tools make it easier than ever to get started, even without technical skills. And if you're already social media savvy, this guide will show you how to leverage that experience to build a cohesive, professional presence for your business brand without getting bogged down in tedious details.

Why Your Business Brand Needs an Online "Home"

Think of your business website as your brand's digital home base: a space you control entirely, where anyone interested in your business or your work can find reliable information straight from the source. Social media profiles are like outposts or networking events (great for reaching people), but a website is your central hub that ties your business brand's online presence together. Realistically, your brand needs both a website and social media to showcase itself effectively nowadays. One without the other can limit your business: a website provides a professional portfolio, storefront, or information center, and social platforms help you reach and engage with your audience. In short, your website establishes credibility (it looks professional to have one), while your social profiles drive traffic and interaction. Used together, they reinforce each other and ensure that people can find the complete picture of who your business is and what it offers.

What About Beginners?

If you've never built a business site before, it might sound daunting, but it doesn't have to be. Gone are the days when launching a website meant coding for months. With today's powerful no-code tools, you can have a business website up in days or weeks, not months. If you grew up using social media, you already have a head start on understanding how online platforms work. We'll keep things platform-neutral (so you can choose what works for your business) and focus on easy, actionable steps.

Launching Your Business Website (Step by Step)

Your business website will serve as your brand's online headquarters, providing a platform to showcase your story, products, services, and content without the limitations of social networks. Here's how to get it up and running the easy way:

Define the Website's Purpose and Content

Before diving into tools, take a moment to decide what you want from your business website. Is it a blog for sharing updates, a portfolio to show your projects, an online brochure, or maybe an e-commerce site to sell products? Defining your goal will guide a lot of your decisions. For example, if you primarily want to showcase your work (such as art, writing, or products), you'll likely want a portfolio section or gallery on your site. If you want to share updates or articles, a blog format might be ideal. And if you plan to sell something, you'll need e-commerce capabilities. Being clear on the site's purpose will help you choose the right platform and organize your content logically.

Equally important is thinking about your business brand and vibe. A business website is all about your brand, so don't be afraid to infuse it with your company's personality. Write in your brand's authentic voice and include a friendly bio or "about us" page that tells visitors who you are in a conversational tone. Include photos of your team, your products, or your work to humanize the site. People connect with people, not just walls of text. Remember, your business is the focus, so let your character shine through. At the same time, ensure the site remains professional and easy to navigate. Whatever you want visitors to see (whether it's your best products, your latest blog posts, or your services), ensure that content is featured prominently (ideally on the homepage or linked in the menu) so nobody has to dig around to find it. In short, showcase your best work upfront and set the tone with an authentic, brand-aligned introduction.

Choose a Domain Name (Your Site's Address)

Your domain name is the web address (URL) where people will find your site (for example, YourBrand.com). It's like your business's digital street address, so you want it to be easy to remember and clearly associated with your company. If the site is for a business or a specific project, use the brand name associated with it. In any case, pick a domain that is short, memorable, and relevant to your business or work. It should ideally match your business name to avoid confusion.

Brainstorm a few options in case your first choice is taken. You can get creative. For instance, adding "shop," "co," or a location, or trying different extensions beyond .com (such as .net, .io, .co) if the .com isn't available. There are online tools (domain name generators) that can help come up with ideas based on keywords you input. Once you have a candidate, you'll need to register it through a domain registrar (services like GoDaddy, Namecheap, SiteGround, etc.). Domains typically cost around $10–20 per year, but here's a reminder. Many website builder platforms will give you a free custom domain for the first year if you purchase a website plan with them. If you're going to use a site-building service, check their offers before you separately pay for a domain.

A quick checklist for a good domain name:

- Easy to spell (avoid tricky words or weird punctuation).

- Short enough to remember.

- Clearly related to your brand name or industry.

If you can say yes to all of these points, you've got a winner. Secure that domain before someone else does. Once registered, it's yours to use, and you can connect it to whatever website platform you choose in the next step.

Pick an Easy Website Building Platform

With your goal in mind and a domain in hand, you're ready to build the site itself. You have a couple of options here, but we'll focus on the beginner-friendly, code-free ways to launch your site:

- **All-in-One Website Builders:** These are services that provide templates, drag-and-drop editing, and hosting all in one package. Popular examples include Wix, Squarespace, Weebly, and Carrd, among others. They are very user-friendly. You don't need to know any coding; you simply pick a design you like and fill in your own text and images. These platforms handle all the technical aspects (such as hosting and security) behind the scenes. For example, if you want a sleek portfolio to showcase your products or designs, a platform like Squarespace can be ideal, as it offers beautiful portfolio templates that you can easily customize. If you plan to sell products, consider platforms like Shopify, which offer built-in shopping carts and payment features that are ready to use. And if you just need a simple one-page brand profile (such as a digital business card or a single-page information site), a service like Carrd is extremely low-cost and straightforward. Many business owners find it "easy to just toss new work up or make adjustments and hit publish" without worrying about technical maintenance. The key advantage of these builders is speed and ease: you can have a site live in a day or two using a template, and many include guided setups.

- **Content Management Systems (CMS) like WordPress:** Another route is to use a platform like WordPress, which powers a huge percentage of websites on the internet. WordPress is a bit more involved than the drag-and-drop builders, especially when using the self-hosted version (WordPress.org). You'd need to arrange for web hosting separately, install WordPress, and pick a theme. However, WordPress also offers an easier hosted option (WordPress.com) where a lot of this is handled for you. WordPress is known for its flexibility, with thousands of plugins and themes, you can make your site do almost anything. If you anticipate needing more custom features down the line (or you want to learn a bit more about websites), WordPress is a solid choice. However, if that sounds intimidating and you want to get started quickly, a classic website builder might be a better choice. Remember, you can always migrate or upgrade your site later as you grow.

No matter which route you choose, stay platform-neutral in your mindset: the goal is to get a site that works for your brand. There's no single "best" builder. The best choice is the one that fits your business and skill level. Many professionals use a combination (for example, a designer might have a Squarespace portfolio because it's easy, and a developer might hand-code their site to show off their coding skills. Choose what aligns with your needs.

Using Templates: The easiest way to design a visually appealing site without design skills is to start with a pre-made template. Virtually all site builders and CMS themes offer templates created by professional designers. Browse through the template gallery of your chosen platform and select one that matches the look and feel you're going for (e.g., a clean, professional vibe, or a bold, creative style). You can usually filter templates by category (portfolio, blog, business, etc.). Don't agonize too long over this. Pick a design that you like and that includes the sections you think you'll need (such as a gallery, contact form, etc.). You can then customize the template with your own content.

After selecting a template, you'll be able to swap in your own text and photos, adjust colors or fonts to match your brand style, and rearrange sections as needed. Play around with the editor. Thanks to the WYSIWYG (what-you-see-is-what-you-get) interfaces, you can usually drag elements around or click to edit text right on the page preview. Most builders also ensure that the templates are mobile-responsive, meaning your site will automatically look good on smartphones and tablets. This is important, as many visitors may access your site from their phones.

As you fill in content, create a few essential pages such as:

- Home (overview of your business and key offers)

- About (your brand's story and values)

- Products/Services (what you do and sell)

- Contact (so people know how to reach you – this can be a simple page with your email or a contact form).

You might also include a Blog or News section if you plan to post updates or articles regularly. A simple one-page site that covers all the basics is perfectly fine to start. The key is to make sure that when someone lands on your site, they can quickly find out who you are, what you offer, and how to take the next step.

Get Your Business Website Live

Once you've edited your brand's template to your liking, it's time to publish! If you used an all-in-one builder, this part is usually just a matter of hitting a "Publish" or "Go Live" button. The platform will either provide you with a temporary subdomain (such as yourbrand.platformname.com) or prompt you to connect your custom domain if you have one. It's worth using the custom domain you should have already secured. It looks much more professional to have yourbrand.com than a long platform sub-address. Most site builders have a straightforward process to connect your domain. Typically, you'd follow their guide to either transfer the domain to their service or adjust your domain's DNS settings to point to your new business site. It sounds technical, but the builder will usually walk you through it step by step. And if you get stuck, customer support or numerous online tutorials can help (chances are that someone has created a YouTube video for your exact platform and question).

If you went the WordPress (or similar CMS) route, there will be a few more steps: you'll need to arrange hosting (services like Bluehost, HostGator, or SiteGround offer one-click WordPress setups), install WordPress (often automated by the host), choose a theme (the equivalent of a template), and then hit Publish from your WordPress dashboard. The good news is that many hosts also offer website setup wizards, and WordPress itself has gotten more user-friendly over the years. Still, it may take a bit longer than a Wix or Squarespace approach. The trade-off is that you get more flexibility and control. If all that sounds like too much, stick with the easier builder for now. You can always switch to WordPress in the future if you outgrow the simple solution.

Before announcing your site to the world, do a quick review: check how it looks on mobile, click all your links to ensure none are broken, review your text for typos, and consider asking a friend to give it a glance. Site builders often have a "preview" mode that shows you how your site will look on various devices. It doesn't need to be perfect. You can (and should) update your site over time, but you want to make a good first impression. Once it's live, congratulations! You now have a home online that your brand fully owns.

Finally, consider adding basic analytics (many platforms have this built-in, or you can connect Google Analytics) so you can see if people are visiting and which pages they view. This is optional for beginners, but it can be motivating to see that people are visiting your business site, and it helps you understand what content is drawing interest.

Setting Up Business Social Media Profiles (and Making Them Shine)

With your business website up, the next step is to either create or refine your brand's social media profiles to build out your online presence. Chances are, your business is already on one or two social platforms (most are). Now you'll be using them a bit more strategically (not just for casual sharing, but to consistently and professionally represent your business brand). The good news is that setting up a profile on platforms like LinkedIn, Twitter (now called X), Instagram, or others is typically straightforward. The great news is that you can leverage all your existing social media know-how. You won't be starting from scratch in learning the ropes. Here's how to do it the easy way:

Pick the Right Platforms

You don't have to be on every social network out there. It's better to focus on the ones that make sense for your brand's goals and audience. For business networking and B2B, LinkedIn is a must. If you're a visual creator (artist, photographer, designer), Instagram or Pinterest might be key places to showcase your work. If you're building a tech or content-driven brand, Twitter/X can be great for sharing insights and connecting with industry peers. If you create videos or want to showcase your expertise, YouTube or TikTok may be relevant options. The idea is to go where your target customers or community hangs out. Since this guide is platform-neutral, we won't tell you exactly which ones to join. However, as examples, many businesses choose a combination like LinkedIn, Twitter, and Instagram, or LinkedIn, a company blog, and YouTube, depending on what aligns with your field.

If your business already has profiles on a platform you intend to use professionally, you may choose to revamp them rather than creating new ones. For instance, you might convert a casual Instagram into a more polished business page by curating the content, or set up a new business profile/page. There's no one right answer. Just be mindful of what each profile will be for.

Ensure Consistent Branding Across Brand Profiles

When setting up your business social profiles, consistency is key. You want someone who finds you on Twitter/X and someone who finds you on LinkedIn to both immediately recognize it's your brand. That means using a consistent business name, logo, and overall style wherever possible. Start with your company logo as the profile picture: use a clear, high-quality logo (if it's a business page) that will serve as your brand's face online. Ideally, use the same logo or brand image across all platforms for recognition. Using the same profile image on all your social media accounts helps establish familiarity. Also, keep your brand name the same (or very similar) across all profiles. If your full brand name is taken or too long on some platforms, consider a consistent handle or username that you can use everywhere (e.g., @BrandNameOfficial).

Next, ensure your business bio and description are consistent across all profiles. You don't have to use identical wording on every platform (since each has its own audience and character limits), but make sure they all convey a coherent image of what your business does. In other words, tell the same story, just tailored for the platform. For instance, your LinkedIn "About" might be a few paragraphs about your company, while your Twitter/X bio is one catchy line, but they should feel consistent in tone and message. Mention your key services, products, industry, or what your brand is known for. Include a brand touch (a tagline or unique value) so you come across as a real, recognizable business, not just a generic profile. Importantly, include a link to your business website in your profiles! Most social platforms allow you to add one hyperlink. Use that to direct people to your site (this is how your site and social profiles will synergize: profiles funnel interested people to the rich info on your business website, and your website will link out to your social profiles, creating a complete loop).

Maintain a consistent tone and style throughout your business profiles' writing. If your brand voice is friendly and humorous, let that show; if it's professional and academic, that's fine too. Just be intentional about it. You want someone scrolling through your Instagram captions, reading your posts, or looking at your LinkedIn posts to get a cohesive sense of your brand's voice and personality. This consistency in how you "sound" builds trust and recognition. And of course, keep it positive and professional, especially on LinkedIn or anywhere partners and customers might check.

Lastly, pay attention to visual branding. If you have specific brand colors or a logo on your website, you can incorporate those in your profile cover images or post graphics for a unified look. Maybe you always use the same two colors in your LinkedIn banner and Twitter/X header that match your website's color scheme. That kind of subtle consistency can give your business presence a polished feel.

Fill Out Each Business Profile Thoughtfully

Let's go through the main elements you'll typically need to fill in, using a platform-agnostic approach (since each social network calls them slightly different things):

- **Profile Picture:** Use your business logo. Consistency across platforms helps people recognize your brand.

- **Business Name and Handle:** Use your registered business name or brand name for the display name on business profiles. For the username/handle (the @ name), try to get a version of your business name. If your exact name is taken, add a word related to your field (e.g., @BrandNameDesign) or use abbreviations. Keep it short and memorable.

- **Bio/About:** This is a crucial section. It's your business elevator pitch for anyone who stumbles on your profile. In a few lines (or a paragraph), explain what your business does, whom it helps, and what makes it different. For example: "Event rentals & decor for unforgettable celebrations | Serving Austin, TX | Let's make your next event shine ✦ ". Utilize industry-specific keywords and a touch of brand personality. On a more formal platform like LinkedIn, you can go into more detail in the "About" section. Perhaps 2-3 short paragraphs covering your mission, expertise, and a personal note from the founder. On all platforms, ensure your bio aligns with your business brand and makes people want to learn more or connect with you. If you have a brand slogan, you can include it as well.

- **Website Link:** There will usually be a field to add a website. Put your business website URL here! This is how you drive traffic from social media to your brand's website. On Instagram and Twitter/X, it's a single link; on LinkedIn, you can add it in the business contact info. Some people use link aggregator tools (like Linktree) if they want to share multiple links, but at this stage, you might not need that. One link to your business site, which itself can list other links, is enough. Make sure the link works (test it).

- **Background/Cover Photo:** Some platforms (Twitter/X, LinkedIn, and Facebook) let you have a big banner image at the top of your business profile. Use this space wisely. It's basically free visual real estate to reinforce your brand. You can create a simple graphic using a tool like Canva or Photoshop that features your business name and tagline against a brand-color backdrop, or use a photo that represents your work or team. For example, a creative agency might use a collage of their top client projects as the cover image. Whatever you choose, ensure it's not distracting or low-quality. It should complement your brand's profile and ideally repeat elements from your website (like your logo, imagery, or colors). As with profile pics, using the same or similar cover image across platforms can help with recognizability.

- **Additional Details:** Fill out any other fields that make sense for your business. If there's a section for your location, add your storefront, service area, or headquarters (especially if being local is relevant to your brand). If there's a section for business specialties, awards, or company story, take the time to fill those in with up-to-date info. On Facebook pages or LinkedIn, you may have a space for a longer description. Use it to expand on your brand's story and mission. These details can enhance your business's credibility.

Connect and Cross-Promote

Now that your business profiles are set up and aligned with your branding, you'll want to connect them together and with your business website:

- **Add Social Links on Your Website:** Make sure your business website includes icons or links to your social profiles. Typically, you'd put these in the footer, header, or on the "About Us" page. This way, someone who lands on your site can easily follow your brand on those platforms to stay updated. Many website templates come with pre-made social icon sections; simply plug in your business URLs.

- **Link to Your Website from Social:** As already covered, add your business website link to every profile's bio. You can also periodically post on your social accounts to invite people to visit your new site. For example, you might announce, "Just launched our new website. Check it out [link]!" Be careful not to spam, though. A pinned post or an occasional mention is enough.

- **Use Consistent Naming:** If possible, use the same name or handle on your website (like in your about page or domain) as your social handles. For instance, if your site is greatbrand.com, ideally, your Instagram and Twitter/X handles are @greatbrand (or a similar variation). This consistency makes it easier for people to find you in searches and ensures they know all profiles belong to the same business.

- **Invite Your Existing Network:** If you've already built up personal or previous business followers, let them know about your new, polished business profiles or pages. For example, if you start a new Instagram for your brand, you can post on your existing pages to invite people to follow the new account, or share your new LinkedIn company page link with professional contacts and ask them to connect or follow. An initial boost of followers from people who know your brand will make your profile look active and credible to newcomers.

Optimize and Professionalize Your Profiles

To truly set up your business profiles "the easy way," address a couple of key housekeeping items: optimization and clean-up. This ensures your business social presence not only exists, but also leaves a strong impression.

- **Optimize for Search:** Many people will find your business social profile by searching (within the platform or on Google). To increase visibility, use relevant industry keywords in your profile. For example, on LinkedIn, if your business is a bakery, including "Bakery" or "Artisan Bread" in your headline and about section helps your brand appear in searches for those terms. On Instagram, the business name field is searchable, so you could do "GreatBrand | Austin Coffee" as your display name, combining your brand and product. Little tweaks like this help your brand's profile get discovered by people who don't know you yet.

- **Professional (but On-Brand) Tone:** Make sure what you post publicly aligns with the business image you want to project. Since this chapter is about setup, we won't delve deeply into business content strategy (that might be a whole other chapter!), but as a general rule of thumb, share content that is relevant to your industry and adds value to your followers. It's absolutely fine (and good) to show some personality, but remember that anyone (including potential clients, partners, or employees) might see what you post. A good mindset is to treat public business posts (and even public personal posts) as part of your brand. Would you be okay with this being associated with your company? If yes, post it. If not, maybe save it for internal communications.

- **Clean Up Old Content:** Now is a good time for a quick audit of what's been posted in the past on business profiles you'll use professionally. You don't necessarily have to delete your entire posting history, but do consider removing or hiding anything that could be misconstrued or seen as unprofessional for a business. This includes obvious things like outdated promotions, off-brand jokes, or content that doesn't match your current message or target customer. If you're repurposing a profile for your business brand, clean up the outliers that don't match the professional image you're building. The goal isn't to look boring. It's to remove anything that doesn't align with your brand's identity.

- **Security and Professionalism:** As you set up new business accounts or refresh old ones, ensure your accounts are secure. Use strong passwords (consider a password manager) and enable two-factor authentication on important accounts. A hacked business social profile can be very damaging to your reputation. Also, use your official brand name (not a personal or casual alias) and ensure all contact info and branding are correct. If you previously mixed business and personal accounts, consider separating them for clarity.

By now, you should have at least a couple of social profiles that are fully aligned with your business brand and link to your business website. That's a huge step in establishing your professional online presence.

First Steps on Each Platform

After the initial business profile setup, it's good to make a "debut" on each platform. This could be as simple as making an introductory post. For example, on a new Facebook account, you might post: "Hello everyone! We're GreatBrand, your go-to source for artisan coffee and fresh pastries in Austin. Follow us for daily specials and behind-the-scenes updates!" On LinkedIn, you could publish a post announcing your business is now open for connections, or share news about your launch. On Instagram, post a great product shot with a caption introducing your brand and what people can expect if they follow you. These introductory posts provide some initial content, so that anyone who checks your profile doesn't see an empty page. It also signals to your existing network and potential customers that your business is active and ready to serve.

Don't worry about getting everything perfect from day one. You will refine your business profiles over time. The key is to start and have that foundation in place. Once you have set up the website and social profiles, you can begin actively using them, posting updates, connecting with customers, and so on, which will help your presence grow organically.

Bringing It All Together: Consistency and Maintenance

Congratulations! You've launched your business website and set up your primary business social media profiles! Now let's talk about keeping them working together for you.

The magic word is consistency. We've hammered on consistency in branding (name, look, tone), but it also applies to how you maintain your business presence. Keep your business information up-to-date across all relevant platforms. If you launch a new product, change services, or finish a new project, update your business website's bio and also update your LinkedIn page (and any other business profile). If you decide to shift your focus (for example, if your brand introduces a new line or changes direction), ensure that your site and profiles reflect this new direction uniformly. This way, no matter where someone finds your business, they're getting current and correct information.

Another aspect is regular activity. Your business website doesn't need daily changes (in fact, many business sites are relatively static), but do consider adding new content once in a while. For example, blog posts, news about company projects, or fresh portfolio pieces will show that your brand is still active. Social media, by nature, rewards regular posting, but "regular" can mean different things on different platforms. Find a sustainable schedule for your business. It could be posting a couple of times a week on Facebook, once a week on LinkedIn, and twice a month on Instagram. Whatever your team can manage without burnout. The key is that you don't want business profiles to look abandoned. If someone sees your brand hasn't posted in a year, they might assume you're not active or serious about it. You don't have to post super often; just keep a heartbeat going.

It's also smart to engage with your audience or community. This means responding to customer messages or reviews, commenting on others' posts, and generally being present. Engagement tends to increase your business's visibility (thanks to algorithms and just general networking). When people interact with your business, it also makes your profiles more dynamic and inviting.

Lastly, periodically do a health check of your business's online presence. Perhaps once every few months, review your business site and profiles as if you were a new customer stumbling upon them: do they still accurately and positively represent your business? Are all the links working? Did you miss updating something? Search for your business name on Google to see what appears. Is it your website and LinkedIn company page? Great. If it's something outdated or unrelated, see if you can improve your SEO or adjust something to get your official business pages higher up. This maintenance step ensures your online business presence remains polished after the initial setup.

Chapter 9 Summary & Key Takeaways

- **Your Website = Your Online Home:** A business website gives your brand a controlled, customizable space to showcase what you do. It adds credibility and lets you present your services, story, and portfolio exactly how you want. Thankfully, creating a business website has become much easier with modern tools. You can use no-code website builders (like Wix, Squarespace, etc.) to get started quickly, without needing programming skills.

- **Step-by-Step to Launch Your Site:** Start by defining your business site's purpose (storefront, service list, blog, portfolio, etc.), then register a memorable domain name that aligns with your brand. Use a site-building platform that fits your needs (drag-and-drop builders for ease, or WordPress for more flexibility). Pick a professional-looking template and fill it with your business's content and images. Focus on essential pages (Home, About, Services/Products, Contact) so visitors immediately see what you offer. With a few clicks to publish (and maybe connecting your domain), your site will be live for the world to see!

- **Social Media Profiles = Your Network Outposts:** Set up profiles on the social networks most relevant to your business goals. Quality over quantity. Ensure each profile is fully filled out and on-brand. Use a consistent business logo, handle, and bio across platforms to reinforce your brand. These profiles should link back to your website, and your website should link out to them, creating a cohesive web of your presence.

- **Consistency and Professionalism:** Treat your online presence as an extension of your business brand. Maintain a consistent tone of voice and visual style across your website and social profiles. Optimize your business profiles by using your brand name, relevant keywords (for searchability), and showcasing your business's strengths in the bio. Ensure that you remove any outdated, unprofessional posts or photos that don't align with the business image you want to project. Customers, partners, and collaborators often review these.

- **Leverage No-Code Tools and Examples:** You don't need to reinvent the wheel. Numerous no-code tools and services are available to handle the heavy lifting (hosting, design templates, etc.), allowing you to focus on your business content. For example, if you want a portfolio site, a platform like Squarespace offers beautiful templates that you can easily customize. Alternatively, if you need a quick one-page intro site, a service like Carrd can be extremely cost-effective and simple. On social media, similarly, utilize built-in features (such as business profile sections, link in bio, and pinned posts) to optimize your business pages with minimal effort.

- **Both Are Necessary and Complementary:** Your business website and your business social profiles serve different purposes and work best together. The website is your anchor. It has all the details someone might seek about your brand. Social media is your amplifier. It's how you engage with people and draw them toward your site or services. As many entrepreneurs find, a website is great for a portfolio and even sales, while social media is great for marketing. You can repurpose content between the two, so maintaining both isn't too much extra work.

With your website launched and your business social profiles polished, you've laid the foundation of a strong online presence. Remember, building your presence is an ongoing journey. You'll continue to add to it and refine it over time. For now, give yourself a pat on the back for creating your digital "home" and claiming your space on the web.

Your Next Steps:

- **Launch Your Site:** If you haven't already, go ahead and publish that business website. Even a simple one-page site is a great start. Share the link with a team member or friend to test it out and get feedback.

- **Secure Your Social Handles:** Register accounts (or update existing ones) on the key social platforms you plan to use for your brand. Use the same name or username whenever possible for consistency. Add your website link to each profile.

- **Polish Your Profiles:** Upload your new business profile logo or photo, write your brand bios, and fill in all the business details you can. Consider what first impression each profile gives and adjust it until you're satisfied.

- **Cross-Link Everything:** Add social media icons/links on your website. On each social profile, double-check that your business website URL is there. This cross-linking helps customers navigate your business's online ecosystem.

- **Announce Yourself:** Make a welcome post or introduction on each platform. Don't be shy. Tell the world your business is online and what you're about! For example, a LinkedIn post about your new site or a post introducing your business brand can kick things off.

By following these steps, you're well on your way to creating a robust online presence for your business. Going forward, keep these assets active by updating your website periodically with fresh content or news, and stay engaged on social media in whatever capacity you can. In the following chapters, we'll dive deeper into growing your audience and creating content, but you've already accomplished the crucial first step: establishing your business presence. Great job! See you in the next part of your journey to building your brand.

CHAPTER 10: SHOW UP IN THE REAL WORLD

You've worked hard to craft your brand's identity and story. Now it's time to bring that brand to life in the physical world. Showing up in the real world means making your business visible and memorable through tangible items and face-to-face interactions. In this chapter, we'll explore how to extend your brand into business cards, packaging, signage, and real-world events. You'll learn how to prepare for in-person opportunities and make a genuine impression on people, even if you're shy or introverted. Let's dive into practical ways your small business brand can shine out in the open!

Business Cards: Your Pocket-Sized Brand Ambassador

Even in our digital age, a great business card remains a powerful tool for small businesses. It's often the first physical representation of your brand that you hand to someone else. A well-designed business card serves as a pocket-sized brand ambassador. It carries your logo, colors, and contact information, all in one handy package.

Designing Your Card: Keep the design simple, clean, and on-brand. Use the same logo, colors, and fonts that define your brand identity so the card is instantly recognizable as yours. Avoid cluttering the card with too much text or graphics. Typically, one side can feature your logo or tagline, and the other side can list your key details. What should you include on a business card? At minimum, have:

- **Your Name and Title:** So people remember who they met and your role in the business.

- **Business Name and Logo:** The company's name (and logo if space allows) front and center.

- **Contact Information:** Phone number, email address, and possibly a physical address if relevant.

- **Website or Social Handle:** A way for people to learn more online. You can list your website URL or a primary social media handle.

- **Tagline or One-Liner (Optional):** If you have a short tagline or a few words that summarize what you do ("Handcrafted Candles with

Love"), this can go on the card to jog the recipient's memory of your specialty.

Make sure the text is readable. Avoid using tiny fonts or hard-to-read script. A plain white background with dark text often works, but feel free to use color as long as it aligns with your brand and the text stands out. For example, if your bakery's brand color is pastel blue, you might have a pastel blue card with white text and your pink cupcake logo. Just ensure there's good contrast.

Quality Matters: Printing your cards on decent cardstock (not flimsy printer paper) shows professionalism. You don't need the most expensive option, but a slightly thicker card with a nice finish (matte or glossy) can give your brand a more established appearance. If your brand is creative or eco-friendly, consider creative touches like a square card, a card with rounded corners, or recycled kraft paper stock. These details can make your card memorable, but only if they align with your brand's personality. For instance, a tech startup might include a scannable QR code on a sleek, minimal card, whereas an artist's handmade business might have a textured, colorful card. Choose what enhances your brand message.

Always Be Ready: Once you have your business cards, use them! Keep a stack with you in your bag, car, or even jacket pocket. You never know when you'll meet a potential customer, partner, or mentor. Whether you're at a conference or just chatting in line at the coffee shop, if someone shows interest in your business, you can confidently hand them your card. It's often more effective than saying "find me on Facebook" because it's a tangible reminder of your business. Plus, it saves people the step of searching for you later.

Digital Business Cards: In addition to physical cards, consider having a digital version of your business card. This could be as simple as a PDF or image of your card that you can text or email to someone you meet online. You might also use a smartphone app or your phone's wallet to create a scannable business card. For example, you can carry a QR code on your phone that, when scanned, loads your contact information or website. This way, if you're at an online networking event or someone prefers digital, you're covered. Another easy win: make sure your email signature includes your name, title, company name, and website, essentially acting as a mini digital business card every time you send an email.

Be Creative and Authentic: Above all, let your business card reflect your brand's personality. If you run a fun, quirky brand, a little pop of color or a witty tagline on your card can spark joy and be a conversation starter. If your brand is very formal and professional, a crisp, classic design with traditional fonts will set the right tone. There are plenty of templates and design services out there, but don't be afraid to inject your own flair. Just remember: the goal is to be memorable and clear about who you are and what you do. A great business card can plant the seed of your brand in someone's mind long after the handshake is over.

Packaging Basics: Extending Your Brand to Your Products

For product-based businesses, packaging is a critical part of your brand's real-world presence. Every box, label, tag, or bag that carries your product is an opportunity to communicate who you are. Thoughtful packaging not only protects your goods, it also delights customers and reinforces your brand identity.

Consistent Look and Feel: Begin by ensuring that your packaging accurately reflects your brand's visual identity. Use your brand colors, logo, and possibly your tagline on packaging materials. This could mean ordering custom-printed boxes or labels, but if you're on a tight budget, don't worry, there are creative, cost-effective options. For example, you can order stickers with your logo and place them on plain boxes or shopping bags. A simple kraft paper bag can be transformed into a branded item with a colorful logo sticker or a rubber stamp of your business name. **Consistency is key.** If your bakery's signature color is mint green, consider using mint green cupcake boxes or adding a mint green sticker. If your soap business features a floral theme in its branding, consider including a small floral pattern on the label or a flower-themed thank-you card inside each package. These touches make your brand instantly recognizable.

Labels and Tags: Product labels (for items such as jars, bottles, or packaged goods) should clearly display your business name or logo, as well as the product name. Design labels with the same fonts and style as your other brand materials so everything feels unified. Include essential product info, but keep the design uncluttered. If you sell clothing or accessories, use hang tags to add branding. A hang tag is the small tag attached to the product. It usually has your logo on the front and perhaps a short message or product story on the back. For instance, a handmade jewelry brand might have a tag with their elegant logo on the front, and the back might say, "Handcrafted in Texas with love. Thank you for supporting our small business!" Along with pricing or care instructions, this little story element connects the customer to your brand's values or origin.

The Unboxing Experience: Think about what a customer sees and feels when they first open your product. That moment of unboxing is a golden chance to create a memorable impression. Big companies do this (imagine the excitement of opening a new smartphone with its sleek, well-organized box), and you can too, on a smaller scale. A few ideas for an affordable but delightful unboxing experience:

- Wrap your product in tissue paper that matches your brand color, and seal it with a small logo sticker. It feels like a little gift.

- Include a thank-you note in the package. It could be a postcard or small card that thanks the customer by name (if possible) or in general for their purchase. You can even print a stack of thank-you cards with a nice message and your social media handles or website on them. This not only shows appreciation but also guides them on how to stay connected.

- Toss in a tiny freebie or surprise if you can. For example, a tea company might add a sample of a new tea flavor, or a boutique might include a branded sticker or a discount code for the next purchase. It's an unexpected treat that can make customers smile and remember you.

- Keep it neat and secure. While being visually appealing is important, never sacrifice safety. Packaging should effectively protect the product. Use appropriate padding (such as paper shreds or bubble wrap), but you can also create on-brand padding (e.g., colored paper shreds in your brand colors).

Branded Packing Materials: If you ship products, consider branding the outer packaging too. Custom-printed shipping boxes or mailers with your logo can be pricey, but as mentioned, a simple logo sticker on a plain box works nicely. Some small businesses use colored poly mailers or boxes that match their brand palette (for example, a bright pink mailer if that's a brand color) so it stands out in the mail. You can also get packing tape printed with your logo or a fun message (imagine sealing a box with tape that says "Thank you for supporting [Business Name]!" along with a tiny logo). This way, even before the customer opens the box, they know it's from you and it builds anticipation.

Don't Overlook Legal and Practical Info: Depending on your product, your packaging might need to include certain information (ingredient lists, safety warnings, expiration dates, etc.). Ensure that you include those elements in a way that doesn't detract from your branding. Perhaps your beautiful label could have a smaller font section on the back or bottom for the less visually appealing details. This way the front-facing part of your packaging focuses on brand and product name, while the back has the required info.

Example - A Memorable Package: Imagine you run a small artisan coffee company. Your bags of coffee have a label with your café's logo, the coffee blend name in your brand's signature font, and maybe a little sketch of a coffee bean character you use as a mascot. Each bag is tied with a tag that says, "Brewed with passion in Austin, TX." When a customer orders online, you ship it in a sturdy brown box sealed with tape that has your logo printed in a repeating pattern. Inside, the coffee bag is wrapped in tissue paper with a sticker that reads "Fresh Coffee, Fresh Start!" and includes a thank-you card, inviting them to tag you on social media when they make their first cup. The customer feels like they've received a gift, not just a product. This kind of thoughtful packaging transforms a simple transaction into a brand experience. It encourages them to remember you, talk about you, or even share a photo of your product unboxing with friends.

Start Small and Adapt: You don't have to nail the perfect packaging experience on day one. Start with the basics: a good label and a thank-you note, and refine as you get feedback. Ask customers if they liked the packaging. Sometimes, you'll find out that a minor tweak (like adding protective padding or using a different sticker placement) can improve things. Your packaging will likely evolve as your business grows, and that's okay. The key is to keep it aligned with your brand personality and make customers feel good about choosing your product. If even your packaging can make them smile or make them feel appreciated, you're doing it right.

Simple Signage: Standing Out with Signs and Displays

Whether you have a physical storefront, a booth at a fair, or a table at an event, signage is crucial for announcing your brand's presence. Effective signage promotes your brand and draws people in. You don't need a giant billboard or expensive light-up display. Even simple signs can be very effective if done thoughtfully.

Why Signage Matters: Think of your sign as the handshake before you get to shake someone's hand physically. It's often the first thing people notice from afar. A clear and attractive sign can pique curiosity and invite people in. If you're at a busy craft market or trade show, you're competing with dozens of other booths for attention. A well-placed banner or poster with your business name can make the difference between someone strolling past or stopping to learn more. In a retail setting, your outdoor sign helps customers find you and sets the mood (e.g., a whimsical painted wooden sign gives a different vibe than a sleek metal one).

Keep It Simple and On-Brand: The best signs are easy to read and aligned with your brand style. Use large, high-contrast text for your business name so it can be read from a distance. Include your logo if you have one, and perhaps a short tagline or a few words describing what you do (especially if your business name doesn't make it obvious). For example, if your company name is "Lunar," a passerby might not know what that is. A tagline like "Handcrafted Jewelry" on the sign clarifies and draws in the right crowd. On the other hand, if your name is "Bella's Bakery," it's already clear, so your sign might just say "Bella's Bakery" with a little cupcake icon. Colors and fonts on the sign should, as you guessed, match your branding. If your brand colors are black and gold, a black banner with gold lettering would look cohesive and consistent. If you have a signature font associated with your logo, use it for the business name on the sign, provided it remains legible at a large size.

Types of Signs: Consider what kind of sign fits your needs:

- **Banners:** A vinyl or fabric banner is excellent for events. You can roll it up and use it repeatedly. For example, a simple 3-foot or 6-foot wide banner with your logo and brand colors can hang behind your booth or across the front of a table. Banners are relatively inexpensive and can be made at print shops or online. Make sure the grommets (the holes for hanging) are sturdy and bring string or zip ties to attach them.

- **Posters or Foam Boards:** If you have a tabletop or wall space, a poster or mounted foam board sign can add more info. You might have a small poster that lists your product menu, prices, or a few photos of your work. Design these to be clear and concise. People should grasp the key points within a few seconds. For instance, a poster might say "Custom Cakes, Made to Order" with a couple of cake photos and your website.

- **Table Signs and Cards:** On your table or booth, you can have little signage like tent cards or picture frames holding mini-signs. These could say "Join our mailing list for 10% off", "Follow us on Instagram @YourBrandName", or highlight a special offer. They're not the main sign, but they reinforce your message once people are up close.

- **Storefront Signage:** If you have a physical location, invest in a decent sign out front. It could be a hanging sign, window decals, or lettering on your door. Ensure it's visible from the street. Also, consider in-store signage, such as a welcome sign at the entrance or section labels for different product areas, all designed to match your brand style. Even small touches, like a sign by the register that says "Thank you for shopping [at Our Store]" add to the experience.

- **Portable Signs:** Consider a lightweight, portable sign like an easel chalkboard or A-frame (sandwich board) if it fits your brand. These are especially useful for sidewalk advertising if you're in a location with foot traffic, or at events to place near your booth. They can be fun because you can update the message ("Today only: Buy 1 Get 1 Free!" or just a friendly "Hello, we're glad you're here!"). If using a chalkboard or whiteboard style, make sure your handwriting or artwork is neat. Practice or use stencils if needed, as it still needs to look professional and consistent with your brand's vibe (a cute, hand-drawn style if that's you, or clean, block lettering if that's more your brand).

Tips for Effective Signage:

- **Readable Fonts:** Fancy scripts or tiny letters might look nice up close, but are hard to read from a few feet away. Test your sign by stepping back and seeing if you can read it at a distance. Strangers walking by won't put in the effort to decipher it. It needs to click instantly.

- **Keep Text Brief:** A sign is not a brochure. Stick to the essentials: typically, your business name, a tagline or product category, and possibly one concise slogan or call to action. If you clutter it with too much info, people's eyes will glaze over. Remember, you can always provide details in person or on handouts. The sign's job is to get their attention.

- **Quality and Durability:** Use materials that won't fall apart, especially if outdoors. A flimsy paper sign taped to your table might flop around or get damaged, inadvertently signaling that you're not very well established or prepared. Instead, laminate a poster or use proper banner material. If you print at home, consider mounting the print on a foam board for sturdiness. If your event is outdoors, ensure your sign can withstand a breeze or a little sprinkle. Carry some clips, tape, or weights to secure things.

- **Branding Consistency:** This bears repeating. Your signage should resemble the style of your website, business cards, and packaging. This unified look helps people remember you. Someone might see your sign at a fair and later visit your website; if the colors and logo are the same, they'll immediately think, "Oh, it's that cool candle maker I saw at the fair!" That consistency builds trust.

- **Budget-Friendly Ideas:** If professional printing is too pricey initially, you can still create decent signage on a budget. For example, print a high-resolution poster of your logo or business name at a local office supply store and display it in a nice frame or on a foam core. Or use premade letters or stencils to paint your business name on a blank banner from a craft store. Just make sure whatever DIY approach you use ends up neat and aligned with your style (it shouldn't look like a last-minute science project poster). As you grow, you can upgrade your signs.

Real-World Example: Imagine a small, handmade soap company attending a local artisan market. The owner brings a banner that reads "Sunrise Soaps" in her sunny yellow brand color with a little rising sun logo. She hangs it on the back of her tent. On the table, she has a framed sign that says "All-natural, aromatic soaps. Try a free sample!" in matching font. Each type of soap has a tiny label sign in front of it describing the scent and price. The cohesive yellow accents and neat signs make her booth look polished. Shoppers' eyes are drawn to "Sunrise Soaps" from down the aisle because of the banner, and once they arrive, the smaller signs help them navigate the products and entice them to engage (who doesn't want a free sample?). This is how simple signage can create an inviting, branded space in the real world.

Showing Up at Events: Preparation, Presence, and Making an Impression

One of the most exciting (and nerve-wracking) ways your brand shows up in the real world is when you and your business attend events. This could be a pop-up shop, a trade show, a local fair, a networking event, or any gathering where you represent your company. In-person events are golden opportunities: people can meet the person (or team) behind the brand, touch and feel your products, and experience your brand personality live. However, success at events stems from thorough preparation and an engaging presence. Let's break down how to get ready, what to bring, and how to leave a lasting positive impression.

Plan and Set Goals: Before the event, clarify *why* you're going and what you hope to achieve. Is it to sell products on the spot? To build awareness and collect emails? To meet potential wholesale buyers or partners? Setting one or two primary goals will help you focus. For example, if your goal is sales, you'll want to bring plenty of inventory and maybe run a special event discount. If it's awareness, you might prioritize handing out samples and brochures and talking to as many people as possible. Having clear goals also gives you a way to measure the event's success afterward.

Prepare Your Brand Materials: Based on your goal, organize your materials well in advance. Here's a quick list of what to gather and prepare for an event:

- **Products or Samples:** Bring enough products if you're selling, or samples if you want people to try out your offerings. It's better to have a little more than to run out early. Display them nicely (consider stands, racks, or baskets depending on the product).

- **Business Cards & Brochures:** Pack a generous supply of business cards. They're one of your most important tools at any event. If you have brochures, flyers, or lookbooks that explain your business or list your products and services, bring those too. Some people love taking something to read later.

- **Signage:** Don't forget the signage we discussed. A banner, poster, or sign for your table or booth is essential. Bring any stands, easels, or clips needed to prop them up. Test your banner hanging at home if possible, so you know how to set it up quickly.

- **Table Setup Items:** If you have a booth or table, consider a tablecloth, ideally in a brand color or a neutral black/white. Many folding tables at events are beat up, and a cloth instantly makes them look nicer. Bring any decor that fits your brand and makes your space attractive. For example, a small floral arrangement for a natural skincare brand, or some product photos, or a laptop slideshow for a web design business. Just don't overcrowd the table. Leave space for visitors to pick up and examine your materials or products comfortably.

- **Tools and Miscellaneous:** Assemble a small kit of event essentials. This might include tape or tacks (to hang signs or secure a tablecloth), scissors, a notepad and pens, a marker, safety pins or zip ties, a portable phone charger (especially if using a phone for payments or demos), an extension cord and power strip if you'll need power, and any device chargers or adapters. If you're processing sales, bring your card reader, receipt book or app, cash change, and any required forms. If you plan to collect contacts, have a sign-up sheet or a bowl for business cards (and pens!). Having these little items on hand can save the day. For example, if your banner needs an extra piece of tape, or your phone battery is dying halfway through the event.

- **Personal Comfort Items:** Events can be long. Bring water, snacks, and maybe a couple of pain relievers or band-aids just in case. Wear comfortable shoes, as you may be on your feet for hours. These aren't "brand" items per se, but if you're tired and thirsty, it's harder to be your enthusiastic best self representing your brand. So, taking care of yourself is part of showing up strong!

Dress and Appearance: You are a walking part of your brand at events. Dress in a way that's both comfortable and reflective of your brand image. This doesn't mean you need a uniform or anything fancy. Just think about the impression you want to make. If your brand is creative and funky, you might wear a bright color or accessory that matches that vibe (maybe even a T-shirt with your logo if appropriate). If your brand is more formal or professional, you'd likely wear business casual attire, possibly incorporating a subtle branded pin or featuring your brand colors in your outfit. The key is to look put-together and approachable. Also, *smile!* A friendly face is part of your "appearance" and can draw people in more than any outfit.

At the Event, Be Approachable: Once you're all set up, focus on your body language and engagement. Stand or sit upright, keep your phone away (nothing is more off-putting than a vendor or representative buried in their smartphone while people wander by), and make eye contact with passersby. You can start with a hello or a warm greeting to anyone who seems remotely interested, or even those just walking past your booth. You might say, "Hi there, how's your day going?" or a simple "Let me know if you have any questions!" to break the ice. Having a bowl of candy or an interactive element (like a product sample to smell or try) on your table can also encourage people to pause and chat. For example, if you sell hand lotions, you could have a tester bottle out and say, "Feel free to try our new lavender lotion!" This invites interaction and starts a conversation.

Tell Your Brand Story (Briefly): When someone shows interest, be ready to share a short and sweet introduction to your business. In previous chapters, you worked on your brand story and elevator pitch. Here's where it comes into play. Explain what your business is about in a sentence or two: "I'm the founder of GreenLeaf Teas, we blend organic teas inspired by my grandmother's recipes." or "Tech Guru Co. helps small businesses by providing affordable tech support, kind of like an IT department for those who don't have one." Tailor it to the event context if possible (at a tech meetup, highlight the tech angle; at a foodie event, focus on the gourmet aspect of your product, etc.). Keep it conversational, not like a rehearsed sales script. The goal is to communicate the essence of your brand and why it's special in a genuine way.

Listen and Engage: Remember, showing up is not just about broadcasting your brand, but also about connecting. Ask questions to the people you meet. What brings them to the event? What are they looking for? This isn't an interrogation, just a friendly chat. If you're at a trade show, an attendee might be shopping around for specific solutions; if you're at a local market, a customer might be curious about how your product is made. Engage in two-way conversations. People appreciate feeling heard, and you might learn valuable information about your potential customers' needs or interests. Plus, for those of us who are nervous talkers, asking questions takes some pressure off you to keep monologuing!

Handling Nerves: It's normal to feel a bit nervous at events, especially if you're new to them. One strategy is to focus on the value you're offering rather than on yourself. Instead of thinking "I have to be a great salesperson," reframe it as "I'm here to help people solve X problem or enjoy Y benefit with my product/service." When you genuinely believe in what you offer, that enthusiasm will be evident. Also, remind yourself that *you* know your brand better than anyone. You're the expert on your business. So even if you get a tough question, there's no need to panic; answer honestly or say, "That's a great question. I think [answer], but I'd also love to follow up with more info after I double-check that." People respect honesty and authenticity over a slick pitch.

Make an Impression: Little details can leave a lasting impression:

- **Be courteous and positive** with everyone, even just the window shoppers. A friendly vibe makes people associate positive feelings with your brand, even if they don't make a purchase right then and there.

- **Use names** if you can. If someone introduces themselves, try to use their name in the conversation ("Nice to meet you, Sarah!"). It makes the interaction more personal. And don't forget to introduce yourself, too, as the face behind the brand.

- **Offer a take-away:** We mentioned business cards and brochures. Ensure everyone who seems interested leaves with something that has your brand on it, so they can follow up or remember you later. It could even be a small freebie with your logo (like a sticker or a magnet). These keep your brand in their mind beyond the event.

- **Collect contacts** if appropriate. For example, you could have a newsletter sign-up sheet or a bowl to drop business cards in for a raffle prize. Make it optional and low-pressure ("Drop your email here if you'd like to stay in touch or hear about our upcoming sales. Totally up to you!"). Building an email list or contact list from events is gold for future marketing efforts.

- **Snap Photos (if allowed):** Take a few pictures of your booth or interactions (with permission). It not only provides you with social media content ("Here we are at the Austin Spring Market!") but also helps you review your setup later to see how you can improve your display.

- **After-Event Follow-Up:** This happens behind the scenes, but it's worth mentioning: after the event, follow up with any promising contacts you made. Shoot a quick email saying, "Great to meet you at the event, thanks for stopping by our booth!" to those who gave you cards or emails. This follow-up solidifies the connection, and often people appreciate the gesture. It shows you remember them as individuals.

Learn and Improve: Treat each event as an opportunity for learning and improvement. Perhaps you've discovered that people keep asking the same question about your product. That might mean making the information more evident in your signage or materials next time. Or you realized you needed an extra extension cord, or more inventory of a particular item that sold out quickly. Make notes after each event about what worked well and what to do differently. This kind of continuous improvement is how even the biggest brands fine-tune their event presence, and you can do it too, getting a bit better each time.

Lastly, have fun if you can! Your attitude is a key component of your brand. If people see you enjoying the event, being passionate about your business, and being genuinely interested in meeting them, they'll remember that positive energy. Not every event will be a home run in terms of sales or leads, but each one presents an opportunity to showcase your brand and build your confidence. Over time, showing up in the real world becomes one of the most rewarding parts of brand building, as you witness real people connecting with what you've created.

Types of Events to Consider for Your Brand

Not all events are created equal. Depending on your business type and target audience, some will be more relevant than others. Here are several types of real-world events and opportunities you might consider, along with why they could be great for your brand:

- **Local Pop-Up Shops:** Pop-ups are temporary retail events, often hosted within another shop or at a special venue, where you set up a mini store for a short time (a day, a weekend, a month). For example, a local clothing boutique might invite your handmade jewelry business to do a weekend pop-up in their store. Pop-ups are excellent for *testing the waters* in new locations or reaching a built-in audience from the host venue. They create a sense of urgency ("we're here only this week!") that can drive interest. They also allow customers to experience your brand in person without having a permanent store. They can touch products, try them on, and ask questions. If you primarily sell online, pop-ups can occasionally give your online brand a physical presence, which can boost your visibility and allow you to gather in-person feedback.

- **Farmer's Markets and Craft Fairs:** These community events are fantastic for many small businesses, especially if you make handcrafted goods, food items, or artisan products. Farmers' markets usually occur weekly and attract people who love local and handmade products. Craft fairs or maker markets might be seasonal or annual events. The vibe at these is usually casual and friendly. It's a chance to meet lots of local customers who appreciate small businesses. If your brand values include local sourcing, handmade quality, or community, these events reinforce that. Plus, they're typically low-cost to join (you might pay a small booth fee or a percentage of sales). You can also network with fellow small business owners in other booths, which can lead to collaborations or support.

- **Trade Shows and Industry Expos:** These are larger, often more formal events where businesses in a specific industry showcase their products and services. Examples include trade shows for tech gadgets, beauty products, and pet supplies. Trade shows typically attract wholesale buyers, distributors, media representatives, and consumers. They can be pricey (booth fees, travel, elaborate displays), so you want to choose carefully. If you have a product and your goal is to get retail stores to carry it or secure media coverage, a trade show can be worthwhile. You'll be among industry peers, which is excellent for learning and making significant connections. Ensure your branding is exceptionally polished here. You're competing with well-established brands on the same floor. The earlier tip about setting goals is crucial. If your goal at a trade show is finding a retail partner, you might tailor your pitch and materials to that angle (e.g., have a line sheet or catalog ready and prepare wholesale pricing). Trade shows can significantly boost brand awareness beyond your local area if done correctly.

- **Networking Meetups and Business Groups:** Sometimes the events you attend aren't about selling on the spot, but about building relationships. Consider joining local business networking groups (like your Chamber of Commerce, industry associations, or entrepreneur meetups). These gatherings might be breakfast meetings, happy hours, or workshops where the focus is on professionals connecting rather than showcasing products. While you might not set up a booth, you show up as the face of your brand. This is where your business card and personal introduction carry the day. The benefit? You could meet potential mentors, partners, or referral sources. For instance, a wedding photographer might meet an event planner at a networking event and later get client referrals, or a home baker might meet a café owner who's looking for a supplier for pastries. Go in with the mindset of mutual support and learning, not just "sell, sell, sell." Networking events build your reputation in the community, and people often prefer to do business with those they know and trust.

- **Workshops, Classes, or Speaking Opportunities:** Depending on your expertise, hosting or participating in a workshop can showcase your brand's authority and personality. If you make craft goods, you could host a small class teaching a simple skill (like a candle-making workshop sponsored by your candle brand). If you're a marketing consultant, you might speak at a local business workshop about branding (showcasing your own brand as a case in point!). These events position you as a helpful expert and help you establish a positive reputation. They're also great for making deeper connections. Spending an hour teaching a group means those people get to know you more intimately than a brief chat at a busy fair. Just ensure any workshop or speaking topic you choose is closely related to your business, so it feels cohesive (for example, a bakery might do a cupcake decorating class, which directly ties to their products).

- **Community Events and Sponsorships:** Keep an eye on community calendars. There may be charity events, school fairs, local festivals, or holiday markets where you can participate or sponsor. For instance, sponsoring a Little League team or having a booth at the town summer festival can increase local visibility. When your brand shows up at community events, it signals that you're invested in the community. Just make sure to choose events that align with your brand values and where your target audience will be. If you run a pet supply store, sponsoring the local animal shelter's fundraiser is a natural fit (and you could set up a table with some products or freebies there). If your brand is committed to sustainability, participating in an Earth Day community event would be a great fit.

- **Pop-In Visits and Guerrilla Marketing:** Apart from organized events, consider informal ways to show up. Could you do a pop-in demo at a related local business? For example, a coffee roaster might arrange a free tasting at a local bakery one morning (with permission, of course). Or use a guerrilla marketing tactic, such as handing out free samples in a busy pedestrian area (again, ensure you have obtained any necessary permissions). These are more one-off and require creativity and confidence, but they can create a buzz if done cleverly. Always bring branding materials to these events (wear a branded apron or display a sign with your name, and include a card or flyer with each sample so people know how to find you later).

Choose What Fits Your Brand: You don't have to do all these types of events. In fact, it's better to choose a few that make sense for your business and do them well. Consider where your target customers are likely to be and which environment will best showcase your brand. If you sell visually appealing products, craft fairs and pop-ups are great because people can see and fall in love with them in person. If you offer professional services, networking events, or workshops where you can talk about what you do, might yield more leads than a general market. Be strategic with your time and resources. It's better to have an amazing presence at two events a year that really matter to your business than to stretch yourself thin doing 10 events that don't connect with the right audience.

Also, consider your own comfort zone and build from there. If the idea of a huge trade show in another state is too overwhelming right now, start with a small local fair to get experience. You can always scale up as you gain confidence and see results. The important thing is that you get out there in some capacity. Don't hide your awesome brand in a shell. The world needs to see it!

Tips for Introverted or Shy Brand Builders

Putting yourself out there can be challenging, especially if you're naturally shy or introverted. Many small business owners are introverts at heart. You might prefer making or planning over pitching and mingling. The good news is that you don't have to transform into a stereotypical extroverted salesperson to show up in the real world successfully. You can leverage your own strengths and still make meaningful connections. Here are some tips to help even the most introverted brand builders shine offline:

- **Leverage One-on-One Strengths:** Introverts often excel in smaller group or one-on-one interactions. Use that to your advantage. At events, rather than trying to draw a huge crowd to talk to at once, focus on **connecting deeply with one person at a time**. A few genuine, quality conversations can be more valuable than dozens of quick chats. The people you connect with will remember the authenticity of your interaction.

- **Prepare Talking Points (and Questions):** It can calm nerves to have a plan. Before an event, practice a brief introduction of yourself and your business (your elevator pitch). Also prepare a couple of open-ended questions to ask others. For example, "What brings you here today?" or "Have you been to this event before?" These questions prompt others to talk, so it's not all on you to carry the conversation. Having a mental script for the first 30 seconds of an interaction can ease the anxiety of the unknown. Once the conversation gets going, you'll naturally find it easier to continue.

- **Use Your Brand as a Conversation Starter:** Sometimes talking about yourself feels hard, but talking about something you created is easier. Let your products, booth, or materials do some of the talking. If you're shy, a friendly way to engage is to point out something about your display: "Have you tried kombucha before? This one we brew has Texas peaches, want a taste?" or "This photo here shows how our software helps track inventory. I can explain more if you're interested." People will ask questions about what they see, which provides a comfortable opportunity to discuss your business. You're effectively talking about your passion, which is usually an easier topic than making small talk about the weather or sports.

- **Set Manageable Goals:** Give yourself a small, achievable goal for each event. For instance, "I will hand out 5 business cards today" or "I will have at least two conversations with new people." This shifts the focus from an amorphous "I have to be outgoing" to a concrete task. Once you meet your goal, you might find you're warmed up and continue further! However, even if you stop short of your goal, you can still consider the event a success for you personally. Over time, you can increase these goals as your confidence grows.

- **Bring a Buddy (if possible):** If events absolutely drain you, see if you can bring a friend, family member, or team member along (someone who knows your business fairly well). Their presence can ease your stress. They can help handle conversations or at least give you a short break when you need to catch your breath. For example, if you run a small bakery and you're shy, bring your outgoing friend who loves your cupcakes to help at the booth. They might naturally jump in to say, "Aren't these cupcakes great? You've got to try the chocolate one," giving you a moment to relax. Ensure that anyone assisting knows the key points to convey about your brand, so they accurately represent you.

- **Find Comfort in Roles:** Sometimes introverts feel more at ease when they have a defined role. At your booth, your "role" is the owner/expert, so lean into that expertise. You might not love bragging about yourself, but you can confidently educate people about your product or craft because you know it inside out. Focus on being helpful by assisting customers in finding what they need, offering guidance, and sharing your knowledge. Shifting from "selling mode" to "helping mode" often reduces anxiety because you're just being of service, which might come naturally to you.

- **Take Breaks to Recharge:** Give yourself permission to step away for a few minutes if you feel overwhelmed (of course, ensure your booth is staffed or safe, or ask a neighboring vendor to keep an eye on it). A quick walk or a moment outside the crowd can recharge your social battery. At a networking event where you can't physically leave, excuse yourself to the restroom or refreshment table for a short breather. It's better to take tiny breaks than to push until you're completely drained and anxious.

- **Use Non-Verbal Tools:** Let your printed materials and environment speak when you need a pause. For example, have a sign that says, "Join our mailing list for a free sample," so people can engage with it on their own. Wear a name tag or branded apparel so people start conversations ("Oh, you're from XYZ company? I've heard of you."). When walking around a networking event, a shirt or tote bag with your logo can draw attention without you having to say a word initially. These silent signals can prompt others to approach you, which is half the battle!

- **Practice in Low-Stakes Settings:** If the idea of networking still sounds terrifying, practice your social brand skills in easier scenarios. Consider volunteering at a community event to get accustomed to the environment, or attend one as a visitor before participating as a vendor. You could also join a small club or take a class where interacting is part of the experience. These can build confidence. It's like a rehearsal for the real business events, but without the pressure of selling anything.

- **Embrace Your Introvert Advantages:** Believe it or not, introverts have superpowers in networking and branding. You are likely a good listener, which means you can make others feel truly heard, a memorable quality. You probably think before you speak, so when you do share something, it tends to be thoughtful and meaningful. These are strengths! Many people are a bit tired of overly pushy salespeople; an approachable, calm, and genuine presence can attract those who appreciate a softer approach. Your authenticity can set your brand apart in a crowded, noisy marketplace.

- **After Socializing, Do Self-Care:** Recognize that showing up in the real world might drain you more than someone who is extroverted. Plan some relaxation or quiet time after an event as a reward. Maybe the night after a big networking meetup, you unwind with a good book or a warm bath, not more socializing. Taking care of your mental energy ensures you don't burn out and start dreading events. We want these experiences to be sustainable and even enjoyable for you over time.

Remember, being introverted is not a weakness in brand building. You might approach it differently, and that's perfectly fine. Many customers (and fellow business folks) you meet will appreciate a low-pressure, genuine interaction more than a flashy sales pitch. By using the tips above, you can step out of your comfort zone in manageable ways and let your brand speak in a style that stays true to you. Each successful interaction will boost your confidence for the next. You've got this!

Reflection and Action: Bring Your Brand to Life

Now that we've explored how your brand can be physically represented, it's time to turn ideas into action. This final section will help you reflect on what you've learned and create a plan to apply it immediately. Use the prompts and checklist below to solidify your next steps:

Reflection Prompt - Your Real-World Brand Presence: Take a moment to envision your brand out in the world and consider these questions:

- How do you currently present your business in person? (Do you have business cards, packaging, signs, or attend events yet?) How does it feel, and is it consistent with the image you want to portray?

- Which aspect of showing up in the real world excites you the most? Which aspect feels most challenging or intimidating? Why?

- Think of a business (big or small) that impressed you when you saw it in person. What did they do that made them stand out, and what can you learn from that example for your brand?

Jot down your thoughts to these questions in a notebook or journal. Being aware of where you stand and how you feel now will help you track your progress as you implement changes.

Action Checklist - Start Showing Up: When you're ready, use this checklist to guide your real-world branding efforts. These steps will help you apply the chapter's lessons one by one:

- ☐ **Design or Refresh Your Business Card:** If you don't have a business card yet, create one that includes your essential info and matches your brand style. If you have one, review it. Does it need an update in design or info? Once satisfied, print a batch and put some in your wallet or work bag right away.

- ☐ **Enhance Your Packaging:** Identify one way to infuse more branding into your product packaging. It could be as simple as ordering logo stickers, printing a thank-you insert to include with orders, or choosing a new packaging color that aligns with your brand. Implement that change for your next batch of products or shipments.

- ☐ **Create a Basic Sign:** Plan a primary sign for your next event or your store (if applicable). It might be designing a banner online or making a neat DIY sign. Ensure it has your logo or name clearly visible. Acquire or make that sign and practice setting it up. Even if you have no event scheduled yet, having a ready-to-go sign will motivate you to use it!

- ☐ **Schedule an Event or Outreach:** Look at upcoming opportunities in your community or industry. Choose at least one event (a market, meetup, pop-up, etc.) in the next couple of months where you can show up for your brand. Mark your calendar and sign up or RSVP. This commitment makes it real.

- ☐ **Prepare Your Event Kit:** Make a list of everything you'll need for that event: products, marketing materials, supplies, and personal comfort items. Start gathering those items in a box or bag so you're not scrambling last minute. **Pro Tip:** Always keep an "event bag" packed with essentials like tape, scissors, pens, and an extension cord.

- ☐ **Practice Your Introduction:** Stand in front of a mirror or with a friend and rehearse a 15-second introduction of your business ("Hi, I'm __ and my company __ does __."). Also, practice asking a friendly question to a stranger. It might feel silly, but it builds muscle memory. When the real moment comes, you'll find the words flow more easily.

☐ **Reach Out for Support:** If you're nervous about in-person interactions, consider identifying a friend, mentor, or fellow business owner to discuss your concerns with. They might join you at an event or offer a pep talk. Sometimes sharing your fears out loud makes them less powerful, and you might pick up a helpful tip or two from others' experiences.

☐ **Set a Post-Event Follow-Up Plan:** Decide now how you will follow up with people after any event. For example, prepare a generic "thank you for visiting" email template, or plan to post a shout-out to the event on social media. Having a follow-up routine means you won't lose the connections you make.

☐ **Celebrate Your Wins:** Finally, each time you take one of these actions or attend an event, reward yourself. It could be as simple as a quiet evening off, a favorite treat, or a shout-out in your journal about what went well. Acknowledging your progress will keep you motivated to continue taking steps forward.

By checking off these items, you're actively building your brand's presence in the real world. Remember, consistency is everything. The more regularly you show up, whether through branded materials or at events, the more people will recognize and trust your business. Your brand grows stronger every time you put it out into the world.

As you work through this checklist, keep the spirit of this chapter in mind: it's about forming genuine connections and conveying the essence of your business through tangible experiences for people. Stay true to your brand identity, be patient with yourself as you gain experience, and keep pushing slightly beyond your comfort zone. You'll find that each effort becomes easier and more rewarding.

Now, take a deep breath and give yourself credit – you've come a long way in building your brand from scratch. Making a presence in the real world is a significant milestone, and you are fully capable of making it a success. The world is ready to meet your brand, in living color. Go out there and shine!

CHAPTER 11: UNDERSTAND YOUR PEOPLE

Building a strong brand extends beyond a visually appealing logo or a clever tagline. At its heart, a brand is a relationship between your business and the people you serve. To nurture that relationship, you must have a deep understanding of your audience: their needs, habits, concerns, and aspirations. Whether you're a brand-new entrepreneur or an established small business owner refreshing your brand, this chapter will help you gain clarity on who you are serving, what problems you solve for them, and how to speak directly to your ideal audience.

In this chapter, we'll explore why understanding your audience is essential and walk through practical ways to get to know "your people." You'll learn how to listen and observe, use simple research tools like surveys and interviews, create customer personas, leverage data from your website and social media, avoid common biases, and tune your brand's language and offerings to fit your audience like a glove. By the end, you'll have actionable strategies (and perhaps a few "aha!" moments) to ensure your brand truly resonates with the people who matter most: your customers.

Let's dive in, with a friendly reminder: every expert in branding started as a beginner who took the time to listen and learn. You can do this!

Why Knowing Your Audience Is Essential

Imagine trying to have a meaningful conversation with a stranger without knowing anything about them. You wouldn't know what topics interest them or what tone of voice to use. The same goes for your brand and its audience. Understanding your audience is the foundation of effective branding. Here's why it matters so much:

- **Stronger Connections:** When you know your audience's values, needs, and pain points, you can create messages and solutions that hit home. Your marketing won't feel like generic advertising; it will feel like a heartfelt conversation. This builds trust and emotional connection. People are far more likely to support a brand that "gets" them.

- **Relevance and Resonance:** Understanding your audience helps you stay relevant. You'll offer products, services, and content that genuinely solve their problems or enrich their lives. Instead of guessing what they might want, you'll know what they want. This means you're not wasting effort on things people don't care about. Every blog post, social media update, or promotion can be tailored to resonate with your ideal customer.

- **Loyalty and Word-of-Mouth:** When customers feel understood, they also feel valued. Meeting their needs consistently can turn one-time buyers into loyal fans. These satisfied customers often become your brand ambassadors, spreading the word to friends and family. Remember, a strong brand is built on people who keep coming back, and who bring others along.

- **Efficient Marketing:** Clarity about your audience means you can target your marketing better. Instead of throwing messages out to the whole world and hoping someone responds, you focus on the specific group of people who are most likely to love what you offer. This saves you money and time, and it increases the impact of every dollar or minute you spend on marketing.

- **Standing Out from Competitors:** In a crowded market, brands that understand their customers can differentiate themselves. If you know exactly what frustrates your customers and none of your competitors are addressing it, you have an opportunity to stand out by doing so. Your brand can become the go-to choice because people see that you *truly* understand them, unlike others who feel distant or out of touch.

In short, without understanding your audience, you don't really have a brand, at least not one that will matter to people. Branding isn't about what *you* say, it's about what your customer *hears* and *feels*. So, let's talk about how to get that understanding.

Listen First: Observing and Hearing Your Customers

The best way to understand people is simple: listen to them. Your customers (and potential customers) are constantly giving off clues about what they want and how they feel, if you pay attention. This doesn't require fancy technology or big budgets. It starts with being genuinely curious and observant in everyday interactions. Here are some informal ways to observe and listen to your audience:

- **Casual Conversations:** If you have direct contact with customers (in a store, over the phone, on a service call, etc.), take a moment to chat. Ask how they're doing, what they're looking for, or if everything was satisfactory. Then really listen to their answers. For example, a hair salon owner might learn a lot by chatting with clients about how they maintain their hair at home or what beauty tips they're curious about. These casual chats can reveal common pain points or desires (like "I wish I could style my hair as well as you did just now", a cue that there's an opportunity for a styling workshop or product recommendation).

- **Online Reviews and Feedback:** Read the reviews people leave for your business, and even for similar companies or competitors. Reviews are a goldmine of unfiltered customer thoughts. Pay attention to what people praise ("The staff always remembers my name") and what they complain about ("Shipping took forever" or "menu is confusing"). You'll start noticing patterns. For instance, if multiple reviews of your café mention that it's a cozy spot to relax, that's a strength you can highlight in your branding. If several reviews of a competitor's product say, "It didn't solve X problem," and that's a problem your product *can* solve, that's insight into how to position your offering.

- **Social Media and Forums:** People often talk about their needs and preferences on social platforms and community forums. Do a little social listening: what are people saying about products or services like yours on Twitter/X, Facebook groups, Reddit, or local community boards? You don't have to spy or be intrusive. Much of this is public discussion. Suppose you run a yoga studio, and you find a local Facebook group where people discuss fitness classes. You might see posts like "I wish there were a beginner-friendly evening class in our area." Bingo! That's great insight for scheduling or marketing your classes as beginner-friendly. Even just monitoring your own social media comments and messages can be illuminating. If someone asks, "Do you offer this in blue?" or "Is it kid-friendly?", those questions show you what matters to them.

- **In-Store or On-Site Observation:** If applicable, observe how customers interact with your product or service in real life. How do they navigate your store? Which items do they pick up and then put back (indicating interest but maybe some hesitation)? Where do they spend the most time? If you own a retail shop, you might notice customers consistently gravitate to a particular display in the back. Maybe that's an opportunity to place a promotional sign or to rearrange the store to make popular items more visible. If you're a consultant meeting clients, notice their body language and reactions when you discuss various offerings; do their eyes light up at certain benefits you mention? All these cues help you understand what they care about.

- **Customer Service Interactions:** Don't overlook the questions and complaints that come through email, phone calls, or customer support channels. If multiple people ask, "How do I do X with your product?" it may mean that your instructions were unclear, or that X is an area that needs improvement or explanation. If certain complaints persist, it indicates a pain point that needs to be addressed. Treat these not as annoyances but as *free product research*. They're telling you what's not working for them and what they need.

Pro Tip: Keep a notebook or digital file of these insights. Jot down recurring themes or surprising comments you hear. Over time, you'll build a clearer picture of your audience's collective voice. For example, you might compile a list like "Several people this week asked if we offer vegan options" or "Noticed many window shoppers drawn to the colorful displays but leaving without buying. Maybe they didn't find what they wanted?" These notes will be invaluable as you refine your brand.

The key in all of this informal research is empathy. Put yourself in your customer's shoes. Be present and attentive. Even a short conversation or a single review can spark a new idea or alert you to something crucial about your audience. Listening is how relationships start, so let your audience know you're listening.

Ask and You Shall Learn: Using Surveys, Interviews, and Polls

While observation is great, sometimes the simplest way to find out what your customers want is to ask them directly. You don't need to be a professional researcher to do this. In fact, some of the most insightful feedback can come from very basic questions. Let's look at a few friendly tools you can use:

- **Surveys:** A short survey can reveal patterns across many customers. You can create surveys easily using free or inexpensive tools

(Google Forms, SurveyMonkey, etc.) and share them via email, social media, or a link on your website. Keep it simple and respectful of your customers' time: a handful of questions is often enough. For example, you might ask, *"What's the biggest challenge you face when [related to your product/service]?"* or *"How did you first hear about us?"* Include a mix of multiple-choice (for easy analysis) and one or two open-ended questions for richer feedback. **Pro Tip:** Offer a small incentive, if possible (such as a coupon code or entry into a prize draw) to encourage responses. Even a dozen responses can give you valuable insights.

- **One-on-One Interviews:** Nothing beats a real conversation for depth of understanding. Identify a few customers (or prospective customers) who might be willing to chat. This could be in person, over the phone, or on a video call. Prepare a few guiding questions, but approach the conversation as a dialogue, not an interrogation. You could ask questions like, *"What problem were you hoping to solve by using our service?"*, *"Can you walk me through how you use our product in your daily life?"*, or *"Have you tried similar services before? How do we compare?"* The goal is to let them talk freely about their experiences and feelings. Follow-up questions often yield the best insights (e.g., "Oh, you mentioned our website was hard to navigate. Could you tell me more about that?"). Make sure to listen more than you speak. You might be surprised. A customer could reveal, for example, that they found a creative workaround to use your product for a purpose you never expected. That could spark a new feature or a new way to market it!

- **Polls and Quick Questions:** If a long survey or interview feels like too much, try quick polls. Social media platforms (Twitter/X, Instagram Stories, and Facebook) have built-in poll features. You can ask fun, easy-to-answer questions like, *"Which new flavor should we launch next: Chocolate or Green Tea?"* or *"What's the #1 thing you look for in a bookkeeping service: 1) Low cost, 2) Personal advice, 3) Time saved?"* People are surprisingly willing to click a poll option when it's simple. While these won't give deep, nuanced answers, they provide directional data and also engage your audience by showing you care about their opinion. It can be as informal as a yes/no question: *"Would you be interested if we offered weekend appointments? Yes or No."* If 90% say yes, well, there's your answer!

- **Feedback Forms:** If you have a website, consider adding a feedback form or a single-question pop-up asking something like *"Did you find what you were looking for today?"* or *"How would you rate your experience?"* Keep it optional and easy. Over time, these tiny bits of feedback add up. Similarly, for a service business, you might send a follow-up email after a project is done: *"Thank you for choosing us! We'd love to know, what did you enjoy and what could we do better?"* Customers appreciate being asked, especially if you frame it as wanting to serve them better.

- **Informal Chat Messages:** Depending on your relationship with customers, sometimes even a casual email or text asking for thoughts can work. For example, a freelance graphic designer might send a quick message to a past client, *"Hey! I'm updating my approach to working with clients. Is there anything you think I could do to make the process smoother?"* The informality can make people comfortable enough to give an honest answer.

When using these tools, keep a few best practices in mind:

- **Be clear and specific** in your questions so people understand what you're asking. Avoid jargon or broad terms. Instead of "How do our services meet your expectations?" you might ask, "Did the service solve your problem?" or "What would you change about your experience with us?"

- **Keep it short.** Respect your customers' time. It's better to get a 5-question survey thoroughly answered than a 50-question survey abandoned halfway.

- **Assure anonymity if appropriate.** People tend to be more honest if they know their feedback won't be linked to their name (especially when completing surveys). You can say, "All answers are anonymous, so please be candid!"

- **Show gratitude.** Always thank people for sharing their thoughts, even if the feedback is hard to hear. If someone took the time to help you understand them, that's a gift. Reply with a thank you message or consider sending a small discount code as appreciation, if possible.

Lastly, don't be afraid of what you'll hear. Sometimes, as business owners, we avoid asking because we secretly fear negative feedback. But knowing the truth is always better than guessing in the dark. If a few interviews reveal that your product isn't solving the problem people thought it would, that's tough to hear, but it gives you a chance to fix it, adjust your messaging, or develop a new solution that *does* meet their needs. It's all valuable information.

By proactively asking your audience to share their opinions and experiences, you open a dialogue. Customers often feel *more* connected to a brand that asks for their input. It shows humility ("we don't assume we have all the answers") and genuine care ("your voice matters to us"). This collaborative approach can transform your audience into partners in shaping the brand, ultimately creating a stronger brand.

Creating Customer Personas: Who Are You Really Serving?

After you've gathered information by listening and asking, it's time to synthesize what you've learned. One powerful technique in branding and marketing is to create customer personas (also called buyer personas or audience profiles). A persona is like a fictional character that represents a segment of your real customers. Think of it as painting a picture of your ideal customer so clearly that you almost feel you know them as a person.

Why do this? Because it's easier to craft messages, products, and services for a specific someone than for a vague "everyone." When you have a persona in mind, you can always ask, *"Would this resonate with [Persona]?"* and it keeps your branding on track.

How to Create a Persona:

1. **Gather Your Data:** Look at all the information you've collected from conversations, surveys, reviews, etc. What common traits do your best customers share? You might notice patterns. For example, let's say you run an online bookkeeping service. You observe that many of your clients are self-employed professionals in their 30s and 40s who say they struggle with finding time for bookkeeping and worry about making tax mistakes. Already, you have seeds of a persona here.

2. **Give Them a Name and Face:** This might feel a bit silly, but it really helps. Give your persona a name that evokes their identity, like "Busy Brenda" or "Entrepreneur Ellis." Some people even find a

stock photo or draw a little sketch to visualize them. For instance, "Busy Brenda" could represent those overwhelmed small biz owners juggling many tasks. Naming your persona makes them feel real and keeps you focused on an individual rather than an abstract concept.

3. **Demographics and Basics:** Outline the basic details about this persona: age, gender (if relevant), occupation, location, maybe family status or income range if those matter to your business. Example: *Brenda is a 38-year-old graphic designer who started her own company. She's married with two kids, lives in a suburban area, and earns about $80k a year.* These details help ground the persona in reality. However, note that not every detail is always relevant. Focus on what matters to the customer's relationship with your business. If marital status doesn't impact how they use your product, you don't need to define it.

4. **Needs, Goals, and Pain Points:** This is the heart of the persona. What is this person trying to achieve, especially as it relates to your product or service? What problems or pain points do they have that you can help solve? Continuing our example: *Brenda's goal is to grow her design business and maintain a good work-life balance. Her pain point is that bookkeeping and managing finances consume time she'd rather spend acquiring new clients or spending time with her family. She's worried about making a mistake with her taxes or not knowing if she's profitable month to month.* These insights come directly from what real customers have told you. If you noticed lots of your clients saying, "I never have time to do my books," put that in the persona's story.

5. **Habits and Behavior:** How does this persona typically behave? Where do they get information? What is their buying behavior? For Brenda: *She finds solutions by searching online and asking for referrals in her professional network. She's pretty tech-savvy, uses her smartphone a lot for work, and she values tools that save her time. She tends to research a service thoroughly before buying, reading reviews, and comparing options, because she can't afford to waste time on the wrong choice.* This part helps you determine where and how to connect with your persona. If Brenda is always on LinkedIn and reads industry blogs, that's where your brand should probably have a presence or advertise. If she values convenience, perhaps an easy-to-use mobile app for your service would appeal to her.

6. **Preferred Brand Interaction:** Consider what kind of brand communication or style this person prefers. Do they like formal and professional interactions, or casual and friendly ones? Are they looking for a supportive guide or an authoritative expert? In Brenda's case: *She appreciates when service providers talk to her in plain English (not heavy accounting jargon) and treat her like a partner. She doesn't like it when she feels talked down to about finances. She responds well to a friendly, helpful tone, like someone who's on her side, helping her succeed.* This insight suggests keeping your brand voice encouraging and clear, rather than overly corporate or technical, when targeting "Brenda."

7. **Give a Scenario or Story:** Sometimes it helps to write a little narrative about a day in the life of your persona or how they might go through the customer journey with your brand. *For example:* "Brenda discovers our bookkeeping service after venting to a friend about her messy finances, and the friend sends her our blog article on 'Accounting Tips for Busy Entrepreneurs.' She skims it at 10 PM after a long workday and realizes we understand exactly what she's feeling. The next morning, she signs up for our free trial. Initially, she's worried it'll be complicated, but when she hits a snag, she uses our live chat support and gets a quick, friendly answer. That relief she feels reinforces that this was the right choice. After two months, she's not stressed at tax time for the first year ever, and she happily refers another friend to us." This mini-story encapsulates how your ideal interaction might go. It's a great test of whether your brand experience is aligning with your persona's needs and expectations.

You can create multiple personas if you serve distinct audiences, but start with one or two core personas: the ones that represent your ideal or most common customers. Each persona should be distinct. If you find yourself trying to stuff too many details into one persona that clearly diverge (e.g., half your customers are "Brenda" but the other half are maybe "Retired Robert" with totally different needs), separate them into two profiles.

Once your personas are created, use them! They're not just a pretty exercise. Share them with your team if you have one, or keep them handy when you're making decisions. When writing your website copy, you might think, *"Would this headline catch Brenda's attention? Would she understand this wording?"* When deciding which new product feature to develop, consider, *"Which feature would make Brenda's life easier?"* If you're deciding where to advertise, ask, *"Does Brenda spend time here?"* Personas provide a target to aim for, making your branding efforts more focused and consistent.

Remember: personas are a tool, not a cage. Real people are more complex than any one profile, and not every customer will fit neatly into one persona. However, even a rough persona is incredibly helpful in keeping your mental image of the customer clear. It shifts your perspective from *"What do I want to say?"* to *"What does my customer need to hear?"*, and that's the key to branding that connects.

Using Data and Analytics to Validate Your Assumptions

Up to now, we've discussed the importance of talking and listening to customers directly, which provides qualitative insights (the stories, the feelings, and the reasons behind their behavior). Another powerful piece of the puzzle is quantitative data: numbers and analytics that show you what people are doing. Using data doesn't have to be intimidating, even for beginners. Think of it as another way your audience is "telling" you about themselves, just in a less personal but more aggregated way.

Here are some approachable ways to use data and analytics to understand your audience and make sure your assumptions line up with reality:

- **Website Analytics:** If you have a website (or an online store or blog), tools like Google Analytics can show you a trove of helpful information. For example:

  - *Traffic sources:* How are people finding you? Is it mainly through Google searches, social media, or referrals from other sites? If you assumed most people find you via Facebook, but the data shows search engines dominate, you might invest more in SEO content or Google Ads.

  - *Popular pages:* Which pages or products get the most views? If your website has a blog, which articles are read the most? This indicates what topics or offerings attract your audience's attention. Say you wrote 10 blog posts, and one of them ("DIY Home Fixes on a Budget") is getting 5x more views than the others. That tells you something: your audience has a significant interest in budget-friendly home fixes. You might then decide to create more content or even products around that interest.

- *User behavior:* See how long people stay on your site, what path they take (for instance, many might view your homepage then click straight to "Pricing" page, indicating interest, or maybe they often go to "About Us" first, perhaps to check credibility). If you notice that users leave (or "bounce") quickly from a particular page, that page may not be meeting their expectations. For instance, if a lot of people click on "Product Features" but then leave immediately, the content may be confusing or not compelling enough. That's a clue to improve it.

- *Audience demographics (if available):* Some analytics tools can give you general demographic info (age ranges, geographic location, device type). While these are broad strokes, they can validate or challenge your persona assumptions. You might think "Brenda" is in her 30s, but your site data shows that the majority of visitors are 45-54. It's time to dig deeper. Perhaps you've been reaching a slightly different crowd than you thought, and you'll want to adjust your messaging or investigate why that older group is more interested.

- **Social Media Insights:** Every major social platform has built-in analytics for business accounts. For example, Facebook and Instagram provide insights into your followers, including their age, gender breakdown, and peak online times. Twitter/X shows which of your posts got the most engagement. Use these:

  - Check if the people engaging with you match your intended audience. If you run a hip skateboard shop aimed at teens, but your Instagram insights show that most of your followers are 30+, that's a red flag that your message or medium might not be connecting with actual teens, or perhaps your target audience needs reconsideration. Maybe it's the parents buying skateboards? Either way, that data is prompting you to ask the right questions.

  - Look at **which posts get the most likes, comments, or shares.** This is a clue to what content resonates. If every time you post a customer success story, it blows up, that's your audience telling you, "we love this!" If your more salesy posts fall flat but your how-to tip videos get shared, focus more on what's working. You don't have to guess; your audience votes with their clicks and comments.

- o Pay attention to the times your audience is online and active. Posting or engaging during those times can increase the chances they'll see and respond to you, which deepens the interaction.

- **Email and Sales Data:** Do you send out newsletters or promotions? Many email marketing tools show open rates and click-through rates on links. This can help you determine which subject lines or content your subscribers are most interested in. *Example:* An online pet supply store notices that any email with the subject line mentioning "training tips" receives a higher open rate than those that say "New Products this Month." That suggests the audience craves helpful tips (so maybe incorporate more useful content in branding, not just product pitches).

  Similarly, look at sales or product purchase data if you have multiple offerings. Which products or services are the top sellers? Is there a particular category that's consistently underperforming? If something isn't selling as expected, it may not be aligned with what your audience truly needs, or it may not be communicated in a way that appeals. Alternatively, your data may reveal unexpected uses (e.g., many customers purchasing a product you considered niche, which could indicate an untapped demand to build upon).

- **Search Queries and SEO Data:** If you have access to Google Search Console or similar tools, you can see some of the search terms that led people to your website. This is literally what people were looking for. For example, a local bakery might discover that many people found their site by searching for "gluten-free cupcakes in [city]." If the bakery isn't already emphasizing their gluten-free options, now they know it's a draw. They might expand that line or market it more, because clearly people are searching for it. On the other hand, if no one is finding you for something you heavily feature, perhaps the wording is off or the demand isn't as high as assumed.

Using data is an excellent way to challenge or confirm your assumptions. It keeps you honest. Sometimes we get attached to a particular idea of our audience or what we think is working. Data will tell you if that's true or if you're a bit off track.

For instance, suppose you assumed your new feature in an app is a big hit, but analytics show only 5% of users are using that feature. That's a sign to investigate why. Maybe they don't see it, or maybe they tried it and didn't find it helpful. You might then survey those who did use it and those who didn't to learn more. See how qualitative and quantitative work together? The numbers raise questions, and the conversations can provide answers, or vice versa.

A Note of Caution: Don't drown in data or try to track every metric under the sun. Identify a few key metrics that relate to your goals. For example, if your goal is to increase engagement with your brand, focus on metrics such as time spent on site, repeat visitors, or social media interactions. If your goal is to understand your customer demographics, pay attention to age and location data. Always tie data back to a question: *"I want to know X about my audience, so I'll look at Y metric, which might inform that."* This way, you use data with purpose, not just for vanity.

Finally, remember that people are more than numbers. Data can tell you what's happening, but not always *why*. That's why we blend analytics with the listening methods discussed earlier. For example, analytics might reveal a high bounce rate on your pricing page (what's happening), and customer interviews might indicate that your pricing packages are confusing or seem too high (why it's happening). Together, you get the whole story and can act on it.

In summary, use analytics as a reality check. It's like getting a bird's-eye view of your audience's behavior to complement the on-the-ground perspective you get from direct feedback. When both perspectives align, you know you're really understanding your people.

Avoiding Assumptions and Bias: Stay Open and Objective

One of the biggest dangers in brand building (and business in general) is assuming you already know everything about your customers or letting personal biases steer decisions. We all have blind spots, and it's easy to see the world through our own lens. In this section, let's discuss how to avoid common pitfalls of assumptions and biases when understanding your audience.

- **Don't assume *you* are your customer:** As a small business owner or solopreneur, you might have started your business to solve a problem you personally had. That's great. It means you empathize with your customers. However, be careful not to project all of your own preferences onto them. For example, you might love an edgy, humorous marketing style, but if your target audience is, say, caregivers looking for daycare services, they might prefer a warmer, more sincere tone. Always test your assumptions by getting feedback from actual customers (not just friends and family, who might share your perspective or be too polite to disagree).

- **Beware of Confirmation Bias:** This is a tendency to notice and trust information that confirms what you already believe, and to ignore information that challenges it. For instance, if you strongly believe "My customers only care about price," you might focus on the one survey comment that says "too expensive" and overlook five other comments that say "I would pay more for better quality." To combat this, actively seek out diverse opinions. If most feedback is positive but one person has a detailed negative critique, resist the urge to dismiss that outlier. Dig in and understand it. It could reveal something important about a subset of customers or a potential improvement.

- **Challenge Stereotypes:** It's human nature to use mental shortcuts, like stereotypes, when thinking of groups of people, but individuals often defy expectations. Let's say you have a notion in your industry like "People over 50 aren't tech-savvy" or "Teenagers have no brand loyalty." If you let those stereotypes guide you, you might alienate or underestimate a portion of your audience. Instead, rely on your actual research. If data shows that many seniors use your app, then they *are* tech-savvy enough and probably appreciate a larger font option, for example. If you see teen customers sticking with your service for a year or more, then they *do* show loyalty when value is delivered. Treat people as multidimensional. Use objective evidence to shape your understanding, and be willing to update your beliefs.

- **Be Cautious of Small Samples:** If you only talk to one or two customers, you might get skewed perceptions. For example, if the last two customers you spoke with happened to hate a new feature, you might assume "everyone hates it," but maybe those two were outliers. That's why combining methods is good. Balance individual anecdotes with larger-scale surveys or data if you can. Conversely, if you send out a survey and only your most enthusiastic customers respond, you might get an overly rosy picture. Try to gather a representative mix: include different age groups, new and long-term customers, etc., in your feedback efforts.

- **Stay Humble and Curious:** Adopt the mindset that you're always learning about your audience. Markets change, people's preferences evolve, and your business might attract new types of customers over time. What was true last year might not be true next year. By staying curious and regularly engaging with your audience, you'll catch these shifts early. A humble approach ("I can always learn more, I can be wrong") gives you a huge advantage because many businesses grow complacent and out of touch. You won't, because you'll be continually checking in with your people.

- **Use Data as a Check, Not a Crutch:** We just talked about analytics, which can feel very "objective," but data can be interpreted in biased ways, too. Two people might look at the same numbers and come to different conclusions depending on what they expect to see. Use data to question your assumptions, not just to confirm them. If you expect a campaign to do well and the numbers say it didn't, resist the urge to rationalize it ("Oh, it was a slow season, never mind..."). Instead, ask *why* it didn't work and what you might have misjudged.

- **Invite Outside Perspective:** Sometimes, to spot your own biases, it helps to get an outside view. This could be a mentor, a colleague, or even some of your customers themselves. For instance, you could run your new marketing idea by a friend in a different field and see if they catch any assumptions, or create a small customer advisory group: loyal customers who'd be happy to give feedback occasionally. They might catch blind spots ("Actually, that tagline doesn't resonate with me because...") before you go live.

The bottom line is, never utter the words "Our customers would never..." unless you've validated it. Keep an open mind. The phrase "Never assume" is a cliché, but it's a wise one in branding. If you ever hear yourself thinking, "I don't need to ask them, I just know," that's a flag to pause and reconsider. There is no downside to asking or verifying; the worst that can happen is you learn something new!

By avoiding assumptions and actively challenging your biases, you ensure that the picture you have of your audience is accurate and up-to-date. That means you'll make decisions based on reality, not just on what *feels* right to you. It keeps your brand genuine and user-centered.

Speak Their Language: Tuning Your Brand to Your Audience

Understanding your audience isn't just a theoretical exercise. It directly informs *how you communicate and what you offer*. Once you've gathered all these insights about your audience, it's time to tailor your brand's language and offerings to match them. When you "speak their language," your brand messages will connect on a deeper level, almost as if you're reading their mind (in a good way!). Also, when you adjust your products or services to meet their needs, you demonstrate that you're not just selling. You're serving.

Let's break down how to apply your audience understanding:

1. Align Your Brand Voice and Tone:
Your brand voice is the personality of your business in communication. Are you formal, casual, playful, authoritative, or compassionate? To decide, consider what will resonate best with your target audience. Reflect on what you learned from them:

- *What words or phrases do they use?* Mirror some of their language in your marketing. For instance, if customers describe your product as "a lifesaver for busy moms," you might incorporate that phrasing in your messaging ("A lifesaver for busy moms. Get more time back in your day!"). It's instantly relatable because it's *their* phrasing.

- *What tone do they respond to?* If your audience is younger and engaged on TikTok, a very informal, trendy tone might click (with memes or pop culture references, if appropriate). If your audience is professionals seeking financial consulting, they may prefer a tone that's friendly yet highly professional and trustworthy. You can still be conversational and encouraging (remember, beginner-friendly tone is our goal), but in a way that respects their context.

- *Be consistent and authentic:* Don't force a tone that doesn't fit your brand's values, even if you think it's what the audience likes. For example, you might see some brands being snarky on social media and getting attention, but if that's not you or not what your audience expects from, say, a healthcare service, it could backfire. Find the overlap between your brand's personality and your audience's preference. Speak with a voice that is true to your mission and culture, yet tailored to engage your audience. A good trick: imagine speaking directly to one of your real customers (or your persona) when writing any communication. What would you say, and how would you say it, to ensure it resonates with them?

- *Use the proper channels:* Speaking their language is also about where you speak. If your audience spends more time reading emails than on Instagram, then an email newsletter might be a better way to "talk" to them. If they love watching video tutorials, consider creating video content on YouTube or TikTok. Your understanding of their habits (from earlier research) guides this choice. Essentially, be where they are, using a style that fits the environment and aligns with audience expectations.

2. Emphasize the Benefits *They* Care About:

Often in branding, we're tempted to shout about the features or qualities *we* think are great. Now that you know what your audience truly needs and values, focus your messaging on the benefits that matter most to them.

- Revisit those pain points and desires you identified. If you know your audience's biggest pain point is "wasting time on bookkeeping" (to use our earlier persona example), then your brand's homepage should probably prominently say how you save them time, rather than leading with something generic like "Innovative Accounting Solutions 2.0." Speak directly to the need: "Take back your time. Let us handle your bookkeeping, accurately and fast."

- Solve problems in your messaging. Make it crystal clear that you understand their problem *and* you have the solution. A formula often used: "You know how [audience] struggles with [problem]? We help them achieve [desire] without [common hassle]." For a lawn care business: "You know how busy homeowners struggle with keeping a green, healthy lawn? We help them get a picture-perfect yard without spending their weekends doing yard work." This kind of messaging resonates because it's grounded in the audience's reality.

- Highlight what they've told you they love. If, through reviews, you learned customers absolutely love your friendly customer service, weave that into your brand story: "At XYZ, you're not just a client. You're family. Our friendly team is here to support you at every step." That way, potential new customers who also value personal support will see that and be drawn in.

- Use testimonials or exact words from your audience if possible. There's nothing more convincing than hearing someone "just like them" praising your brand. Quotes on your website or social proof in marketing materials can double as both evidence and as reinforcement of the language that resonates. If a customer wrote, "This software is a game-changer for my small business; it's like having an assistant," you might feature that quote or incorporate the idea of "your virtual assistant" into your taglines.

3. Adapt Your Offerings (Products/Services) to Fit Their Needs:
Understanding your people might reveal gaps between what you offer and what they need. Tuning your brand isn't only about words; it's also about actions and offerings.

- You might discover you need to tweak a product feature. For example, a bakery discovers that many of its customers are dairy-free due to allergies, so they start offering more dairy-free baked goods. Or a mobile app developer learns that users wish the app could do X, Y, or Z. Maybe adding one of those features will make your product significantly more valuable to them.

- It could mean changing how you package or deliver your service. If your research reveals that clients appreciate your consulting but struggle to afford the upfront cost, consider introducing a payment plan or a scaled-down offering. Or if you learn that customers would use your cleaning service more if it were available on weekends, consider adjusting your schedule or staffing to meet that demand.

- Sometimes it means introducing an entirely new product that aligns with an unmet need you discovered. Suppose you run a pet supply store and, through engaging with your community, you learn many of your dog-owner customers also desperately need good grooming services. If feasible, you could expand to offer grooming services, or perhaps partner with a local groomer, thereby addressing a holistic need of your audience (a one-stop shop for pet care).

- On the flip side, it can mean letting go of offerings that your audience doesn't care about. If you have a service that consistently has low uptake and your audience feedback is, "it's nice but not necessary," you might put more energy into what truly provides value. This focus ensures every part of your brand offering is aligned with solving problems or bringing joy to your ideal customers.

4. Personalize Where Possible:
Modern consumers appreciate brands that feel personal. Use your audience's knowledge to personalize experiences:

- Address them in a way that feels personal. For example, use "you" in copy ("You deserve a break today" vs. "Customers deserve a break"). This subtle shift in language makes each reader feel seen.

- Segment your communication if you have slightly different sub-audiences. Let's say you identified two personas: "Busy Brenda" and "Retired Robert." In your email marketing, you might have different lists or at least tailor sections of your newsletter to speak to each. (e.g., "For our entrepreneur readers, here's a time-saving tip... And for those of you enjoying retirement, here's how our service can simplify your finances so you travel more worry-free...") People will gravitate to the parts that speak to them.

- Reference things you know they know. If your audience is really into local sports, a playful reference in your social content about the local team's recent win could delight them. Or if they're primarily parents, a nod to back-to-school season challenges (with a solution your brand offers) can be very effective. It shows you live in the same world they do and understand their context.

5. Maintain a Feedback Loop:
Tuning your brand to your audience isn't a one-time task. It's an ongoing process. After you make adjustments, continue to listen to how people respond. Are things improving? Did that new tone or offering resonate? Continue to gather feedback and data. This creates a loop: *Learn about audience → make changes → see audience's reaction → learn more → refine further.* Over time, your brand becomes increasingly attuned to the people it serves, which is a recipe for sustainable success.

To illustrate all of this, consider a short example:

Imagine a fictional company, GlowGarden, that specializes in selling organic skincare products, primarily online. Initially, their branding was very generic: "High-quality organic skincare for everyone!" They noticed that sales were okay but not growing significantly, and they had a mix of customers. The team decided to dig into understanding their best customers. Through reviews and some social media polls, they discovered their most passionate customers were women in their late 20s to 40s who love outdoor activities (hiking, beach, etc.), and who choose GlowGarden because the products are eco-friendly and particularly good at repairing sun-exposed skin.

Armed with this insight, GlowGarden created a persona named "Outdoor Olivia," who is 35, health-conscious, loves hiking, and wants effective skincare that aligns with her natural lifestyle. They tuned their brand language to speak to Olivia. Instead of generic lines about "quality skincare," they now say things like "Love the sun, but not what it does to your skin? We've got you covered." Their website and social media posts began featuring women on hikes, using GlowGarden after a day outside, accompanied by messages about nourishing and protecting their skin *while* enjoying nature. They added a blog section with tips on "skincare for adventurers" and "how to pick reef-safe sunscreen" (since their audience cares about the environment). They also introduced a new product: a compact, travel-size skin repair balm designed for hikers and campers.

The result? Their target audience felt *seen*. GlowGarden's engagement increased because their content resonated directly with those who identified with Olivia. Customers started sharing stories like, "This is perfect for my post-surf routine!" (something GlowGarden now highlights in testimonials). As hoped, sales increased, especially for the travel balm, because it met a specific need they had uncovered.

This example shows how aligning your brand messaging and offerings with your audience makes your brand much more compelling. You go from talking *at* people to having a conversation *with* people.

In essence, tuning your brand means shaping what you say, how you say it, what you sell, and how you deliver it based on what your audience has told you (directly or indirectly). It's the payoff for all the listening and learning you've done. When done right, your ideal customers will read your brochure or website and think, *"Wow, it's like this was made for me!"* because in a way, it was, and that feeling is incredibly powerful. It's the difference between a forgettable brand and one that earns a place in your customer's life.

Reflection and Action: Get to Know *Your* Audience (Checklist & Prompts)

Congratulations on diving into the world of understanding your people! We've covered a lot, so let's bring it all together. This final section gives you some actionable steps and questions to reflect on. Use these as a checklist or journaling prompts to turn ideas into practice for your own business. You don't have to do everything at once; even small steps can make a big difference over time.

Checklist: Building Audience Understanding

☐ **I have identified the core problem I solve for my audience.**
(*In one sentence, describe the main pain point you address. E.g., "I help busy moms save time on weeknight dinners with pre-planned meal kits."*)

☐ **I know where and how to listen to my customers informally.**
(*List 2-3 places you will pay attention to customer voices: e.g., "Read new Yelp reviews weekly," "Join the local parenting Facebook group and observe discussions," "Spend an hour a week on the shop floor talking to customers."*)

☐ **I have decided on a simple way to ask my audience for input.**
(*Choose at least one: Will you send out a short survey this month? Schedule one customer phone interview a week? Post a poll on social media? Write your plan here and a target date to do it.*)

☐ **I have created at least one customer persona.**
(*Write the name of your persona(s) and a few key traits. If not yet, schedule a time to sit down and create it from your notes. It's worth it!*)

☐ **I have verified my assumptions against the data or feedback.**
(*Note one assumption you held that you will verify: e.g., "I assume my audience is primarily millennials. I will check my Instagram and Google Analytics age data to confirm or adjust this."*)

☐ **I'm aware of a bias I need to be mindful of.**
(*Acknowledge one potential bias: e.g., "I love feature X, but I'll verify if customers use it as much as I think," or "I tend to ignore feedback about price because I think it's worth it, but I'll pay attention and see if cost is a real barrier."*)

☐ **I have ideas to adjust my brand voice or offerings based on what I learned.**
(*Jot down one or two changes you want to implement: "Tone: Make our website copy more casual and friendly, like how customers talk." Or "Offering: Add a beginner package since many expressed they feel overwhelmed starting out."*)

☐ **I have a system in place to continually learn about my audience.** *(Plan how often you will gather feedback or review analytics. Maybe "Quarterly persona update meeting (even if it's just me and my notebook)" or "Monthly deep-dive into website stats and social comments." Consistency is key.)*

Reflection Prompts:

1. Imagine your ideal customer walking into your store or visiting your website. What's the first thing they see or hear that tells them "This brand is for you"? How can you make that signal stronger?

2. Think of a time you, as a customer, felt a brand really understood you. What did they do to make you feel that way? How can you recreate that feeling for your own customers?

3. What are three questions you would love to ask your audience right now if you could sit each one down for coffee? (Now consider how you might actually ask those questions, via email, social, etc.)

4. Finish this sentence: "I know I truly understand my audience when I can clearly see that they _____ and that my brand _____." (For example, "...when I can clearly see that they *struggle with keeping their plants alive* and that my brand *offers them an easy, guilt-free way to enjoy houseplants*.") Fill in the blanks for your situation.

5. Envision your business five years from now with a loyal community of customers. What kind of relationship do you have with them? What do they say about your brand? Use this vision to identify what understanding you need to build *today* to make that a reality.

Take a moment to celebrate the progress you've made in thinking about your audience. Even reading through this chapter means you're committed to putting people at the center of your brand, which is honestly half the battle. Many businesses skip this step and end up wondering why their marketing efforts aren't effective, but you're building a brand on understanding, empathy, and service. *That* is a recipe for success.

Moving Fautionorward: Treat understanding your people as an ongoing journey, not a one-time project. Your audience may evolve, and you will too. Keep your ears and eyes open. Keep asking, listening, and observing. Your brand will thank you for it, as it grows stronger and clearer with each insight you gain.

Remember, your brand exists in the minds and hearts of your customers. The more you understand those minds and hearts, the more effectively you can inspire them. Continue to learn about your people, and let that understanding guide every aspect of your brand building efforts. You've got this! Here's to creating a brand that truly speaks to those it serves.

PART IV - CONNECT AND GROW

CHAPTER 12: SHARE YOUR STORY

Every small business has a unique story to tell. Sharing your story is about making genuine connections with your audience, and you don't need a big marketing budget to do it. In this chapter, we'll explore creative marketing and content strategies that make a significant impact without a hefty price tag. By now, you've crafted your brand identity and voice. It's time to broadcast that voice across a variety of channels. From old-fashioned word-of-mouth and community events to modern email newsletters and partnerships, you have many ways to get the word out. The key is to focus on authenticity, consistency, and creativity. This chapter will show you how to leverage a wide range of channels (beyond just social media), including email marketing, community outreach, events, partnerships, print materials, and organic word-of-mouth, to share your story far and wide.

We'll break down each channel with friendly, actionable advice. You'll find examples that apply to both product-based and service-based businesses, so you can see how the ideas work in real life. Along the way, look for checklists and reflection prompts to help you apply what you learn. Remember, marketing isn't about who spends the most money. It's about who tells the most relatable and engaging story. Your story is your superpower. Let's make sure the world hears it!

Social Media: Engage and Inspire Your Audience

Social media is often the first thing small businesses try for marketing, and for good reason. It offers free (or low-cost) access to a broad audience and lets you interact with customers directly. The trick is to use social platforms not just to advertise, but to engage and inspire people with your story. Rather than obsessing over follower counts, focus on building a community that cares about your brand.

Tell your story authentically: Share posts that highlight why you started your business, what you're passionate about, and the behind-the-scenes moments. For a product-based business, this might mean showing how you design or create your products or introducing the people who make them. For a service business, you might share a personal anecdote about a client success (with permission) or a "day in the life" of your work. These kinds of posts resonate more than polished ads because they feel human and relatable.

Choose the right platform: You don't have to be everywhere at once. Identify where your target customers are. If you run a boutique or bakery with a lot of visual appeal, platforms like Instagram or Facebook could be ideal for sharing photos and stories. If you're a B2B service provider or consultant, LinkedIn may be a more suitable platform for sharing industry insights and your professional journey. A home décor store or a fitness coach could even leverage Pinterest or YouTube for how-to content. Pick one or two platforms to start, rather than stretching yourself thin across all of them.

Engage with your community: Social media is a two-way street. Encourage interaction by asking questions, responding to comments, and even asking your followers to share their stories. For example, a café owner could ask followers to post their favorite morning routines (coffee cup photos are welcome!), or a pet groomer might invite customers to share pictures of their pet transformations. User-generated content is like gold. When customers post about your business, it spreads your story to their friends for free. Repost or celebrate these customer stories (with credit) to show you value your community. This not only provides you with free content but also builds social proof that real people love your brand.

Stay consistent and approachable: Consistency builds recognition. Use your brand voice and visuals uniformly so that people instantly recognize a post as yours. Post regularly. It could be a few times a week or whatever schedule you can maintain, so that you stay on your audience's radar. Maintain a friendly tone and respond to messages or comments in a timely manner. Imagine social media as a casual conversation with your customers: share updates, celebrate milestones (like your shop's birthday or a customer testimonial), and even acknowledge challenges or express gratitude to customers for their support. This openness makes people feel connected to the person behind the business.

Quick Tips for Social Media Success:

- **Provide value:** Aim for posts that either entertain, inspire, or inform. For instance, a home cleaning service might share a "5 Quick Decluttering Tips" infographic (informative), or a toy store might post a funny behind-the-scenes video of staff testing new toys (entertaining).

- **Use hashtags and local tags:** Make your content discoverable by using relevant hashtags (especially on Instagram or Twitter/X). If you're local, use location tags or city and neighborhood hashtags so nearby customers find you.

- **Leverage Stories & Reels:** Short-lived content like Instagram/Facebook Stories or TikTok Reels can humanize your brand. You could do a quick "meet the owner" video or a time-lapse of a product being made. These formats are informal and great for storytelling.

- **Collaborate online:** Consider teaming up with a complementary business or a local micro-influencer for a social media collaboration. For example, a local bakery could partner with a coffee roaster for a joint Instagram Live about pairing flavors. Collaboration exposes your story to another group of followers and creates a fun dynamic that viewers enjoy.

- **Monitor and adjust:** Pay attention to what types of posts get the most engagement (likes, comments, shares). This is feedback from your audience about what content they enjoy. Do more of what works, and don't be afraid to experiment with new ideas.

Reflection Prompt: What part of your business journey or day-to-day life could you share on social media this week? Jot down one authentic story or moment (big or small) that might give your followers insight into your world. How can you present it in a post?

Email Marketing: Connect Directly via the Inbox

Email marketing is a powerful yet budget-friendly way to share your story and keep in touch with people who genuinely want to hear from you. Unlike social media, where algorithms control who sees your posts, emails land directly in your subscribers' inboxes, a space they check every day. Building an email list might sound old-school compared to the latest social app, but it's one of the most cost-effective marketing channels around. Even better, it's *your* list. You own that direct relationship with your customers or prospects.

Build your list with value: Start by encouraging customers and website visitors to sign up for your email list. Give them a good reason to subscribe. This could be a one-time discount for new subscribers, a complimentary resource, or simply the promise of valuable and engaging content. For example, a handmade soap business could offer a "Skincare Tips PDF" as an incentive for signing up, or a financial planner might promise a helpful monthly money-saving tip. Always obtain permission (never add people without their consent) and make it easy for them to sign up: via your website, in-store clipboard, or a simple "join our newsletter" button on social profiles.

Tell a story through newsletters: Once you have subscribers, nurture that relationship. Your emails shouldn't just be sales flyers. They should feel like receiving a note from a helpful friend. Use a conversational tone and provide content that readers find interesting or beneficial. You can certainly discuss your products or services, but present them in a compelling story or helpful context. For instance, instead of an email that says "30% off this week!", a home décor store could send an email titled "A Cozy Reading Nook on a Budget" where they share 3-4 tips on setting up a comfy reading corner, mentioning a lamp or throw pillow they sell as part of the solution. A fitness coach might send out a short weekly "Monday Motivation" story, perhaps sharing a personal anecdote or a client success (with permission), along with a workout tip of the week.

Personalize and segment: Address your subscribers by name if possible ("Hi Maria," feels warmer than a generic hello). Most email tools let you do this easily. As your list grows, you can also segment it to send more targeted content. For example, if you run a pet supply store, you might have separate lists for dog owners and cat owners, to send each group tips and products relevant to their pets. Personalization shows you understand and care about your customers' interests, which keeps them opening your emails.

Keep it consistent (but not spammy): Determine a consistent email schedule that you can adhere to. It could be weekly, bi-weekly, or monthly. The key is consistency, so subscribers come to expect and look forward to your messages. At the same time, respect their inboxes. Quality beats quantity. It's better to send one value-packed email a month than to send something dull every few days. Always include an easy way for people to unsubscribe in your emails (reputable email services do this automatically), because a smaller list of genuinely interested readers is far more valuable than a massive list of people who ignore or resent your emails.

Use affordable tools: Good news! Many email marketing services have free plans for small lists. Mailchimp, Sendinblue, MailerLite, and others offer free tiers up to a certain number of subscribers. These platforms provide templates, scheduling, and list management, so you don't need technical expertise to start. All you need is your content and a bit of time to craft the emails. Take advantage of these tools to automate welcome emails (for example, when someone joins, send a friendly welcome message that tells your brand's story or shares your best tips). Automation can save you time and make your tiny operation feel just as polished as a big company.

Effective Email Content Ideas:

- **Welcome Series:** Create a simple welcome email (or a short series of 2-3 emails) for new subscribers. In the first email, share your story: why you started this business and what mission drives you. In the second, perhaps offer a helpful tip or a customer story that illustrates your values. In the third, you might include a special offer or invite them to connect with you on social media or at your shop. This series helps new fans get to know you beyond a simple "Thanks for subscribing."

- **Educational or Entertaining Content:** Plan regular emails that aren't just promotions. For example, a bakery could send a "Recipe of the Month" newsletter, sharing a simplified recipe and a note from the baker about why it's special. A marketing consultant might send a monthly case study or a "quick tip" email addressing a common client question. Think about what expertise or unique perspective you have, and share a piece of it in each email.

- **Exclusive offers or first peeks:** Reward your email subscribers by giving them insider perks. Announce your sale to them first, or offer them an exclusive discount code occasionally. If you wrote a new blog post or are launching a new product, let your email list be the first to know. This makes subscribers feel special and part of an inner circle.

- **Strong subject lines:** All your great content won't matter if nobody opens the email. Craft subject lines that pique interest. They should be clear but intriguing. For instance, instead of "June Newsletter," try something like "Meet the Hero Who Inspired Our New Product," or instead of "Tips for Car Care," say "5 Secrets to Make Your Car Shine This Summer." Think about what would make *you* click amid a sea of emails.

- **Call-to-action:** Every email should have some purpose. Perhaps you want readers to read a blog post, shop a new collection, provide feedback, or simply smile at a story. Whatever it is, invite them to take that small next step. Include a clear link or button for any action (e.g., "Shop the Fall Collection," "Read the full story on our blog," or "Reply and share your thoughts"). Don't overwhelm them with too many different links. Keep it focused.

Reflection Prompt: Imagine you're writing an email to your customers. What's a story or tip you'd genuinely love to share with them? Outline one email idea. Include a subject line, a brief description of content (story, tip, or offer), and what outcome you'd want (e.g., readers learning something new, visiting your site, or replying to you).

Community Outreach: Build Local Connections

One of the advantages of being a small business is being *part of a community*. Community outreach means getting involved in your local area or a community of interest in a meaningful way. Not only does this spread the word about your business, but it also builds trust, goodwill, and loyalty. People love to support businesses that give back to the community. Plus, these efforts often cost little more than your time and genuine enthusiasm.

Be a local champion: Consider the community that matters most to your business. If you're a local storefront, it's your town or neighborhood. If you serve a specific group (say, rock climbers or pet owners), it might be a community of those people, whether locally or online. Find ways to give back or get involved. This could include anything from volunteering, sponsoring, donating, or simply lending a hand. For example, a restaurant or grocery store might donate food to a local shelter or sponsor a youth sports team (with your logo on the jerseys, the parents and spectators will notice!). A tech repair shop might volunteer at a school's "Family Tech Night" to help parents set up parental controls. A freelance graphic designer might give a free workshop at the community center on basic design tips for non-profits. These actions contribute positively to your area and naturally draw attention to your business *in a good way*.

Leverage local events and causes: Keep an eye out for community events like fairs, festivals, charity runs, school events, or holiday markets. Participating in these events serves a dual purpose: you're supporting the event and simultaneously promoting your business. You can set up a booth, donate a prize, or help with the organization. For instance, a local boutique could coordinate a neighborhood "Spring Sidewalk Sale" involving multiple shops (collaboration + community fun), or a cleaning service might sponsor the town 5K run by providing water bottles with their logo on them. If there aren't relevant events, consider hosting one for a cause, like a charity drive (e.g., a bookstore hosting a book donation for a local literacy program) or a "Customer Appreciation Day" where a portion of sales goes to a charity.

Network within your community: Building relationships with other local business owners and community leaders can organically lead to word-of-mouth referrals. Join your local Chamber of Commerce or a small business association if one is available. These groups often host mixers, workshops, or joint marketing opportunities (like a local business directory or festival). If you're in a neighborhood with a merchants' association or downtown alliance, get involved. You'll stay informed about community happenings and often receive free or discounted marketing opportunities through their initiatives. For a service provider who might not have a storefront, attending community meetups (like a local entrepreneur meetup, Rotary Club, or industry-specific networking events) can connect you with potential clients and referral partners. The more people in the community who know you and what you stand for, the more they will mention your name when someone needs what you offer.

Show you care (authentically): Consumers are savvy. They can tell when a business is just doing token outreach versus truly caring. Focus on causes or activities that honestly align with your values and your brand's mission. If you run an eco-friendly product line, consider getting involved in a park cleanup or recycling drive. If your business is all about family, support local schools or kid-friendly events. Your passion will shine through, and that's infectious. Additionally, when appropriate, share information about these community involvements on your marketing channels (such as social media and email). It's not bragging. It's inviting your customers to see what matters to you. They may even want to join in! For example, posting "We had a blast volunteering at Saturday's beach cleanup. Thanks to our team and customers who came out to help!" not only spreads the word about the cause but also associates your business with positive action.

Ways to Get Involved Locally:

- **Sponsor or support a local team/event:** Consider low-budget sponsorships like providing refreshments for a school event, donating a gift card to a charity auction, or sponsoring a hole in a charity golf tournament. In return, your business name gets mentioned in programs, T-shirts, or signage.

- **Host community gatherings:** If you have a physical space (store, office, café), offer it for community use occasionally. For example, a bookstore might host a reading by a local author, or a café could host an open-mic night. A yoga studio could hold a free class in the park. These events draw new faces and generate goodwill.

- **Collaborate on community projects:** Join forces with other businesses or community groups on a project. A few businesses could collectively organize a "Shop Local Day" festival. Or partner with a nonprofit for an awareness campaign (such as a salon hosting a breast cancer awareness day, where a portion of the proceeds goes to a cancer charity).

- **Offer a helping hand where needed:** Sometimes, outreach is as simple as doing something kind in your community. A bakery might donate unsold bread at day's end to a food pantry. A construction contractor might volunteer to fix the playground equipment. Such deeds often get noticed and remembered.

- **Publicize gently:** It's okay to let people know about your community involvement. It might inspire others to join or support those causes. Use a light touch: a photo on Facebook of your team at the charity walk, or a blog post about why you chose to partner with that nonprofit. This becomes part of your brand story ("we're the company that cares about X"), which attracts like-minded customers.

Reflection Prompt: What local cause, event, or group resonates with you or aligns with your business's values? Identify one opportunity to get involved (big or small). How could you participate in a way that's genuine and helpful? Write down one action, like "email the organizer of __ to offer help" or "put up a flyer offering my shop as a meetup space for __".

Events: Create Memorable Experiences

Sometimes the best way to share your story is to meet people face-to-face and let them experience your brand in person. Events give you that chance. Whether you're hosting your own gathering or joining an existing event, the goal is to create a memorable experience that gets people talking (and thinking fondly) about your business. Don't worry. An event doesn't have to be a massive, expensive production. Even a small, simple event can have a significant impact, and there are numerous low-cost ways to make a lasting impression.

Local festivals and markets are excellent places to share your story in person. Setting up a booth or table is an affordable way to meet new customers and introduce your brand to them.

Attend markets, fairs, and shows: One of the easiest ways to get started is by participating in events that are already happening. Think local craft fairs, farmer's markets, holiday bazaars, trade shows, or industry conventions. These events draw crowds of people looking to discover something new, making them a perfect opportunity for you to shine. For example, if you sell products (such as handmade goods, food items, or artwork), renting a stall at a weekend market can put you in front of hundreds of new customers for a relatively small fee. Service businesses can benefit too: a landscaper or home organizer might set up a table at a home and garden show, a wedding photographer can exhibit at a bridal fair, or a game developer might demo at a local tech expo. Come prepared with visuals (banners or samples), business cards or flyers (so interested folks remember you later), and most importantly, a friendly story to tell every visitor. *Pay attention to the print materials section coming up!* People will remember the passionate soap maker who shared Grandma's recipe with them, or the personal trainer who told them about overcoming her own health struggles and now helps others. Those human elements stick in the minds much more than a generic sales pitch.

Host your own event: Hosting has its perks. You get to design the experience, and you're the star of the show. Consider what type of event would both appeal to your target audience and showcase your brand's personality. Here are a few ideas:

- **Open House or Shop Anniversary Party:** Invite locals to come check out your space, with light refreshments and maybe a one-day discount or door prize. It's a casual way for curious neighbors to step inside and finally meet you. A salon might host an open house with free mini consultations, or a bookstore might celebrate its anniversary with a story time for kids and cake for all.

- **Workshop or Class:** People love to learn, especially if it's free or low-cost. If you're knowledgeable about a relevant topic to your business, consider offering a short workshop. A bakery could host a cupcake decorating class, a garden center could run a free "spring planting 101" workshop, and a marketing agency might offer a small business marketing seminar at the library. These position you as an expert and draw in folks who are likely interested in what you offer.

- **Product Launch or Demo Event:** If you're launching a new product or service, turn it into an event. A fashion boutique might host a "New Collection Reveal" night featuring a small fashion show. A tech gadget seller could host a demo day where people can try the latest devices. This not only generates buzz but makes attendees feel special about getting a first look.

- **Community Meet-and-Greet:** Not every event has to be about selling. You could organize a meetup that aligns with your brand's theme. For example, a board game café might host a weekly game night tournament, an outdoor gear shop could host monthly hiking meetups, or a language tutor could start a casual language exchange evening. These gatherings build community around your brand.

Make it memorable: Whatever the event, think about the touches that will stick in people's minds. This doesn't mean spending a fortune. It could be the ambiance you create (playing music, decorating with balloons or your branded colors), a small freebie (like goodie bags with samples or a useful trinket), or an interactive element. An interactive element could be a contest (raffle for a prize, "guess how many candies in the jar" kind of fun) or a photo booth corner with a nice backdrop and your logo. People will take pictures and share them, giving you extra exposure. If you run a pet shop and host an adoption day event, set up a cute "puppy kissing booth" for photos. Attendees will remember that! The more senses and emotions you engage, the more your event will create a positive memory associated with your brand's name.

Plan and promote: Successful events require a bit of planning. Choose a date and time that are convenient for your audience (weekends for families, weekday evenings for working professionals, etc.). If you're hosting, spread the word through all your channels: social media, email, flyers on community boards, and word of mouth with your regular customers. If you're participating in someone else's event, still promote your presence ("Come see us at Booth 12 at the Spring Fair this Saturday!"). This not only boosts attendance but signals that your business is active and vibrant. On the day of, be sure to capture some photos or videos. These can be shared afterward, thanking those who attended and showing those who missed it what a great time it was (so maybe they'll come next time). After the event, follow up where you can. For instance, send a thank-you email with a special offer to everyone who signed up for your mailing list at the event, or personally thank the new followers you met there on social media. This follow-through turns a one-day encounter into a lasting relationship.

Event Success Tips:

- **Start small & partner up:** If hosting alone is too daunting, consider co-hosting an event with another business or community group (this overlaps with our Partnerships discussion!). For example, a coffee shop and a local artist might team up for an art showcase night at the café. The artist brings art and followers, the café provides space and snacks, and both benefit. Sharing the load makes it easier and usually splits any costs.

- **Make a checklist for event day:** List what you need to bring or set up. For example, a table, a tent, signage, products, samples, a mailing list signup sheet (or a tablet for digital sign-ups), and plenty of business cards, among other essentials. Being prepared prevents last-minute scrambles and expense.

- **Engage visitors:** Don't sit back passively. Actively greet people. Smile and say hello to passersby if you're at a fair. Welcome folks warmly to your shop event. Have a short opening line ready, like "Have you heard of [Your Business]? We do X" or even just "Thanks for coming out! Let me know if you have any questions." If you're shy, remember, nobody knows your business like you do. Your genuine enthusiasm will overcome any nerves. You might even prepare a fun demo or talking point: a skincare seller might offer free hand lotion massages, while a 3D-printing business could showcase the machine in action. When people are engaged, they tend to stay longer and form a stronger memory.

- **Collect contacts:** Events are prime for finding new leads. Offer a simple way for interested individuals to leave their email address (perhaps in exchange for entering a raffle or receiving a small coupon). That way, you can continue the conversation via email or social media later. A fishbowl for business cards or a digital signup form on a tablet works well. Just be sure to follow up within a few days while the memory is fresh ("It was great to meet you at the Spring Fair! Here's the 10% off coupon I promised. We hope to see you again soon.").

- **Learn and improve:** After any event, reflect on what went well and what could be better next time. Did people seem interested in one product more than others? Was your table layout inviting? Did you run out of brochures or find that your event timing was off? These insights are gold for making your next event even better.

Reflection Prompt: Imagine participating in or hosting one event in the next few months. What kind of event would best showcase your business and attract your target customers? Describe your idea (the theme, location, what you'd do) and one step to get started (e.g., "Research local craft fairs coming up" or "Email two fellow business owners about co-hosting a workshop").

Partnerships: Collaborate for Mutual Growth

Remember the saying, "If you want to go fast, go alone. If you want to go far, go together."? Partnerships embody that idea. By teaming up with others, whether it's businesses, organizations, or even influencers, you can reach new audiences and share resources, all without a hefty budget. A smart partnership is a win-win: you promote them, they promote you, and both of you grow. In this section, we'll explore how to identify good partners and creative ways to collaborate.

Find the right partners: A great partner complements your business rather than competes with it, and shares a similar audience or values. Think about what else your customers are interested in or need. If you sell baby clothes, new parents might also be interested in photographers (newborn photos), toy stores, or family cafés. The opportunities are there. If you're a personal trainer, your clients might also appreciate the services of a nutritionist or a local athletic wear boutique. For a local example, a bridal dress shop could partner with a wedding cake baker, a florist, and a photographer to refer clients to one another or create a joint package. If you're an online artisanal tea seller, you could partner with a pottery maker who crafts teacups, bundling a cup with your tea as a special set. List out a few businesses (or community organizations) that target a similar demographic but offer something different. Don't forget, partnerships can also be within your industry if you specialize. For instance, a portrait photographer might partner with a wedding photographer to refer jobs that suit each other's niche.

Cross-promote each other: One of the simplest partnerships is exchanging promotions. This can be as easy as trading flyers or business cards to display in each other's locations. A local coffee shop might have a bulletin board that features a nearby bookstore's events, while the bookstore has a stack of the coffee shop's loyalty cards at the checkout. Online, you could do shout-outs on social media for one another ("Today we want to appreciate our friends at X Yoga Studio. If you need to unwind, they're the best in town!" and they post something similar about you). You can also swap spots in each other's email newsletters or blog posts. For example, a travel blogger and a local tour guide might collaborate by writing guest articles for each other. The key is that each partner introduces the other to their customer base with an implied endorsement. Because it's coming from a trusted source (their favorite business recommending you), new customers are more likely to give you a chance.

Collaborate on marketing campaigns: Pooling resources can enable you to undertake marketing efforts that might be costly to undertake solo. Consider sharing the cost of an advertisement or direct mail campaign that features both businesses. Joint flyers are common. For example, a cleaning service and a lawn care service might create a combined "Spring Home Care" pamphlet, splitting printing costs and distributing it to the neighborhood. You could even run a co-branded contest or giveaway on social media: "Follow both of our accounts and tag a friend to win a prize bundle from [Business A] and [Business B]!" This way, both businesses gain new followers and exposure. Collaboration can also extend to content creation, such as filming a joint how-to video or hosting a podcast together to discuss a topic you both know. Sharing expertise in this way elevates both of your profiles.

Co-host events or workshops: Partnerships and events often go hand in hand. If hosting an event alone seems too much, consider finding a partner to do it with. As mentioned earlier, complementary businesses can attract a bigger crowd by combining forces. Consider a local example: a wine shop and a cheese shop hosting a wine-and-cheese tasting night together. Each brings their customers, who get to enjoy the whole experience. Or a gym and a health food store teaming up for a "New Year New You" wellness fair. Perhaps a few local boutiques band together to put on a joint fashion showcase in the street. By sharing the planning and costs, everyone benefits from a larger event that creates buzz for all involved. Plus, it's often more fun to do it with others!

Consider influencer or affiliate partnerships: In today's world, not all partners are traditional businesses. An influencer partnership can be highly effective when approached thoughtfully. This doesn't mean you need a celebrity. Often, a micro-influencer (someone with a modest but engaged following in your niche) is affordable and impactful. For instance, a local food blogger with 5,000 loyal followers might be delighted to feature your restaurant in exchange for a complimentary meal and an engaging conversation with the chef. A parenting vlogger could review your educational toy line on their YouTube channel. Always choose influencers whose style and audience align with your brand. Their followers are your potential customers. Agree on what each party will do (free product, commission on sales, or paid fee on your side; a certain number of posts or an honest review on their side). Similarly, affiliate programs (where someone earns a small commission for referring sales to you via a special link or code) can incentivize others to share your story, effectively turning loyal customers or bloggers into partners who market for you.

Keep partnerships mutually beneficial: The foundation of any good partnership is that both sides feel they're gaining. Be upfront in communication. Perhaps you have the space, and they have the audience, or you have marketing expertise, and they have a great product. When proposing a partnership, emphasize how it benefits them as much as it benefits you. For example, "I have a mailing list of 500 local families who might love your kids' music classes. What if we offer a discount for them, and you let your students know about my toy store? We could both get new customers." Ensure the workload and costs are shared fairly, and maintain good communication throughout. A thank-you note or small gift to your partner after a successful collaboration can go a long way to solidify the relationship for future projects.

Partnership Ideas:

- **Product bundles:** Team up to create a combined offering. For example, a bakery and a flower shop offer a "Valentine's Day Package" (cakes and bouquets) at a special price. A salon and a spa offer a "Ultimate Pamper Gift Card" that is redeemable at both locations.

- **Referral program between businesses:** Set up an agreement where you refer clients to each other and maybe offer those referred customers a little perk. For instance, a bike repair shop offers a free accessory with a tune-up to anyone referred by the nearby bike rental store, and vice versa. Track referrals and acknowledge your partner (even a simple thank you email, a small referral fee, or a gift can sweeten the deal and keep referrals coming).

- **Shared space or swap:** If you have a physical location, could you lend part of it to a complementary business occasionally? Perhaps a local artisan pops up in your store on weekends (attracting their fans to your shop), and in return, you get to place a small display in their store. Or a coffee truck parks outside a busy retail shop with permission. The shop benefits from more foot traffic, and the coffee truck gets a prime location.

- **Joint content:** Write a guest blog post for a partner's website and have them do the same for yours. Or feature each other in a "spotlight" in your newsletters ("Partner Spotlight: Meet ____ , they do awesome work in ___!"). It enriches your content and shows you're community-minded.

- **Braintrust and support:** Not all partnerships are public-facing. Simply forming a small group of fellow business owners to share advice and even cross-promote informally is valuable. For instance, a cluster of neighboring shops could meet monthly to plan how to drive more traffic to their block (maybe through seasonal window displays or a collective sale day). By supporting each other, you create a rising tide that lifts all boats.

Reflection Prompt: *Think of one business or person that reaches a similar audience but isn't a direct competitor. How could you collaborate? Write down the name of a potential partner and one idea for a partnership (however simple or grand). Next, outline how both parties would benefit. This will prepare you to propose the idea in a way that's exciting for them, too.*

Print Materials: Make a Tangible Impression

In our digital age, it's easy to overlook print marketing, but tangible materials still have a significant impact, especially for local marketing and events. There's something memorable about a physical object someone can hold on to. The great news for small businesses is that print materials can be done very inexpensively and still look professional. This section will cover classic print channels, such as business cards, flyers, brochures, and more, and explain how you can use them creatively to share your brand's story.

Business cards. Small but mighty: A business card is often the first piece of print marketing a business creates. It's your pocket-sized ambassador, ready to hand out at networking events, pin to bulletin boards, or tuck into packaging. Make sure your card isn't an afterthought. Include your logo, the key contact info (don't overload it with every detail, just the main ways to reach you or find you online), and maybe a tagline or brief description if your business name doesn't make it obvious what you do. For example, if your company is called "Smith & Co.", adding "Custom Woodworking" on the card clarifies your trade. A well-designed card can leave a great impression. If you want to stand out, consider a card that reflects your personality. A yoga instructor might use a calming color palette and maybe a subtle lotus graphic, while a party planner might opt for a fun, bright design. Always carry some cards with you. You never know when you'll meet a potential customer or someone who asks, "Do you have a card?" You want to be prepared and look professional.

Flyers and posters. Spreading the word: Flyers are a low-cost way to advertise events, promotions, or just general awareness of your business. You can design simple flyers using templates (many free tools like Canva offer nice layouts). Post them on community bulletin boards (libraries, coffee shops, community centers, and grocery stores often have these), in apartment buildings (with permission), or distribute them door-to-door in your target neighborhoods if appropriate. A cleaning service might do a door hanger or mailbox flyer offering a first-time discount for local residents. A tutoring service might post posters on college campuses or community boards at local schools. Keep the design clean and ensure the key message and call-to-action (what you want the reader to do) are clear and large enough to read at a glance. For instance, "Grand Opening! 20% off all weekend at [Your Store Name]!" with the dates and address in bold, plus maybe a photo of your best product. **Pro Tip:** Include a little bit of your story or something distinctive on print materials to make them engaging. Instead of a generic "We fix computers, call us," a computer repair flyer could say "Neighborhood Nerd since 2010. Keeping Your PCs Happy. John at TechFix can help with any computer woes, no jargon, no hassle." That touch of personality can make a reader smile and remember you.

Brochures or catalogs. Tell a bigger story: If your business has a lot to explain or showcase, a brochure can be a helpful tool. This could be a tri-fold pamphlet or a small booklet. Brochures make sense for service businesses that need to list services or provide education (like a brochure for a financial planner describing their offerings and some client success vignettes) or for product-based companies at trade shows (maybe a catalog sheet of your best-selling items with photos and prices). When crafting a brochure, organize it into sections with headings so it's easy to skim. Use visuals whenever possible, such as images of your work, charts, or graphics that align with your brand. And definitely weave your story into the design: one panel of a tri-fold could be titled "About Us - Our Story," featuring a friendly paragraph that explains why you started the business or what mission drives you. People do read these, especially if they pick up a brochure out of interest. It's more intimate than a website because they're holding it in their hands without digital distractions.

Signage and physical presence: Your storefront sign, window display, banners, and even your vehicle signage (if you have branding on your car or truck) all count as print or traditional marketing. They silently tell your story to anyone who passes by. Even if you don't have a physical location, you can invest in a simple banner or sign to use at events or on a table when you're selling at a market. Make sure your branding is consistent: use the same logo, colors, and tone of messaging as you do elsewhere. For example, if your brand voice is warm and humorous, a sandwich board outside your caféte might say something like "Life happens, coffee helps. Come on in!" which conveys your friendly vibe and invites people in. If you're a serious, professional law office, your signage would be more elegant and straightforward to build trust. Good signage is an upfront cost, but typically lasts a long time and is essentially free advertising every day.

Print advertising (strategically): Placing ads in local newspapers, community newsletters, or niche magazines can sometimes be effective and affordable. Many small towns have local papers or city magazines that don't charge too much for a small ad, and they reach a targeted local audience. If you have a specific demographic (say, senior citizens for a home healthcare service), consider the publications or places (church bulletins, senior center newsletters) that cater to them. The key with paid print ads is to ensure you have a clear message and possibly a special offer to track responses (like "Mention this ad for a free consult" so that when someone does, you know the ad worked). Only do this if the budget allows and you suspect a decent reach. Otherwise, there are plenty of free print options as we've discussed.

Leverage your packaging and print inserts: If you sell physical products, the packages you send out or the bag you put items in at your shop is a great storytelling canvas. Print packaging doesn't have to be fancy custom boxes (though if you can, that's nice branding). Even a thank-you card or a little story tag goes a long way. For example, a candle maker could include a small card in each box that says, "This candle was hand-poured by us in small batches. We started our studio in 2022 to bring calm and coziness to homes like yours. Thank you for supporting our dream! - Jane & Amanda from Glow

Candle Co." That feels personal and reinforces your story at the moment the customer receives their item. A clothing boutique might print fun tissue paper or stickers with a quirky message that aligns with their brand ("You've got great taste! Enjoy your new finds from [Shop Name]"). These touches are relatively low cost but make the unboxing experience share-worthy (hello, word-of-mouth!) and memorable.

Cost-Saving Tips for Print:

- **DIY where possible:** You don't need a professional designer for basic materials. As mentioned, tools like Canva, as well as templates from Microsoft Word, Publisher, or Google Docs, can help you create decent-looking cards, flyers, and more. Use high-quality free stock images or your own photos. Keep it simple for a clean look.

- **Bulk printing and deals:** If you know you'll use a lot of something (like business cards or flyers), printing in larger quantities often reduces the per-piece cost significantly. Also, watch for promotions from online print services (Vistaprint, Staples, local print shops). They frequently offer sales or special deals for first-time customers. However, avoid over-printing materials that might date themselves (like an event flyer). Print only what you need, as it will be obsolete after the date.

- **Use standard sizes:** Custom sizes or fancy finishes can increase cost. Typically, sticking to standard postcard, flyer, or business card sizes will be more economical. You can still be creative within that. For instance, you could print a bookmark with your business information on it as an alternative to flyers, if you're a bookstore. It's a standard size and useful for the recipient.

- **Ask for local print partnerships:** Since we're on partnerships, see if there's a local printer or office supply store that might sponsor some printing for you in exchange for credit or if you agree to be a reference. Sometimes, local B2B businesses will support community businesses, particularly for community events or charitable causes. ("Printing of this flyer donated by XYZ Printing Co." on the bottom of a community event poster gives them a bit of promotional value, too.)

Essential Print Materials:

- **Business Cards:** Do you have an up-to-date, good-quality business card? (If not, design and order some. They're inexpensive and invaluable.)

- **At least one Flyer or Poster:** Create a simple flyer for either your general business or an upcoming promotion. Keep some at your location and post on community boards. Refill as needed.

- **Brochure or Menu of Services:** If applicable, have a handout that details your offerings. Useful for consultations, events, or to leave with someone who's interested.

- **Branded Stationery:** This could be as simple as a template for invoices/letterhead with your logo or thank-you note cards you use for customers. It adds a professional touch to any communication in print.

- **Signage Check:** Ensure your signage (store sign, window, vehicle decal, etc.) is visible, clear, and reflective of your brand. If you don't have any signage (for example, if you operate from home), consider at least a magnetic car sign or a banner for event use.

- **Packaging/Insert:** If you ship products or hand over items, include a little something (business card, thank-you note, or small flyer about your loyalty program or next event).

Reflection Prompt: Take stock of your current print materials. Do they tell your story and match your brand vibe? Identify one print item you could create or improve. Perhaps it's designing a fresh business card or making a flyer for the service you offer that people often don't know about. How will you distribute or use this material effectively?

Organic Word-of-Mouth: Let Your Customers Tell the Tale

We've saved one of the most powerful (and budget-friendly) marketing strategies for last: word-of-mouth. This is when people naturally talk about your business to others, recommending you to friends, family, or colleagues because they had a great experience. Word-of-mouth is marketing you *can't buy* in the traditional sense. It has to be earned. The trust level of a personal recommendation is sky-high. Think about it. You're far more likely to try a new restaurant if two of your friends have been raving about it, right? For small businesses, cultivating positive word-of-mouth can lead to a steady stream of new customers without incurring any advertising costs. Here's how to nurture this golden channel.

Deliver an experience worth talking about: This is the foundation. If you consistently delight your customers, they'll become your unofficial ambassadors. Focus on excellent customer service and quality in whatever you offer. This doesn't mean you have to be perfect or fancy. It means you care, and it shows. A friendly, personal touch can turn a routine transaction into something memorable. For example, an auto repair shop that takes the time to explain issues in plain language and maybe throws in a free car wash at the end is going to get talked about: "They were so honest and helpful, and they cleaned my car!" A bakery that remembers a regular's favorite muffin or a hairstylist who follows up with a text to check if you're happy with your new cut. Those little extras stick in people's minds. Aim to under-promise and over-deliver whenever possible. If you quote a project to be completed by Friday and finish it by Wednesday, your client will be pleasantly surprised. If you told a customer their special-order cake would be a particular design and you added an extra decorative flourish at no charge, they'll notice. These are the kinds of things people mention to their friends.

Encourage referrals and reward them: Sometimes people need a friendly nudge to refer others. You can make it explicit by creating a referral program. For instance, a home cleaning service might say, "Refer a friend and you both get 20% off one cleaning." A gym could offer a free extra training session to members who bring in a new member. If you rely on appointments or bookings, consider giving loyal customers a couple of your business cards with a special "new client" promo code on the back. Tell them to share with someone who might need your service. Many satisfied customers are eager to share their positive experiences. A small incentive reinforces the behavior and shows appreciation. Be sure to genuinely thank anyone who refers someone to you (even if you don't have a formal program, a personal thank-you note or a little gift card is a classy touch when you learn a particular customer sent new business your way).

Make it easy for people to review and recommend you: In today's world, word-of-mouth often happens online, too. Encourage satisfied customers to leave reviews on platforms such as Google, Yelp, Facebook, or industry-specific sites (e.g., TripAdvisor for tourism, Zillow for real estate agents). Many people trust online reviews as much as personal recommendations. When you finish a job or make a sale and the customer is beaming, that's a great time to politely say, "I'm so glad you're happy! It would mean a lot to us if you could share your experience in a review. It really helps a small business like ours." You can provide a direct link or instructions to make it simple. Also, keep an eye on social media mentions. If someone shouts you out on Twitter/X or Instagram, drop in and thank them. Engaging with these public mentions shows that you're attentive and grateful. Potential customers who see how you handle feedback (even negative feedback) can be swayed. Always respond kindly and helpfully to reviews, especially if someone had an issue. A graceful handling of a complaint can actually impress onlookers and restore trust.

Foster a sense of community among your customers: If appropriate, create channels where your customers can interact and celebrate their connection to your brand. This could be a Facebook Group for your business (for example, a bookstore might have a "Book Club" group for patrons to discuss reads, or a crafting shop could have a community forum to share projects made with their supplies). By facilitating these connections, you deepen loyalty and encourage them to bring friends in. Hosting a "customer appreciation event" (even a virtual one, such as a special sale or a thank-you live stream with Q&A) can also galvanize your base and make them feel part of something special, which they'll likely mention to others. Some businesses name their loyal fans (think "VIP members" or even fun names like how Starbucks lovers are just Starbucks fans, but some communities have nicknames). When people feel like they belong to your brand's family, they naturally advocate for you.

Tell *their* stories: A clever way to spur word-of-mouth is to highlight your customers' stories in your marketing. People love recognition. You could do a social media post featuring a "Customer of the Week" and their experience. For example, a cookware store might share a mini-story and photo of a customer who's a passionate home chef, concluding with how they use the store's products. When you feature someone, guess what? They're likely to share that post with all *their* friends and family ("Look, this store featured me!"), thereby introducing your business to new folks. It's flattering for the customer and effective for you. Similarly, testimonials are powerful. Ask for testimonials and then display them (on your website, in flyers, or on social media). When Jane Doe gushes that your interior design service changed her home life for the better, she'll likely share that testimonial, and it provides concrete assurance to new customers reading it.

Consistency and integrity count: Word-of-mouth, good or bad, grows from the consistent reputation you build. Stay true to your word in all dealings. If you claim to value customers, demonstrate it in every policy and interaction. Over time, you'll build a strong reputation that precedes you. In a small community or niche industry, people talk. Being known as "that café with the friendly barista who remembers everyone's name" or "the mechanic you can trust not to rip you off" is priceless. It also means if ever there's a mistake (we're all human), addressing it quickly and generously can even turn a potential negative into a positive story ("They accidentally shipped the wrong item, but when I told them, they immediately fixed it and even included a bonus for the trouble. I'm so impressed!"). Protect your reputation by treating every customer interaction as important.

Summary: How to Spark Positive Word-of-Mouth:

- **Be remarkable in some way:** It could be your exceptional service, unique product, cozy atmosphere, or your personal charisma. Find what makes you stand out and lean into it. Give people a reason to remark about you.

- **Ask for the share:** Sometimes a simple "If you're happy, please tell a friend" goes a long way. People don't always think to promote you. A gentle ask (in person, or at the bottom of an email signature, or a sign by the register saying "The best compliment is a referral!") can plant the seed.

- **Build referral mechanisms:** Set up a formal referral reward if it suits your business, or at least track how new customers found you. When you hear "my friend Jake said you're great," make sure to thank Jake next time. That acknowledgement reinforces the behavior.

- **Engage in the conversation:** Stay active in your community, both offline and online. That means being friendly with neighboring businesses (they'll mention you to their customers if they know and like you) and participating in local social media groups. Many towns have Facebook or Nextdoor groups where people ask for recommendations. Being known there helps your name come up.

- **Patience and persistence:** Word-of-mouth doesn't skyrocket overnight. It's an accumulation of all the little things you do right. But once it reaches critical mass, it becomes like a flywheel. It keeps bringing in new business with minimal ongoing effort, allowing you to rely less on paid advertising.

Reflection Prompt: Who are your top 2-3 happiest customers (or friends/family who love your business)? Have you ever explicitly asked them for a review or referral? Think of one way you could encourage them to spread the word, whether it's giving them some extra business cards to share, a referral discount code, or simply a heartfelt request for a review. Also, consider this: what story will your customers tell about your business after their experience? Write down in one sentence the ideal thing you'd love a customer to say about you to someone else. That "ideal quote" can guide you in delivering that experience every time.

Bringing It All Together: Your Story, Everywhere

We've covered a lot of ground, from emails and Instagram posts to local charity events and partnership promotions. The overarching theme is that sharing your story as a small business owner is about making genuine connections across diverse channels. You don't need to use every channel at once. It's wise to prioritize what aligns best with your business and where your audience is most reachable. Perhaps you can start by improving your social media presence and asking for reviews, then gradually add hosting an event or collaborating with a neighboring business. That's perfectly fine. The goal is to create a marketing mix that works for you and feels authentic to your style and bandwidth.

A few final pointers to keep in mind as you put this chapter's advice into action:

- **Be consistent in your message:** While you adapt content to each channel (you might be more playful on Instagram and more formal in a brochure, for instance), your core story and values should shine through everywhere. Consistency builds trust and brand recognition. Over time, people should be able to hear a particular phrase or see a specific color palette and think of your business. Repeating your key messages (your mission, unique selling points, and slogan, if applicable) across channels solidifies your identity in customers' minds.

- **Quality over quantity:** It's better to have a strong presence on a few channels than to stretch yourself thin trying to do it all. A beautifully written monthly newsletter and active engagement in a local Facebook group can yield more loyal customers than half-hearted daily posts on five social networks. Choose what you enjoy and can maintain. Your enthusiasm (or lack thereof) will be evident. If designing print materials isn't your forte but you love chatting with customers in person, focus on the latter and keep the former simple. There's no one-size plan. Tailor the strategies to your strengths.

- **Budget-friendly creativity:** Throughout this chapter, we emphasized low-cost ideas. As you implement them, track what actually brings in business or engagement. That way, you can allocate any budget or time to the things that work best. Maybe you find that the community trivia night you sponsor brings in more new faces than the ads you tried. That's valuable insight. Marketing is an experiment. Learn from each attempt, and don't be afraid to be creative and even a bit bold. Small businesses often win hearts with charm and ingenuity rather than polished, big-budget campaigns. A witty chalkboard sign might attract more walk-ins than a pricey billboard, and makes people smile!

- **Stay adaptable:** Trends change, communities evolve, and what worked great one year might slow down the next. Keep listening to your customers. Perhaps a new social media platform gains popularity with your audience, or a local neighborhood blog becomes the go-to source for news. Be prepared to adjust your channels accordingly. The beauty of being small is that you can pivot quickly. If something isn't yielding results after a fair try, you can shift focus without wading through corporate red tape. Continually ask yourself: "Where are my customers? How can I reach them effectively and meaningfully?" Then adjust your strategy based on the answers.

- **Keep the enthusiasm alive:** Sharing your story should ultimately be fun and rewarding, not a dreaded chore. Yes, it's work, but it's work that directly feeds into the passion that made you start your business. When you see a response, such as a customer emailing back saying, "I loved your newsletter tip!" or a crowd showing up to your event, take a moment to savor it. That's the magic of connection. Your story is touching lives, and that's something to be proud of. Whenever marketing feels tough, reconnect with why you're doing this: you have something valuable to offer, and the world deserves to know about it. With that mindset, even the hustle of promoting can feel like an extension of your purpose rather than a distraction from it.

Finally, here's a handy **Share-Your-Story Checklist** to wrap up this chapter. Use it as a quick reminder of action items as you plan your marketing activities:

- ☐ **Elevator Pitch Ready:** I can articulate my business's story or mission in 2-3 sentences with enthusiasm, and I'm ready to share it whenever there's an opportunity (e.g., networking, social bio, etc.).

- ☐ **Social Media Active:** I have chosen at least one social media platform to focus on, and I regularly engage with content that reflects my brand personality and story.

- ☐ **Email List Building:** I am actively collecting customer emails (with permission) and have a plan to send out valuable content on a consistent schedule.

- ☐ **Community Presence:** I participate in at least one community outreach effort (such as an event, charity, or local group) that aligns with my values, keeping my business visible and involved in the local community.

- ☐ **Upcoming Event:** I have either hosted, planned, or signed up for an event or meetup to connect with potential customers in person (or virtually), providing them with a memorable experience of my brand.

- ☐ **Partnerships Identified:** I have identified (and potentially reached out to) at least one potential partner for cross-promotion or collaboration, which will help expand my reach in a budget-friendly manner.

- ☐ **Fresh Print Materials:** My business cards, flyers, and other print materials are updated, on-brand, and readily available for distribution. I've placed or posted them where my target audience can find them.

- ☐ **Review/Referral System:** I've put a system in place to encourage happy customers to leave reviews or refer others (and I make sure to acknowledge or reward them for it).

☐ **Consistent Branding:** Across all channels (online and offline), I maintain a consistent look, tone, and message, ensuring customers receive a cohesive impression of my brand story.

☐ **Monitor and Adapt:** I have a straightforward approach to tracking which marketing efforts are yielding results (by asking new customers how they found me, monitoring social engagement, etc.), and I'm willing to adjust my strategy based on the insights I gain.

Sharing your story is an ongoing journey, not a one-time task. As your business grows and evolves, so will your story, and you'll find new ways to tell it. Keep this chapter as a reference and inspiration whenever you need fresh ideas or a motivational boost. You have a story worth sharing, and now you have plenty of tactics to share it far and wide, without breaking the bank. So go ahead and let the world know what you're all about. Your future customers are waiting to hear from you! Good luck, and enjoy the process of watching your small business's presence blossom.

CHAPTER 13: SELL WITHOUT THE SLEAZE

Selling is an essential part of growing your business, but it doesn't have to be sleazy or pushy. In fact, many customers today are turned off by high-pressure sales tactics. They crave authenticity and want to buy from businesses they know, like, and trust. In this chapter, we'll explore how you can turn interest into paying customers through trust and authenticity, rather than relying on pressure. Whether your business is product-based or service-based, and whether you sell online or in person, the principles remain the same: build genuine relationships, offer clear value, and guide people to a decision without tricks or traps.

If you've ever felt awkward about "selling," take heart. You don't need a flashy persona or hard-sell gimmicks to succeed. By the end of this chapter, you'll see that selling can be as warm and honest as helping a friend. Let's explore practical strategies for selling with integrity and converting more customers by being genuine.

Rethinking Sales: From Pressure to Trust

Selling doesn't have to feel slimy. The first step is to rethink what "sales" means. Instead of viewing sales as the art of convincing someone to do something (often against their hesitation), view it as the art of helping someone solve a problem or fulfill a need. The old stereotype of the fast-talking, pressure-dealing salesperson is outdated. Not only do pushy tactics make customers uncomfortable, but they also often backfire. People may buy once under pressure, but they rarely come back. Worse, they might leave negative reviews or warn friends to stay away if they feel they were manipulated.

Why do high-pressure tactics hurt more than help? Because they erode trust. Imagine a salesperson following you around a store, urging you to buy now, dropping buzzwords, and not listening to a word you say. You'd likely find an excuse to leave, feeling stressed or even irritated. Now contrast that with someone who greets you, lets you browse, answers your questions honestly, and maybe offers helpful advice with no immediate pressure to buy. In which scenario are you more likely to make a purchase *and* feel good about it? Clearly, the second.

Trust is the currency of modern sales. Customers have more choices than ever and access to an endless amount of information online. If they sense insincerity or deceit, they can swiftly click to a competitor or walk out the door. On the other hand, if they trust you and feel you genuinely understand their needs, they'll *want* to buy from you. They might even pay a bit more or wait a bit longer, because they know you'll deliver value and treat them well. As the saying goes, people love to buy but hate being sold to. Your goal is to create an environment where customers feel safe and empowered to make a purchase, rather than feeling pressured.

Replace the "close at all costs" mindset with a "serve and support" mindset. When you prioritize the relationship over the immediate sale, something magical happens: you often get *more* sales in the long run. Customers stick around. They refer their friends. They become repeat buyers. An authentic approach turns a one-time transaction into a long-term revenue stream and genuine loyalty. So, take the pressure off yourself as well. You're not out to trick anyone. You're here to help, and if what you offer truly benefits them, the sale becomes a natural conclusion.

Focus on Relationships, Not Just Transactions

Think of your favorite businesses or brands. Chances are, you keep going back to them because of how they make you feel, not just because of what they sell. Building relationships with your customers is far more rewarding (and profitable) than chasing a quick buck through one-off transactions. When customers feel seen and valued as people, not walking wallets, they develop an emotional connection to your business. That connection is what keeps them coming back and bringing others along.

So, how do you build genuine relationships in a business context? Here are a few key approaches:

- **Be genuine and approachable:** Let your personality and values shine through in your business. You don't have to put on a "sales mask." In fact, being yourself is a competitive advantage. It's something no other business can copy. Whether you're chatting in person or writing online, use a natural, friendly tone (just as you would with a good friend). Authenticity is disarmingly compelling. For example, if you run a boutique, you might share your honest excitement about a new product: "I absolutely love this scarf because it reminds me of my trip to Paris, and I think it would look great with your outfit," rather than a scripted pitch. Let customers see your human side.

- **Take a genuine interest in them:** Good relationships are two-way. Ask your customers questions and listen actively to their answers. If you're selling in person, this might mean learning a bit about what brought them in or what problem they're trying to solve. If you're selling online, this could mean engaging with comments or emails thoughtfully. The key is to show that you care about *them*, not just the sale. Small personal touches go a long way. Remembering a regular customer's name, their previous purchase, or noting a client's key goal for their project shows that you value them as individuals. For a service business, for instance, you might start a consultation by asking, "What prompted you to look for help in this area?" and listen to their story.

- **Build rapport through empathy:** Empathy is your superpower in relationship-building. Try to put yourself in your customer's shoes and understand their emotions and perspectives. If a customer expresses a concern, validate it before you address it. Simple phrases like "I understand how you feel" or "I've heard others ask about that too" can make someone feel heard. For example, if you offer home remodeling services and the client worries about the project timeline, empathize: "It's totally understandable to be concerned about the timeline. Living in a construction zone is stressful. Let's talk about how we minimize disruptions for you." This approach makes the customer feel like you're on their side, working *with* them rather than just trying to sell to them.

- **Nurture over time:** Not every interested person will buy immediately, and that's okay. Relationship-focused businesses find ways to stay in touch and nurture leads over time without being pushy. This could mean following up periodically with a helpful note or a useful piece of information, rather than a repetitive "Are you ready to buy now?" For example, if someone visits your website and downloads a free guide, you might send a friendly follow-up email a week later: "Hey, I hope you found the guide useful! I'm here to answer any questions you have." No hard sell, just an offer to help. We'll discuss specific tools, such as email newsletters, for nurturing leads in a bit. Still, the idea is to build the relationship gradually, much like you wouldn't ask someone to marry you on the first date. You also wouldn't ask a new prospect for a huge commitment right away. Instead, create a path of small engagements (such as following you on social media, joining your email list, or attending a free webinar) that build up to a purchase when they're ready.

Remember, relationships turn customers into lifelong fans. By focusing on making a positive connection rather than just "closing," you transform the sales process into something enjoyable and meaningful for both sides. This doesn't just feel better. It leads to more sustainable business growth. A customer who trusts you will buy from you again and again and recommend you to their friends. That lifetime value far exceeds any one tricky "close" you might force with pressure. So, invest in relationships the way you'd invest in a friendship: with time, care, and authenticity.

Serve First: Educate and Add Value Before Selling

One of the most effective ways to sell more without feeling salesy is to shift your mindset from "selling" to "serving." Instead of approaching potential customers with the question, "How can I convince them to buy?" ask, "How can I help them or improve their life *right now*, even before they buy anything?" By providing value upfront (through education, valuable content, or small, helpful actions), you build trust and goodwill. You demonstrate that you actually care about the customer's needs, and you showcase your expertise in the process.

Educate, don't just pitch. Sharing your knowledge freely is a powerful way to build trust. For example, if you run a product-based business, you might educate customers with how-to videos or blog posts. A local gardening store could write a blog post or email newsletter about "5 Tips to Prepare Your Garden for Winter," genuinely helping readers (while subtly showcasing that the store owner is knowledgeable, which will likely lead readers to the store when they need gardening supplies). Similarly, a software company might host a free webinar teaching businesses best practices that relate to their software, positioning their product as a helpful tool within a larger solution. In a service business, education might take the form of a free initial consultation or assessment. For instance, a personal fitness coach could offer a complimentary 15-minute fitness assessment and email a personalized tip sheet to each prospect. During that session, the coach is actively helping the person, whether or not they sign up, and establishing credibility and trust.

Give value through content and resources. Content marketing is essentially the art of selling by helping. By producing valuable content (articles, videos, podcasts, infographics, etc.), you attract people who are interested in what you do and prove your value before money ever changes hands. Consider starting an email newsletter that shares genuinely helpful tips or insights related to your field of expertise. If you're a tax advisor, your newsletter could provide seasonal financial tips or a simple checklist for tax prep. If you sell eco-friendly home products, your newsletter could share "DIY green living" hacks or showcase creative ways to use your products. The key is consistency and generosity. Send value regularly. Over time, readers start to see you as a helpful friend or mentor in your domain. So, when they have a need, *you* are the one they trust and turn to as a paying customer. And don't worry, sending valuable content doesn't mean you never mention your products or services; it just means the overall tone is educational rather than salesy. You can include a light call-to-action ("P.S. We just stocked a new line of organic gardening tools if you're interested") after delivering value, and it will feel natural rather than pushy.

Host events or demos that serve your audience. For product-based businesses, product demonstrations, workshops, or free trials are golden opportunities to let people experience value firsthand. Imagine you create artisanal cooking gadgets. Instead of simply saying, "Our blender is the best, please buy it," you could host a live cooking demo (either in-person at a local market or virtually via a live stream) to demonstrate how to make a tasty recipe using the blender. During the demo, you're teaching attendees a new recipe (value!) and subtly highlighting the blender's benefits. Even if someone doesn't make a purchase immediately, they leave with a positive impression and valuable knowledge, which keeps the door open for a future purchase. Similarly, a cosmetics brand might offer a free makeup class or skincare workshop, allowing people to learn techniques and try products in a no-pressure environment. The attendees have fun, gain skills, and often end up purchasing the products because they saw how well they work, and they don't feel forced. They genuinely want them.

Service businesses can offer something equivalent, such as consultations, free sessions, or community Q&As. A consultant or coach might offer a free 30-minute strategy session or hold an "Ask me anything" hour on social media. An interior designer could host a free webinar on "Small Space Design Tricks" or volunteer to do a short talk at a community center about color choices in home decor. These events position you as a helpful expert, allowing people to experience your style and knowledge. When they have a bigger need that requires paid help, who will they think of? The person who has *already helped them for free*. This approach not only generates warm leads, but it also filters in the right customers: those who resonate with your approach and are likely to be great long-term clients.

Be involved and give back. Another way to sell through service is by community involvement. Participating in community events, local charities, or industry forums (online or offline) can indirectly boost your sales in a non-sleazy way. For example, a local bakery might sponsor a charity bake sale or donate treats to a community fundraiser. They're not directly advertising their products with a hard sell. They're demonstrating their values and generosity. People notice and develop a positive impression of the brand. Down the line, when those community members need a cake or bread, they'll remember the bakery that cares about the community. For a service example, consider a real estate agent who volunteers to run a free first-time homebuyer workshop at the library. They're educating and giving back. Attendees of the workshop may later choose that agent when they're ready to buy a house, as trust has been established in a genuine setting.

The overarching principle is to give value before asking for it. When you consistently serve your audience by informing, educating, inspiring, or assisting them, you create a sense of reciprocity. People see that you're not just out for yourself, and in turn, they feel good about supporting you. By the time you present a paid offer, it feels like the next logical step in an ongoing relationship, not a cold pitch out of the blue. You become the guide and helper in their eyes, rather than "just another vendor trying to sell something."

Listen and Consult: Helping People Make the Right Decision

Selling without sleaze means making the sales conversation about the customer, not about you. One of the most effective ways to achieve this is to adopt a *consultative approach*. Essentially, act like a consultant or advisor who is there to help diagnose and solve the customer's problem. This begins with listening more than talking.

When you're face-to-face with a potential customer (or on a call/Zoom), resist the urge to launch straight into a pitch of features and benefits. Instead, begin with questions and genuine curiosity. Ask open-ended questions that invite the person to share their situation, needs, or concerns. For example, if you sell web design services, you might ask, "What do you feel isn't working about your current website?" or "What goals do you have for your business online?" If you run a pet supply store and a customer comes in, you might ask, "Tell me about your pet. Any specific needs or challenges you're looking to address?" These kinds of questions prompt the customer to talk about themselves. Your job then is to actively listen. Pay close attention not only to their words, but also to their tone and body language, especially if you are meeting in person. Are they anxious about the price? Overwhelmed by choices? Excited about a new opportunity? Encourage them to elaborate by nodding, saying "I see," or asking follow-ups like "Can you tell me more about that?"

Show empathy and understanding. As they share, acknowledge their feelings or challenges. Something as simple as, "I hear you. Choosing the right solution can definitely be confusing," goes a long way. You might even gently repeat or paraphrase their key concerns to confirm you got it right: "So, it sounds like reliability is your biggest concern, and you've had some bad experiences with appliances breaking down. Is that right?" When the customer hears their own concerns reflected back, they feel understood and validated. This builds trust quickly. They see that you're *listening*, not just waiting for your turn to talk.

Once you have a clear understanding of their needs, frame your product or service as a solution to *their specific problem*. Focus on how you can help them, using what they've told you. For instance, instead of a generic sales pitch like "Our accounting software has XYZ features," you could say, "From what you've described, you're spending too many hours on bookkeeping. Our software can help by automating monthly reports, which means you'll get several hours of your time back every week. How does that sound?" Here, you're directly linking their stated problem (too much time spent) with your solution (automation giving time back). It feels personalized because it *is*. You've tailored your explanation to what matters to them.

Address objections with honesty. Inevitably, customers might voice hesitations: perhaps it's the price, uncertainty about whether it's right for them, or a feature they wish you had. Never dismiss or ignore these objections. Old-school sleazy salespeople might try to bulldoze past objections or use high-pressure rebuttals ("You say it's expensive, but what's the cost of *not* buying it today?!"). In a trust-based approach, you do the opposite: you encourage the customer to voice concerns, and you tackle them openly and honestly. If someone says, "I'm not sure if this service will work for my situation," don't get defensive. Instead, explore it: "That's a fair concern. Let's talk about your situation in more detail to see if this is truly a good fit. If it isn't, I'll be the first to tell you." Imagine the relief a customer feels when they hear that! You are signaling that you're not going to twist their arm if it's not right. Often, this level of honesty convinces them *more* that you're trustworthy and might actually make them comfortable buying.

Being honest might even include recommending a more affordable option or an alternative if that serves the customer's best interests. For example, if you own a pet store and a customer is looking at a very expensive dog food but you know a mid-priced brand is just as nutritious for their breed, you might say, "Honestly, you don't need the ultra-premium for a healthy two-year-old Labrador. This other brand has very similar nutrition and costs less. Many of our customers have great results with it." That kind of integrity wins customers for life. You just proved you care about their wallet and their needs more than squeezing a few extra dollars out of them *right now*. In many cases, they will trust your recommendation and buy the item you suggested. Even if they stick with the expensive one or leave without buying, you've planted a seed of trust that can bloom later.

Help them envision success. Part of consulting with the customer is painting a picture of how their life or business will be improved after using your product or service. This isn't about hype. It's about connecting the dots for them in a realistic, positive way. Use vivid but honest examples or stories. "Once we redesign your website, you'll likely notice visitors spending more time browsing. We had a client in a similar industry who saw a 20% increase in online inquiries after their site revamp. I can imagine you getting more quote requests like they did, which is exactly what you're looking for." Here you're educating them on outcomes through a relatable example, not just saying, "It'll be great, trust us." You're helping them make an informed and confident decision.

Finally, honor their autonomy. A true consultative seller guides the customer, leaving the decision up to them without exerting pressure. Sometimes, after all the discussion, the best close is, "Let me know what you think would be the best next step. I'm here to support your decision." You can offer a recommendation if appropriate ("Given everything we discussed, I honestly think the mid-tier package is a good fit because of X, Y, Z benefits. But of course, it's your call and I want you to feel comfortable."). By empowering the customer to choose, you remove the adversarial tension. It's no longer you vs. them; it's *you and them* on the same side, figuring out the best solution together. This is how you help people make a purchase rather than pushing them to buy.

Honesty and Transparency at Every Step

In a world where skepticism is high, one of the simplest ways to stand out is by being radically honest and transparent with your customers. Nothing builds credibility faster. Think of transparency as shedding light on anything that a customer would want to know to make a wise decision. When you hide or gloss over details, customers sense it, and trust erodes. But when you proactively share important information, even if it's something that might lose you a quick sale, you gain trust that can win you many more sales down the road.

Start with the basics: be clear about what you're offering and at what price. If you provide a service, clearly explain your packages or fees upfront in plain language. If you sell products, make sure pricing is easy to find and understand (no hidden "gotcha" fees at checkout). Customers sincerely appreciate knowing what to expect. For example, if your photography service charges extra for prints or travel, be sure to mention this upfront when discussing the package. You might say, "My standard package is $X and includes A, B, C. If we need to add anything like an extra hour or travel outside the city, I'll let you know in advance what that cost would be so there are no surprises." This kind of clarity is unfortunately rarer than it should be, and it immediately differentiates you as someone who respects the customer's right to know precisely what they're getting into.

Never make promises you can't keep. It's tempting to say "yes" to every request or to exaggerate what your product can do when you're eager to close a sale. Overpromising is a cornerstone of sleazy sales, and it almost always leads to disappointment and damaged reputations. If your product has limits or your service has boundaries, be upfront about them. Honest selling might sound like: "I want to set the right expectations. Our app will greatly simplify your workflow, but it won't eliminate all manual steps completely. You'll likely still need to do X or Y occasionally." Or, "I can certainly expedite this project, but to be transparent, it may incur a rush fee because we'll need to allocate extra resources to meet the two-week deadline. Let me know if that's okay, or if a normal timeline is better for you to avoid that fee." These kinds of statements might seem risky to a traditional salesperson ("What if mentioning a limitation scares them off?!"), but in truth, customers value honesty so much that it often increases their confidence in buying from you. They know they're dealing with a straight shooter.

Transparency also means admitting what you don't know or can't do. If a question comes up that you're unsure about, it's far better to say, "That's a great question. I want to be sure I give you accurate information, so let me check on that and get back to you," rather than bluffing through an answer. Customers can tell when someone is BS-ing. Admitting a gap in knowledge doesn't make you look weak. It makes you look trustworthy, and it gives you a chance to follow up later with the info, which is another touchpoint of service.

In addition, consider being transparent with social proof and feedback. For instance, many businesses showcase testimonials and reviews, which is great, but also be willing to acknowledge less-than-perfect feedback if it exists. If a customer brings up a critical review they saw, don't get defensive or dismissive. Address it calmly: "Yes, I did see that review. The customer had an unusual situation, and we've since made some changes to address that issue. I reached out to them afterwards to offer a solution. I understand how that part of the review could be concerning, and I want you to feel comfortable, so let's talk it through if you have any worries." By being open about it, you remove the scare factor. It shows you're not hiding anything, and you care about getting it right.

For product-based businesses, transparency can also involve sharing the story behind the product (materials, sourcing, and process), especially if customers might care about ethical or quality aspects. For example: "This furniture costs a bit more because it's made with solid wood and is hand-finished. I want to be transparent that you can find cheaper options, but the trade-off is durability. We guarantee ours for 10 years. I'm happy to show you how it's constructed so you know what you're paying for." Such openness about price and quality considerations helps customers make informed decisions and shows that you respect them.

A special note on integrity: Always align your sales messages with the truth of what you deliver. If you say "customer satisfaction is guaranteed," mean it, and have a clear, fair policy to honor that guarantee. If you say a course will have 10 modules, don't deliver 8. These might sound obvious, but customers have been burned enough times that they often listen for any hint of overinflated claims. Stick to honesty as your policy, and you'll never have to worry about remembering any "tricks". You speak the truth about your business.

Transparency builds long-term trust and loyalty. Customers remember when a business was upfront with them. Even if they don't buy immediately, they may come back later precisely because you were the one honest voice among others trying to make a quick sale. Internally, selling with honesty feels so much better. You can close a deal and sleep at night knowing you did right by the customer. That peace of mind is priceless, and it's the foundation of a brand built on authenticity.

Gentle Persuasion: Using Soft Calls to Action

Selling with authenticity doesn't mean you never ask for the sale. It simply means doing it in a gentle, non-pushy manner. This is where the concept of soft calls to action (CTAs) comes in. A soft CTA is an invitation or suggestion that guides the customer toward the next step, rather than a hard demand for an immediate purchase. It creates an opportunity for the customer to engage further without feeling like they're being shoved through a door.

Consider the difference between these two approaches on a website or in an email:

- **Hard Sell:** "BUY NOW! LIMITED TIME OFFER! Don't miss out!!!"

- **Soft Sell:** "Interested in learning more? Get a free demo," or "Take a tour," or "Start a free trial. No obligation."

The hard sell might spur a few impulse actions, but it will also turn many people off with its aggression and potentially create mistrust ("Why are they so desperate for me to buy right now?"). The soft sell, on the other hand, respects the customer's pace. It's saying, "Here's something useful or low-risk you can do next if you're interested." It's a friendly nudge, not an elbow in the ribs.

Use CTAs that emphasize helping or informing. Phrases like "Learn more about how this can help you" or "Schedule a free consultation to see what we can do for you" are effective because they promise *value* or clarity as the next step. You're essentially saying, "Let's continue the conversation" instead of "Commit this second." For instance, a consultant might end a helpful blog post with, "Curious how these tips could apply to your business? Let's chat. Book a 15-minute free consultation." A product seller might have a button on their site labeled "See it in action," which leads to a video or a live demo sign-up. These CTAs guide the customer toward purchase in a gradual, comfortable manner.

In person, a soft call to action might be as simple as asking, "Would you like to try it out?" if you have a product they can handle or sample. If you've been discussing a service, your soft close could be, "I'd be happy to send you a proposal with all these details for you to review. Would that be helpful?" Notice that you're not cornering them with, "So, can I sign you up right now?" Instead, you're offering to give them more information or an easy next step. Another gentle prompt in person or on a call might be, "How are you feeling about this so far? Is there anything else you'd like to know?" This invites them to express any remaining doubts. Quite often, the customer will say something like, "No, I think it sounds good," which opens the door for you to say, "Great, should we go ahead and schedule/start/prepare the paperwork?" Now it's collaborative.

Scarcity and urgency, done ethically. A common sales tactic is to use urgency ("Only 2 left!" or "Sale ends today!") to prompt people to act. Used excessively, this can come off as sleazy, especially if it's fake urgency or constant. However, urgency can be communicated sincerely if there is a truly time-sensitive aspect, but it should be used sparingly and honestly. If your offer genuinely expires or you have limited slots, you can softly communicate that: "We have a few spots left for the November workshop, and I wanted to give you a heads-up in case you'd like to join." This informs the customer so they can make an informed decision, rather than using it as a pressure tactic. Always avoid false urgency. Savvy customers will see through it, and it will permanently erode trust.

Encourage small commitments. Earlier, we mentioned nurturing leads and not jumping straight to the "big ask." Soft CTAs often align with this by encouraging small "yeses" first. For example, asking someone to subscribe to your newsletter or follow your social media is a very low-pressure CTA, and it keeps them connected to you. Once they're in your world, you continue providing value and occasional offers. Another small commitment might be a free trial or sample. "Try our service free for 14 days" or "Come to a free class this Saturday" are CTAs that imply, *"Experience it, see if you like it, no pressure."* If your product or service truly shines, these trial experiences can effectively convert people without any heavy selling at all. Their own experience convinces them.

Be patient and positive. When you make a soft offer, be okay with the customer taking their time to respond. Sometimes a customer will take the info and say, "Let me think about it." Your response should be along the lines of, "Absolutely, please do. This is an important decision. Take as much time as you need. I'm here if any questions come up." Maybe ask if it's alright to check back in a few days or a week, which is still gentle: "I can send you a follow-up email in a week just to see if you need anything else, does that work for you?" Most people will appreciate this considerate approach. And crucially, when you do follow up, keep that same calm, helpful tone. For example, "Hi, just touching base to see if you had any more questions after our chat. I'm happy to clarify anything, or when you're ready, we can take the next steps. No rush. I want you to feel completely comfortable." This kind of follow-up reinforces that you care about *them*, not just the sale.

By using gentle persuasion techniques, you lower the resistance that customers often have when they sense a sales push. Instead, they feel in control and respected, which ironically makes them *more* likely to move forward with you. It creates a buying environment where the customer says "yes" because they want to, not because they were strong-armed, and that makes all the difference in how they perceive the purchase and how loyal they'll be afterwards.

Leveraging Tools Without Losing the Personal Touch

In both online and in-person sales, there are plenty of tools and systems that can assist you, from email automation software to customer relationship management (CRM) systems to sales scripts for conversations. These tools can be incredibly helpful in implementing the strategies we've discussed. However, it's important to use them in a way that enhances your personal, authentic approach rather than replacing it. Technology and prepared materials should serve your relationship-building strategy, not turn your interactions into mechanical or generic experiences.

Email automation and newsletters: Staying in touch with potential and existing customers is crucial (remember nurturing leads over time), and email is one of the best ways to do it. If you have a growing list of interested contacts, you can't personally email each one on a regular basis. This is where an email automation tool shines. You can set up a welcome email series for new subscribers that introduces your brand story and provides helpful content. You can schedule a weekly or monthly newsletter that is sent to everyone. The key is to write these emails in a personal, friendly tone, as if you're writing to one person, not a faceless crowd. Even though it's automated, a well-written email can feel like a note from a friend. Use the person's first name if possible (most email tools allow you to personalize that), and share helpful information, stories, or tips as we discussed earlier. For example: "Hi Jane, I was reflecting on a client story this week and thought it might resonate with you. Have you ever felt overwhelmed by social media marketing?..." This doesn't feel like a mass sales email. It feels human. Avoid overly slick, marketing-speak emails that sound like an infomercial. If you do mention a product or a sale in an email, sandwich it with genuine content. Don't bombard people either. Respect their inbox. A helpful email every so often will be read and appreciated, while a daily barrage of "offers" will just get you ignored or unsubscribed.

Landing pages and websites: Your online presence can do a lot of selling for you, especially for product-based businesses or service providers who gather leads online. A landing page is a dedicated page that guides a visitor to take one action (like signing up for something or making a purchase). When designing these pages or your website in general, carry forward the "sell without sleaze" principles. That means your web copy should be clear, honest, and customer-focused. Highlight the benefits and value to the customer, use testimonials for trust, and include those soft CTAs ("Contact us for a quote," "Get started with a free trial," etc.). You can mention promotions or limited offers here, but keep the tone friendly and factual. For instance, it's fine to say "20% off until June 30" if that's a genuine promotion. Just don't layer it with high-pressure flashing banners and countdown timers that stress people out the moment they arrive. Also, use your website to educate as much as you're selling, perhaps through a blog, FAQ section, or resources page. That way, visitors feel they've gotten something useful, even if they don't buy immediately. The ultimate goal is that browsing your site or landing page feels like interacting with a trustworthy guide, not a hard-selling listing.

Customer Relationship Management (CRM) tools: If you manage a large number of clients or leads, a CRM system is invaluable for tracking interactions and preferences. However, the power of a CRM in ethical selling lies in how you utilize the information. Use it to remember personal details that show you care. Did a client mention their daughter was starting college? Make a note. The next time you talk, you can genuinely ask, "How did your daughter settle into college?" This isn't fake friendliness. It's a genuine recall of something important from a past conversation. People are often pleasantly surprised and touched when you remember these small details. It shows you see them as a whole person. A CRM can also remind you of follow-ups at appropriate intervals. For example, you might set a task to follow up with a prospect a month after submitting a proposal. When that time comes, you can reach out personally: "Hi, just checking in as promised. How are you feeling about the plan we discussed? I'm here for any questions." The tool ensures no one falls through the cracks, but you are the one crafting a warm message.

Scripts and sales templates: Many businesses use scripts or templates for sales calls and meetings, and there's nothing wrong with having a guideline. In fact, having a prepared outline or key talking points can ensure you don't forget to mention important benefits or ask critical questions. The danger is when a script is followed rigidly, regardless of the actual conversation. That *does* feel sleazy and robotic. To avoid that, think of your script as a flexible roadmap. Customize it to each client or context, and be prepared to deviate when the conversation naturally takes a turn. For instance, your script might have a series of questions, but if the customer brings up an important point early, you might jump to address that section of your script out of order, which is perfectly fine. Maintain a conversational tone. If you have specific phrases you like to use (maybe to explain your pricing or to describe a feature), practice them enough that they come out sounding natural, not read. It can also help to acknowledge the conversation openly rather than trying to stealthily "lead" it with a script. For example: "I have a few questions to understand your needs better. I jotted them down so I don't forget any of them. Mind if I go through those with you?" This is a polite way to use your prepared list while making the customer a partner in the process. They usually appreciate your thoroughness.

Personalize wherever possible: Whether online or offline, look for opportunities to tailor the experience to each individual. Online, this could involve using the customer's name in communications, recommending products or content based on their previous clicks or purchases, and segmenting your email list so that people receive relevant messages. (For example, a pet store might send different tips to cat owners vs. dog owners.) In person, it's things like greeting a repeat customer with, "Good to see you again, how did you like that roast coffee you bought last time?" or sending a handwritten thank-you note after a client purchases from you. These personal touches are far from sleazy. They are heartwarming. They show that even as you utilize tools and processes, you still see the human being in front of you.

In summary, tools and systems should amplify your care, not replace it. Automations can keep you consistent, scripts can keep you focused, and digital platforms can extend your reach, but the warmth, integrity, and authenticity must still come from you. Always review your automated messages or marketing materials with a human eye. Does this sound like something I'd appreciate as a customer? Does it align with the trust-based experience I want to create? If you can say yes, then you're leveraging these tools the right way to sell more effectively without ever losing the personal touch that makes your brand special.

Selling by Serving: Examples in Action

To see how all these principles come together, let's look at a couple of scenarios where a business "sells without the sleaze" in practical ways. These examples (one product-based and one service-based) will illustrate how educating, serving, and building trust can directly lead to more sales.

Example 1: Product-Based Business - The Helpful Home Goods Store: Meet Elena, who owns a small home goods store that sells kitchenware and décor. In the past, Elena tried typical sales tactics: big discount signs, "limited time" coupons, and upselling every customer at checkout. She noticed it didn't foster loyalty. People would buy during a sale and disappear, and some seemed uncomfortable with the pushy upsells. So, Elena revamped her approach to focus on service and trust.

First, she started an email newsletter called "Home Comfort Tips." Each month, she emails subscribers seasonal home advice, such as how to organize your pantry in spring or cozy décor trends for fall, along with a simple recipe or DIY project. The newsletter feels like a friendly magazine, not an ad. Readers love it and forward it to friends. Of course, Elena includes a section at the bottom highlighting a couple of products (e.g., "Featured: Our handwoven baskets that make pantry organization a breeze"). Still, it's always after providing genuine tips. Over time, subscribers begin to visit the store, mentioning something from the newsletter, feeling like they already know Elena as a helpful expert. Sales increase, but interestingly, *so does the amount of time people spend in the store chatting and asking questions*. It's become a community hub vibe.

Next, Elena started hosting free workshops and product demonstrations in the store on weekends. One weekend, it's a knife skills workshop in the kitchen section (co-hosted by a local chef friend). Another time, it's a "decorate your mantel" mini-class using items she sells. These events are casual, fun, and zero-pressure. Attendees are explicitly told, "This is just about learning and enjoying. Of course, if you see something you love in the store, we're here, but today is about having a good time." Because people are encouraged to experience things, they *interact with the products* more than they would on a normal shopping trip. They chop veggies with those high-end knives, and they arrange candlesticks and vases on a sample mantel. And guess what? Many of them end up falling in love with the items through use. A customer might say, "Wow, this pan heats so evenly," and Elena will smile and offer, "You're welcome to take one home today if you like it, but no pressure. I can also order one for you later if you decide." More often than not, they purchase it on the spot *because they genuinely want it*, remembering the positive experience rather than feeling like Elena "sold" it to them. Those who don't buy still walk away with new knowledge and a good impression, which makes them more likely to return.

Elena also engages in community activities. She sponsors a booth at the town's annual food festival, not directly selling products, but giving out a helpful pamphlet, "Ultimate Kitchen Cheat Sheet," with measurement conversions and cooking tips (branded with her store name subtly). Attendees flock to her booth for the free cheat sheet and sample some snacks she made using her store's cookware. She chats with dozens of locals, never pushing sales. In the following weeks, many of those people visit her store. They feel like they've met a friend at the festival, and they're curious to see more of what she has to offer. Sales keep growing, and Elena realizes she hasn't had to use a single sleazy tactic. By educating and engaging, she's created a loyal customer base that trusts her. People have even started asking Elena for advice on home projects, giving her ideas for new workshops and content: a virtuous cycle of trust and sales.

Example 2: Service-Based Business - The Trustworthy Tech Consultant: Now consider Raj, an IT consultant who provides tech support and system setup for small businesses. Initially, Raj struggled because he was soft-spoken and found it hard to make the aggressive pitch that some competitors used. He didn't like the approach of pushing clients into long contracts or making grand promises. So, he decided to lean into his natural strengths: listening, teaching, and problem-solving.

Raj's primary marketing strategy became education through content. He began writing simple, jargon-free blog articles, such as "5 Free Tools To Make Remote Work Easier" and "How to Protect Your Business from Phishing Scams - A Quick Checklist." He shared these on LinkedIn and local business forums. This began attracting an audience who saw him as a knowledgeable and generous expert. Some readers reached out with questions, which Raj always answered patiently without immediately trying to sell his services. In fact, he'd often end his advice with, "If you need more help, let me know, but hopefully these tips get you started!" This approach surprised people. He wasn't hooking them with a sales pitch. He was truly helping. As a result, many ended up hiring him when the free tips weren't enough or when they needed a trusted professional to handle things.

For more direct interactions, Raj offered a free tech audit for local businesses. Instead of a typical sales call, he'd come on-site and spend an hour looking over their setup, then write up a short, no-obligation report of recommendations. In the report, he'd clearly outline "Here are 2-3 critical issues to address (e.g., weak Wi-Fi coverage, outdated firewall) and some suggestions on how to fix them." He even noted which tasks the business owner could potentially handle themselves and which might require professional assistance. Many owners were impressed by this clarity. Some did try to implement the easier fixes themselves. Raj was okay with that, since they often called him later for the tougher parts. Most owners, however, were busy running their business and saw that Raj already understood their situation and had a plan, so hiring him was an easy next step. They didn't feel pressured. They felt *grateful* for the insight and confident that Raj would do a good job (after all, he basically diagnosed the issues for free, demonstrating his expertise and honesty).

Raj also made sure to listen and adapt in each consultation. For example, one client was hesitant to upgrade their computers due to the cost. Instead of pushing, Raj empathized: "I get that budget is tight. Let's prioritize. Perhaps, replace the two oldest PCs this quarter, which will resolve the immediate slowness issue at your front desk, and plan the rest for next year. We can also look at refurbished units to save money." The client's relief was palpable. Raj had talked the client *into spending less money* for now, which is the opposite of a greedy sale. Still, that client became one of his longest-term accounts, trusting every recommendation thereafter and providing many referrals. Raj's willingness to be transparent about costs and offer phased solutions proved he cared about the client's best interest.

To maintain relationships, Raj set up an automated system to send quarterly tech tips via email to all past and prospective clients. These were short, friendly notes ("Happy Spring! It's a good time to clean dust out of your computers. Here's how") with no sales pitch, just his contact information at the bottom. This kept him on their radar in a helpful way. When those businesses faced a tech crisis or finally had a budget for improvements, who did they call? The guy who had been kindly advising them all along.

Through these examples, you can see a pattern: educate, help, and be patient. Both Elena and Raj leveraged educational content, free value offerings, and authentic relationships to generate sales. They utilized tools (such as newsletters, events, and audits) and techniques (including listening and offering soft suggestions) that aligned with a trustworthy brand image. Most importantly, they enjoyed their work more because they weren't dealing with the anxiety of forcing anyone's hand. Customers walked away happy, whether they made a purchase or not, and that goodwill translated into more business over time.

You can apply these ideas to your own business context. The specifics might differ. Perhaps you'll conduct livestreams instead of in-person workshops, or maybe your free value is a downloadable guide rather than a consultation. Still, the core principle remains the same: you win sales by prioritizing the customer's needs and demonstrating how you can meet them, not by wearing them down with pressure. Selling with service at the forefront creates a positive experience that people remember. It may not always yield the instant gratification of a high-pressure close, but it lays the foundation for a stable, growing business fueled by loyal customers and referrals.

The Payoff: Loyal Customers and Lasting Success

It's worth underscoring what you stand to gain by selling without the sleaze. When you invest in trust and authenticity, you're building more than just sales. You're building a reputation and a brand that people believe in. The payoff comes in multiple forms:

- **Loyal customers:** A customer who had a positive, pressure-free buying experience is far more likely to come back. They remember that you treated them with respect and helped them make the right choice. This means repeat business. Over time, the lifetime value of a loyal customer far exceeds that of someone who was browbeaten into a one-time purchase. Loyal customers also tend to be more forgiving if something ever goes wrong, because you've built up goodwill. They trust that you'll make it right.

- **Word-of-mouth and referrals:** When people truly love how you operate, they tell others. They'll say, "You know, if you need a ____, you should go to [Your Business]. They are so honest and helpful, it's a totally different experience." This kind of referral is gold. It brings you warm leads who already have positive expectations based on what they heard. Because the referral source is often a friend or colleague, they come in with a high level of trust in you from the start. You can't buy that kind of advertising. It has to be earned through genuine interactions. Conversely, pushy tactics can also spread by word-of-mouth, but in the form of warnings ("Don't go to that place, they'll hound you to buy stuff"). We want to be on the positive side of people's stories!

- **Higher conversion rates over the long run:** It may seem counterintuitive, but easing off the pressure can lead to *more* people eventually saying yes. Why? Because the ones who walk away today on their own terms feel okay coming back tomorrow. A hard "no" under pressure often means "never again," whereas a "not right now" under friendly conditions usually turns into a yes later. By nurturing leads, educating them, and giving them space, you capture many sales that would otherwise be lost. It might happen on the customer's timetable instead of yours, but a sale next month is still a sale, and likely a more enthusiastic one.

- **Stronger brand image:** Selling with integrity becomes part of your brand identity. In a marketplace full of hype and noise, you become known as the breath of fresh air. This differentiation is priceless. Customers crave businesses they can trust. If your brand is consistently authentic, from marketing to sales to customer service, you'll attract customers who share those values and repel those who expect or respond to sleaze. (And honestly, having fewer high-maintenance, distrustful customers is another hidden payoff!) Your business can proudly market itself on honesty and customer-centric service, which in 2025 and beyond is a huge selling point in itself.

- **Personal satisfaction and confidence:** Finally, let's not overlook how this approach affects *you* as the business owner or salesperson. When you sell without sleaze, you can feel proud of how you conduct business. You're building genuine relationships and seeing firsthand how your product or service helps people, because you've taken the time to understand and witness the impact. This feels rewarding. It keeps you motivated through the ups and downs because your work has purpose and positive feedback loops. On a practical level, when you're confident that you're offering value and not tricking anyone, your sales conversations become more confident, too. There's no guilt or second-guessing in the back of your mind. You can fully stand behind your offers. That sincere conviction often shines through, making your sales approach even more effective.

As you apply the trust-based methods from this chapter, remember that patience is key. Building relationships and a solid brand might take more time than blitzing people with high-pressure tactics, but it yields greater rewards that also last longer. You're not just aiming for a spike in sales this week. You're building the foundation for years of success. Each authentic connection is like planting a seed. Some seeds sprout quickly (resulting in an immediate sale), while others take time to bloom (yielding a sale months later or a referral). If you nurture your garden of customers with care and consistency, you'll enjoy a continuous harvest.

Selling without the sleaze is not about being passive or timid. It's about being strategically patient and people-focused. You still guide customers toward making a purchase, but you do it in the same way you might guide a friend: with advice, support, and respect for their free will. In doing so, you create not just customers, but fans and friends of your business. That's the true win-win. They get the solution or product that improves their life, and you get a thriving business built on goodwill and trust.

As we conclude this chapter, challenge yourself to embrace this approach wholeheartedly. Let go of any tactics that don't sit right with your conscience or your brand's values. Double down on serving your audience. Be bravely authentic. It will attract the right people to you. The more you sell in this way, the easier and more natural it becomes. You'll start to see sales opportunities everywhere, not because you're scheming, but because you're listening and empathizing. Every conversation, online post, or event can organically lead to business when you approach it with the intent to help.

In the next chapter, we'll delve into delivering magical service, but before that, take a moment to reflect on how you can implement "selling without the sleaze" in your own world. Below are some prompts to help you think and some key takeaways to remember as you transform your sales approach into one that feels good and delivers results.

Reflection Prompts

- **Think of a bad sales experience:** Recall a time you felt pressured or uncomfortable as a customer. What specific tactics or behaviors made it feel "sleazy"? Jot down what *not* to do in your own sales approach. How could that experience have been improved with a trust-based approach?

- **Assess your current approach:** Be honest. Are there any sales tactics you're currently using (or considering) that don't align with a "serve first" mentality? For instance, do you send overly aggressive follow-up messages or lean on discounts instead of value? How can you tweak these tactics to be more customer-friendly and authentic?

- **Plan to provide value:** Identify two or three ways you could offer value to potential customers before asking for a sale. This could be content (like a how-to guide, checklist, or short workshop) or a personal touch (like a free consultation or helpful demo). What will you create or do in the next month to serve your audience? Schedule it in your calendar.

- **List common customer questions/concerns:** What are the typical hesitations or objections people have about your product or service? Write them down. Now, brainstorm honest and empathetic responses to each. Consider how you can address these proactively, perhaps through a FAQ on your website, a section in your sales presentation, or casual conversation points.

- **Envision the long-term relationship:** Choose a current prospect or a recent new customer. Imagine not just closing a one-time sale with them, but building a five-year relationship. What would that look like? What would you do in the coming weeks, months, and years to keep earning their trust and business? This perspective can shift how you approach your next interaction with them, focusing more on the relationship than the transaction.

Key Takeaways

- **Selling is helping:** The most effective sales mindset is to help the customer genuinely. When you focus on solving their problems and addressing their needs (instead of just pushing a product), you naturally build trust and make sales feel effortless, not forced.

- **Relationships over pressure:** Prioritize building relationships and rapport. A loyal customer who trusts you is more valuable than dozens of one-time customers pressured into a quick sale. Relationship selling leads to repeat business, referrals, and a positive reputation.

- **Educate and add value first:** Offering value upfront, through education, free tips, demos, or helpful content, establishes you as an expert and a trusted ally. Customers appreciate the value you give and are more receptive when you eventually present a paid offer.

- **Listen and tailor your approach:** Take the time to listen to your customers' stories, questions, and concerns. Use a consultative approach: ask open-ended questions, empathize with their situation, and then explain how your product or service can specifically help them. This personalized approach makes the "pitch" feel more like a friendly recommendation.

- **Be authentic and transparent:** Honesty truly is the best policy in sales. Be upfront about pricing, capabilities, and limitations. Never mislead or overhype. Customers will trust you more when you're candid, and trust is the foundation that turns hesitant prospects into confident buyers.

- **Gentle guidance works best:** Encourage customers to take the next steps with soft calls to action, not aggressive ultimatums. Invite them to learn more, try a sample, or start with a small step. This gentle guidance respects their decision-making process and often leads to a "yes" because they never felt cornered.

- **Use tools to enhance the personal touch:** Leverage email automation, websites, and even sales scripts as tools to support your relationship-building, but always keep the communication feeling human and tailored. Technology can amplify your reach and consistency. Ensure your authentic voice and care shine through in every automated message or planned interaction.

- **The payoff is long-term success:** Selling without sleaze may take patience, but it yields loyal customers, positive word-of-mouth, and a strong brand reputation. You'll not only sell more in the long run, but you'll also feel proud of how you're doing it. Each sale will feel like a win-win, which is exactly how sustainable business growth is meant to be.

As you implement these approaches, remember that every business and customer base is a little different. Keep learning from your own experiences. Notice how people respond when you take a trust-first approach and do more of what works. You're building a brand rooted in authenticity and service, which is one of the most valuable assets you can have as a business owner. Selling with trust and integrity isn't just about making sales. It's about building a community of customers who believe in you as much as you believe in what you're selling. Embrace this, and you'll never have to cringe about "sales" again. Happy selling!

CHAPTER 14: DELIVER MAGICAL SERVICE

Every interaction your business has with a customer is an opportunity to build your brand's reputation. Think about the last time you were delighted as a customer. Perhaps a store owner remembered your name, or a support agent went above and beyond to resolve your issue. Those magical moments weren't just pleasant surprises. They became stories you probably told friends or posted online. In today's world, where one glowing review or personal recommendation can bring in a dozen new customers, delivering exceptional service is not just a nice-to-have. It's a critical part of building a brand that people love and rave about.

This chapter is all about how you can deliver magical service in your own business. We'll explore ways to create memorable customer experiences through both consistent systems and spontaneous personal touches. Whether you run a service-based business or sell products, you'll find practical tips here to make your customers feel valued and excited to do business with you. By the end of this chapter, you'll have ideas for systematizing excellent service (like smooth onboarding and follow-ups) and for adding that extra spark (like surprise gifts or personalized notes) that turns ordinary transactions into unforgettable experiences. Let's dive in and start creating those rave reviews!

Why Memorable Customer Experiences Matter

Imagine a customer walking away from your business not just satisfied, but genuinely happy and impressed. That feeling is gold for your brand. Memorable customer experiences matter because they create an emotional connection between your customer and your business. People might forget the fine details of what they bought, but they will remember how you made them feel. If you make them feel appreciated and taken care of, they're far more likely to come back and bring their friends along next time.

For new businesses, delivering excellent service can help you stand out from larger competitors. If you're a beginner, focusing on customer experience is a smart way to build loyalty when you don't yet have the marketing budget or brand recognition of larger companies. For more experienced business owners, leveling up your customer service can refresh and reinforce your brand's reputation in the market. In both cases, excellent service turns customers into enthusiastic ambassadors for your brand.

Word travels fast when people are excited. In the age of online reviews and social media, word-of-mouth marketing is a powerful tool that money can't easily buy. When customers have a remarkable experience, they tend to share it by leaving a five-star review, posting on Instagram, or simply telling their friends and neighbors. On the other hand, if the experience is poor or forgettable, there's nothing positive to share (and in the worst case, they share complaints instead). This is why creating positive, memorable moments is so important. It not only keeps the customers you have, but also organically attracts new ones through the stories and recommendations of those happy customers.

Finally, memorable experiences build trust and loyalty. Customers who feel valued and delighted are more forgiving of the occasional hiccup. They see your business as one that cares about them, not just their money. Over time, this trust means they'll stick with you even if a cheaper or closer alternative comes knocking. In summary, giving your customers an extraordinary experience isn't just about being nice. It's a strategic investment in your brand's long-term success.

Systematize Your Customer Experience

Delivering magical service starts with getting the basics right every single time. The most heartwarming personal touch won't mean much if the overall experience is sloppy or inconsistent. That's where systematizing your customer experience comes in. By creating simple systems and processes for everyday customer interactions, you ensure that every customer gets a consistently excellent baseline of service. Let's examine a few key areas where a little planning goes a long way: onboarding new customers, following up after sales, and providing comprehensive support (such as FAQs and help channels).

Make a Great First Impression with Onboarding: Onboarding is the process of warmly welcoming and educating your customer right after they decide to do business with you. A smooth onboarding flow helps new customers feel confident that they made the right choice. For a product-based business, onboarding might involve a confirmation email with details about their order, shipping updates, and perhaps tips for using the product. For example, if someone buys a kitchen gadget from your online store, your follow-up email could include a short guide or a video on how to get the best results with it. If you run a service-based business, onboarding may involve a personal phone call or email to outline the next steps. Let's say you're a freelance web designer. After a client signs the contract, you might send a welcome packet explaining your design process, timelines, and how the client can prepare (along with a friendly "thank you for choosing me" note). In either case, the goal is to communicate clearly and enthusiastically. Welcome your customer, let them know what to expect, and provide any necessary information to help them get started happily. A well-thought-out onboarding process reduces confusion and anxiety, replacing it with excitement and trust.

Maintain Momentum with Follow-Up: Great service isn't over when the sale is done. It's only just begun. Setting up a follow-up process ensures that you continue to care for customers after their purchase or project. This can be as simple as a check-in message a week or two after delivery, asking if everything is going well or if they have any questions. For a product business, you might send an email saying, "We hope you're loving your new purchase. Do you need any help with it? We're here for you." Many e-commerce platforms allow you to automate these emails, but be sure to maintain a personal and genuine tone. For a service business, a follow-up could be a phone call or a personalized email. For instance, if you're a personal trainer who has just finished a month-long program with a client, you could follow up to see how they're feeling, address any post-program questions, and perhaps offer a few complimentary tips to help them stay on track. Follow-ups demonstrate that you care about your customers' experience beyond the transaction. It's also an opportunity to catch and resolve any issues. If something isn't right, a prompt follow-up and quick fix can often turn a mildly dissatisfied customer into a grateful and loyal one. People are usually pleasantly surprised when a business proactively checks on them, because it's still all too rare! By building a habit of following up, you send a clear message: your satisfaction matters to us.

Be Ready to Help: FAQs and Support Systems: When customers have questions or need help, how easily can they find answers? A key part of magical service is reducing friction when a customer seeks assistance. Setting up an FAQ page or a support center on your website is a simple, effective way to do this. Think about the most common questions customers tend to ask about your product or service. Things like "How do I reset my password?" or "What's your return policy?" or "How long does delivery take?" should be answered in one accessible place. A well-written FAQ not only helps customers self-serve quick answers at any hour, but it also shows that you understand their needs and care enough to address them upfront.

Beyond FAQs, ensure customers know how to contact you (or your team) for more specific assistance. This might mean having a clear "Contact Us" page with an email address, phone number, or live chat option. If you're a solo business owner, you might list business hours during which you respond to inquiries. If you have a support team, ensure they are trained to be friendly, patient, and solution-oriented. Speed matters too. Aim to respond to customer messages promptly, even if it's just to say, "We got your request and we're on it." Quick, helpful responses make customers feel valued and relieve any frustration they might have had. For example, if a customer of your online apparel store writes in about an order issue, responding within a few hours with an apology and an action plan ("So sorry about that mix-up, we're sending the correct size out today with express shipping at no cost to you") can turn a potential complaint into a positive experience. The bottom line is that robust support, through FAQs, guides, and responsive communication, gives customers confidence that if they need anything, your business will be there to help. Peace of mind is a massive part of a great customer experience.

By systematizing these key aspects of your business (onboarding, follow-ups, and support), you establish a reliable foundation for customer satisfaction. Think of these systems as the stage on which you'll add the finishing touches of magic. When the basics run smoothly, you have more time and energy to add the extra delight that elevates "good" service to truly magical service.

Surprise and Delight: Personal Touches that Build Loyalty

With a solid base in place, it's time to discuss the fun aspects: those personal touches and surprises that make customers exclaim, "Wow!" and remember you for all the right reasons. "Surprise and delight" is a phrase often used in customer service, and it really captures the idea. You surprise customers with something positive and extra, delighting them in a way they weren't expecting. These touches reveal the human side of your business and make people feel valued and special. Let's explore some ways you can add personal flair, whether you sell products or offer services.

Handwritten Notes and Messages: In our digital age, a simple handwritten note can feel like a rare treasure. For product-based businesses, consider slipping a thank-you card into your packages. It doesn't have to be long. Even a few sentences thanking the customer for their purchase and wishing them well can leave a strong impression. For example, if you run an online boutique that sells home décor, you might include a little postcard that says, "Thank you for inviting our product into your home, [Customer Name]! - From the team at [Your Business]." If you have a service business, you can still use the power of the pen. A consultant or coach might mail a handwritten thank-you note to a client after a big project wraps up, or send holiday cards to their top clients each year. The key is that it's *personal and thoughtful*. The customer feels valued as an individual, not just a number. Handwritten notes are inexpensive and only take a bit of your time, but to the customer, they can feel as delightful as receiving a note from a friend.

Surprise Upgrades or Freebies: Everyone loves getting more than they expected. Adding a little unexpected bonus can turn a standard transaction into a memorable experience. If you have a product business, this might mean occasionally including a small free sample of another product in the customer's order, or upgrading their shipping speed for free. Imagine you sell gourmet coffee beans online. You could toss in a couple of single-serve samples of a new roast with a note, "Thought you might enjoy trying our new blend! Cheers from [Your Company]." If you're in a service business, think about an extra perk you can give. A photographer could include an extra printed photo or two beyond the package the client paid for, as a surprise "gift." A house cleaning service might do a small extra task they noticed, like organizing a messy shoe rack, without charging more, something to make the customer's day a bit easier. These surprise upgrades work well because they feel like a gift. The customer realizes you didn't have to do it, but you did, which makes them feel valued. It's essential to note that you don't have to give away huge things or do this every single time. You still need to watch costs and keep it reasonable. However, sprinkling in surprises now and then, or for loyal customers, builds goodwill that's hard to forget.

Personalized Interactions: A personal touch can also be incorporated into your interactions, extending beyond physical gifts. One of the simplest yet most powerful ways is to remember and use the customer's name and any preferences they've shared. In a service setting, such as a local pet grooming salon, you know one of your client's dogs is nervous around loud dryers, taking the time to use a quieter approach for that dog, and mentioning to the owner "I know Bella doesn't like the noise, so we gave her a extra gentle drying in a quiet room," shows attentiveness. For product businesses, personalization may take the form of tailored recommendations. If you run a bookstore (online or brick-and-mortar) and a regular customer loves mystery novels, you might personally email or tell them when a new thriller comes in that you think they'd enjoy. These kinds of gestures cost nothing but attention and care. They show that you pay attention to *who* the customer is and what they like.

Another example: Many businesses celebrate customer milestones or special occasions. A day spa might send a small gift or a discount for a client's birthday. An online app might pop up a cheerful message when a user hits their one-year anniversary of signing up, maybe even unlocking a minor new feature as a thank-you. These personal touches, whether it's remembering a birthday, acknowledging a repeat customer's loyalty, or simply customizing your service to their needs, all send the message: you matter to us as a person.

Real-World Example - Small Business Magic: Let's tie this together with a couple of short, real-world-style examples for inspiration. Consider a small, handmade soap business that sells its products online. They decide to implement a "surprise and delight" policy where every 20th order gets something extra. One customer opens their package to find not only the soaps they bought, but also a beautiful little soap dish included as a gift, along with a note: "Surprise! As a token of our appreciation for being a valued customer, we have included a complimentary soap dish. Enjoy! - The [Soap Company] Team." You can bet that customer is going to remember that experience and likely tell friends or post a rave review. For a service example, imagine a wedding photography business. After the big day, while delivering the final photo album, the photographer also includes a framed print of the couple's favorite shot as a gift. The clients expected just digital files or an album, but that extra framed photo (with a handwritten note congratulating them again) becomes a cherished surprise. It's these little "extras" that often earn enthusiastic thank-yous, referrals, and glowing testimonials without even asking.

The beauty of personal touches is that they can be highly creative and tailored to your specific business. Think about what would pleasantly surprise your customers. If you run a café, maybe it's occasionally giving a regular customer a free pastry with their coffee, or creating latte art of something you know they love (like their favorite sports team's logo) and saying, "I tried something fun with your latte today!" If you have a software business, maybe the CEO (if that's you) personally emails new sign-ups to welcome them and offer help. People are often shocked (in a good way) when a company's founder reaches out personally. These gestures leave a deep impression.

The common thread is genuineness. A personal touch only works if it feels sincere, not forced. Customers can tell when something is done out of genuine care versus when it is done grudgingly or as a pure gimmick. So, choose touches that fit your style and truly make you happy to do as well. When you genuinely enjoy delighting your customers, it shines through and creates a positive feedback loop: they're happy, you're encouraged by their joy, and it motivates you to keep raising the bar. This is how loyalty is built over time, through one joyful, unexpected moment after another, layered on top of consistent, reliable service.

Great Service, Rave Reviews: The Word-of-Mouth Connection

By now, you've put a lot of heart into delivering great service, from crafting smooth systems to adding those magical personal touches. So, how does this tie into marketing your business? In a word: powerfully. Exceptional customer service is directly linked to word-of-mouth marketing and positive reviews, which are among the most credible and cost-effective ways to grow your brand.

Think about the last time you raved to someone about a business that really impressed you. When customers have a "wow" experience, they often become unpaid ambassadors for your brand. They'll tell their friends, family, or anyone who will listen about how great you are. These personal recommendations carry significant weight because they come from a place of genuine enthusiasm and trust. A friend saying, "I had an amazing experience with this company," is far more convincing than any advertisement you could buy. In the context of branding, this is gold. Your brand's reputation starts to sparkle in the community thanks to happy customers spreading the word.

Online reviews are the digital version of this phenomenon. Potential customers frequently check reviews on Google, Yelp, Facebook, or industry-specific sites before deciding whom to give their business to. If your service is truly magical, you'll naturally accumulate rave reviews that do the selling for you. "Five stars. They went above and beyond!" is the kind of headline that draws new people in. That said, there's nothing wrong with *encouraging* reviews, either. After you've delivered a great experience, it's perfectly fine to gently ask the customer to share their feedback in a review or testimonial, if they feel comfortable doing so. Many will be happy to do so, especially if you make it easy (for example, providing a direct link to your Google review page in a follow-up email). Be sure to thank anyone who takes the time to leave a review. It shows you're listening and appreciative.

There's also a link between how you handle problems and your public image. If a customer does have a less-than-magical experience, the way you respond can turn the situation into a positive story. By addressing issues promptly and effectively, you demonstrate your commitment to customers in a highly visible manner. For instance, suppose a customer writes a lukewarm comment online about slow shipping or a service mix-up. By publicly replying with an apology and a promise to make it right (maybe offering a refund or a discount on the next purchase), you aren't just fixing it for that one customer. You're showing everyone else who sees that interaction that your business cares and acts with integrity. People often cite "great customer service" in reviews, not just when everything went perfectly, but also when something went wrong and the company handled it professionally. In other words, every interaction, whether good or bad, is an opportunity to reinforce your brand values.

One more point to consider: great service can reduce your need for expensive marketing. Your customers are your most powerful marketing engine. The best businesses often grow primarily through referrals and repeat business driven by customer satisfaction. When you consistently deliver magical service, you might find you don't have to spend as much on ads or promotions to attract new customers. Your existing fans do a lot of that work for you by spreading the buzz. This is especially helpful for small businesses with limited budgets. Instead of pouring money into advertising, pour effort into your service. The returns may very well be greater in the long run.

In summary, there's a direct line from service to reputation to growth. By delighting your customers, you create a ripple effect. Each happy customer can bring you more customers, either directly or indirectly. This word-of-mouth engine builds a brand that people trust, because they hear about it from sources they trust (their peers). So, as you work on delivering magical experiences, remember that you're not only making one person happy in the moment. You're also planting seeds for your business's future success, one rave review at a time.

Checklist: Delivering Magical Service

Use this checklist to ensure you're covering the basics and adding the extras when it comes to customer experience. These action points will help you create memorable moments at every stage of the customer journey:

- ☐ **Welcome Every Customer Warmly:** Develop a friendly onboarding process. For example, send a welcome email or have a welcome call that thanks the customer and lets them know what to expect next.

- ☐ **Set Clear Expectations:** Ensure customers understand how your product or service works and what is included. Provide instructions, timelines, or a "getting started" guide to prevent confusion.

- ☐ **Make Help Easy to Find:** Create an FAQ page or help sheet that answers common questions. Clearly list the various ways customers can contact you (email, phone, chat) and ensure a prompt response when they do.

- ☐ **Follow Up After the Sale:** Check in with customers after purchase or project completion. A simple "How's everything going with X? Let us know if you need anything" shows you care about their experience.

- ☐ **Personalize Where Possible:** Use customers' names in your communication and remember their personal details and preferences. Small touches, such as referencing a past purchase or conversation, make interactions feel more human.

- ☐ **Add a Surprise or Extra:** Identify one way you can occasionally go the extra mile. This could be a handwritten thank-you note, a small free sample or upgrade, a birthday greeting, or any unexpected treat that will make the customer smile.

- ☐ **Empower Your Team (or Yourself):** If you have employees, encourage and train them to resolve customer issues and offer small extras without needing approval for every minor detail. If you're on your own, permit yourself to do what's right for the customer, even if it means a little extra effort.

- ☐ **Handle Mistakes with Grace:** When something goes wrong, apologize sincerely and make the necessary corrections promptly. Include a thoughtful touch, if possible (such as a discount or bonus), to turn the situation around. This can transform an unhappy customer into a loyal one.

- ☐ **Encourage the Positive Buzz:** After a successful interaction, don't be shy about asking for a review or referral. For instance, in your follow-up email, you might say, "If you're happy with our service, we'd love it if you could share your experience in a review!" Make it easy by providing a direct link.

- ☐ **Stay Consistent:** Ultimately, ensure that every customer, not just a select few, gets treated with care and respect. Magical service isn't a one-off event. It's a consistent mindset. Use your systems and your personal touches together to deliver excellence every time.

Reflection Prompts

Take a moment to reflect on how you can apply the principles of magical service to your own business. Use these prompts to spark ideas and identify opportunities for improvement:

1. **Recall a Magical Experience:** Think of a time when you, as a customer, were truly delighted by a business. What did they do to make it special? How did it make you feel? List one or two elements from that experience that you could emulate in your own customer interactions.

2. **Onboarding Evaluation:** How do you currently welcome new customers or clients? Is there an introduction or onboarding step in your business that could be improved or made more memorable? Jot down one change you will make to create a better first impression.

3. **Your Personal Touch List:** Brainstorm at least three personal touches or surprises that would fit your business and customers. For each idea, ask: Would *I* be delighted by this if I were the customer? Circle the one idea you can implement right away and make a plan to do it.

4. **Consistency Check:** Are all your customers receiving a consistently great experience, or does it depend on the day or who serves them? Identify any gaps or weak points in your customer experience (for example, maybe weekend customers don't get follow-ups because you're off, or your response time slips during busy periods). What systems or solutions could you put in place to tighten those gaps?

5. **Empowering for Service:** If you have a team, consider whether they feel empowered to deliver magical service. Do they know they can offer a small freebie or spend extra time to help a customer without fearing reprimand? If not, how can you foster a culture that prioritizes customer happiness? If you're solo, ask yourself: Do I allow enough time and resources to go the extra mile, or am I cutting corners that might affect the customer experience?

6. **Envision the Rave Review:** Imagine a customer is writing a rave review about your business. What specific things would you love for them to mention? ("They really cared about me as a customer," or "The little extra touches blew me away," for example.) Now, think honestly: are you currently doing those things consistently? If not, what steps will you take to make that rave-review vision a reality?

7. **Plan for Word-of-Mouth:** How easy do you make it for customers to refer others or leave reviews? Consider one way to gently encourage or reward referrals and reviews, *after* you've delivered great service. For instance, could you implement a referral discount or ask satisfied customers to share their experience with others? Write down a strategy for leveraging the goodwill you'll be creating.

By reflecting on these questions, you'll uncover practical ways to embed magical service into the DNA of your business. Remember, delivering memorable customer experiences is a journey of continuous improvement. Keep putting yourself in your customers' shoes, and keep looking for those little opportunities to wow them. Your brand will reap the rewards in loyalty, love, and lots of rave reviews. Here's to creating those unforgettable experiences that set your business apart!

CHAPTER 15: GROW YOUR COMMUNITY

Customers today aren't satisfied with just a one-time transaction. They crave connection, belonging, and a sense of community. Think about brands that have die-hard fans who proudly recommend them to everyone they know. Those businesses have transformed ordinary buyers into enthusiastic believers. In this chapter, we'll explore how you can do the same: build loyalty, spark referrals, and turn your customers into a supportive tribe of lifelong fans. Whether you're launching a startup or running an established company, growing your community will amplify your brand's reach and impact. We'll cover strategies for engaging people online and in person, providing plenty of actionable tips, examples, and reflection prompts to help you put these ideas into practice. By the end, you'll know how to turn transactional relationships into genuine loyalty and fan-driven excitement for your brand.

Encourage User-Generated Content and Conversation

One of the most powerful ways to build a community is to invite your customers into the conversation. User-generated content (UGC) (things like customer reviews, social media posts, photos, or videos featuring your product or service) is like word-of-mouth on steroids. When real people share their experiences with your brand, it creates authenticity that no marketing copy can match. For example, a small bakery might start an Instagram hashtag for customers to share photos of creative ways they enjoy its pastries. Soon, customers will not only be having fun posting their foodie pictures but also interacting with each other, swapping flavor tips, and celebrating the brand together.

To encourage UGC, make it easy and rewarding for customers to share their content. You could run a contest or challenge (e.g., "Share a selfie with our product for a chance to win a gift card") or spotlight customer content on your official pages. Many product-based businesses feature a "customer of the week" or repost fan photos, giving public credit to the creators. Service-based businesses can do this too. A personal trainer might share a client's inspiring progress story (with permission), or a consultant might post a testimonial from a happy client on LinkedIn. These gestures show your audience that you value their input and experiences. They also motivate others to join in. **Action Tip:** Create a unique hashtag for your brand or campaign and encourage customers to use it when they post about you. Over time, this creates a snowball effect: customers see their peers getting involved and want to participate as well. The result is a lively online community where customers create content, celebrate one another, and spread the word about your business without needing to be asked.

Reward Loyalty and Incentivize Referrals

Loyal customers are the heart of any strong community. To grow that heart, you need to recognize and reward loyalty, and encourage those loyal fans to bring others into the fold. A straightforward way to do this is by establishing a referral program. People naturally trust recommendations from friends and family, so when a happy customer refers someone new, that newcomer arrives with built-in positive vibes about your brand. You can amplify this effect by offering incentives for referrals. For instance, a salon might give a client $10 off their next appointment for each new customer they refer (and perhaps the new customer gets a welcome discount too). An online software company might give referrers an upgraded feature for free when a friend signs up. By rewarding both the referrer and the friend, you create a win-win that motivates everyone to spread the word.

Alongside referrals, consider implementing a loyalty program to cultivate long-term engagement. Loyalty programs make customers feel part of an exclusive club. They can be as simple as a digital punch card (buy nine coffees, get the 10th free) or as elaborate as a tiered points system with increasing perks. The key is to offer meaningful rewards that show appreciation. Product-based businesses may offer early access to new releases or exclusive discounts to their members. Service businesses might offer a free consultation or bonus service after a certain number of purchases. Modern loyalty programs often extend beyond just purchases. You can also reward community-building actions. For example, you could give points for writing a review, sharing a social post about the brand, or attending a brand event. This encourages customers not only to buy more but also to engage more. Over time, these loyal customers start to identify as part of your brand's family. They feel valued because their support is acknowledged and repaid. The result: higher customer retention, more frequent referrals, and a community of people who stick with you because they genuinely enjoy the relationship, not just the transactions.

Build Emotional Connections with Your Brand

At the core of every strong community is an emotional bond. Think of the brands you love. Chances are, it's not just about the product, but how that brand makes you feel. Building emotional connections with customers means showing the human side of your business and aligning with the values you and your audience care about. Begin by sharing your brand's story and mission authentically and genuinely. Why did you start this business? What do you stand for beyond making a profit? When you communicate this, you invite people to rally around a purpose. For example, a sustainable fashion boutique might frequently highlight its commitment to eco-friendly materials and fair trade, attracting customers who share those values. Those customers aren't just buying a dress. They feel like they're supporting a cause and a community they believe in.

Emotional connection also grows when customers feel heard and involved. Make your communication a two-way street. Ask for feedback, listen to ideas, and respond personally whenever possible. Some companies even involve their community in decisions. For instance, a craft brewery might let fans vote on the next seasonal beer flavor, or a tech company might gather user input to shape a new feature. When people see their suggestions taken seriously or implemented, they feel a sense of ownership in the brand's journey. Even simple interactions matter. Remembering a repeat customer's name or preferences, or sending a personalized thank-you note that isn't just a template, can leave a strong, positive impression. Show appreciation publicly as well. Highlight your customers' stories and achievements related to your product or service. A fitness coach might post a shout-out to a client who ran their first 5K thanks to the training program. A cookware brand could share a photo of a beautiful meal a customer created using its pans. This kind of recognition makes people feel valued as individuals, not just sales figures. It strengthens the emotional bond, transforming casual customers into brand friends. When your customers feel emotionally connected, they transition from being mere buyers to becoming advocates who *want* to see you succeed, because your success feels like *their* success, too.

Host Events and Create Exclusive Experiences

Online interaction is wonderful, but never underestimate the power of bringing people together in the real world (or live online gatherings). Events and exclusive experiences provide your community with opportunities to form personal connections and create lasting memories associated with your brand. For a product-based business, this could involve hosting a launch party for a new product, a workshop on creative product usage, or an open-house celebration for your store's anniversary. Imagine running a home décor shop that hosts a free monthly DIY class where customers come in to learn creative crafts using items from your store. Strangers who attend start chatting, complimenting each other's creations, and suddenly, you've facilitated a room full of like-minded people who feel connected to each other and to your brand. They're likely to come back, bring friends next time, and share that fun experience with others.

Service businesses can also benefit from events. If you're a consultant or run a service company, consider organizing networking mixers, panel discussions, or community meetups related to your industry. A local marketing agency might host a small business networking night, inviting clients and prospects to share tips and stories over refreshments. An online service could host a live webinar or Q&A session, allowing customers to interact in real-time. These events not only provide value (people learn something or enjoy themselves) but also humanize your brand. Customers get to meet the faces behind the business and each other, which builds trust and camaraderie.

In addition to events, consider offering exclusive experiences or perks that make community members feel valued and special. This could include a VIP rewards tier that offers early access to new offerings, a private online group for top customers, or exclusive sales and content for members. For example, a skincare brand might have an "insiders club" where members receive a quarterly gift box of samples and an invitation to a live online chat with the product developers. A catering service might offer loyal clients an invitation to an annual tasting event where they can preview new menu items. These exclusive touches deepen the sense of belonging. Your customers feel like they're part of an inner circle. Importantly, exclusivity doesn't have to mean it's only for a tiny elite group. It can simply mean "everyone who has joined our free loyalty program gets access to X that the general public doesn't." The goal is to reward people for being part of your community with experiences or perks that others miss out on. Not only will this keep your current fans engaged, but it will also attract new customers who hear about these great experiences and want to be part of the fun.

Follow Up and Nurture Relationships Over Time

Building a community isn't a one-off campaign. It's an ongoing commitment to nurturing relationships. One of the simplest yet most effective community-building practices is consistent follow-up with your customers. After someone makes a purchase or uses your service, reach out to thank them and ask how things went. A personalized thank-you email (or a handwritten note for a pleasant surprise) can make a customer feel truly appreciated. If you promised to deliver value, check in to ensure they're getting it. For example, a week after delivering a graphic design project, a freelance designer might email the client to ask if they need any help implementing the files or if everything is working as expected. This kind of follow-through shows professionalism and care, qualities that turn a neutral transaction into a positive relationship.

Over time, keep the conversation going. Share useful information, tips, or updates that your customers will find interesting, not just promotional content. Perhaps you run a pet supply store. You could send monthly pet care tips or fun pet challenges to engage your audience beyond just "Here's what's on sale." If you offer a service, consider sending occasional check-ins or resources related to the service you provided. The key is to provide value in your communications so that when customers see a message from you, they want to read it because they know it's not always a sales pitch. You might also segment your follow-ups based on customer behavior, for instance, sending different content to your long-term VIP customers than to newer customers who are still exploring your offerings.

Don't forget to invite past customers into your community spaces. Encourage them to join your online group, attend your events, or subscribe to your newsletter for insiders. By doing so, you're transitioning them from a one-time customer into an ongoing community member. Also, be responsive when customers reach out to you, whether it's a comment on social media or an email with a question. How you handle these interactions can either strengthen or weaken their loyalty. Prompt, helpful, and friendly responses tell customers, *"You matter to us."* Over the course of months and years, these small touches add up significantly. They create a feeling that your brand is not just a business but a team of people who genuinely care. When customers feel cared for, they stay longer, engage more deeply, and often bring others along for the experience. In essence, consistent nurturing transforms your customer base from a list of buyers into a vibrant, living community of brand advocates.

Reflection: Your Community-Building Action Plan

Building a community around your brand is a journey, and every journey begins with a few concrete steps. Take a moment to consider how you can apply the ideas from this chapter to your own business. Here are a few prompts to get you started:

- **Shared Purpose:** What core values or mission does your brand stand for, and how can you share that story to attract like-minded customers? List one way you will communicate your brand's purpose to strengthen emotional connections with your audience.

- **Customer Involvement:** Identify one way your customers can actively participate in your brand's story. Will you create a hashtag for them to share content, start a user forum or Facebook group, or host a local meetup? Jot down a plan to encourage more customer interaction, either online or in person (or both).

- **Rewards and Referrals:** Design a simple reward that you can offer to thank customers for loyalty or referrals. For example, what incentive could you give someone for referring a new customer to you? Consider a discount, a free bonus, or an exclusive perk, and outline how you'll introduce this to your customers.

- **Follow-Up Routine:** Think about your post-purchase experience. How will you follow up with customers to make sure they're happy and engaged? Draft a quick timeline (for instance: thank-you message at purchase, check-in after two weeks, monthly newsletter with tips) to ensure no customer falls through the cracks.

As you answer these questions, you're crafting a roadmap for a thriving brand community. Remember, you don't have to do everything at once. Begin with one or two actions and build upon them. Over time, these efforts will compound. You'll notice customers becoming more than just customers. They'll become friends, supporters, and champions of your brand. When you make people feel valued and connected, they reward you with loyalty that money can't buy. Grow your community, and you'll grow a network of lifelong fans who help lift your brand to new heights. Good luck, and happy community-building!

CONCLUSION

CHAPTER 16: NEXT STEPS - YOUR BRAND BUILDER ROADMAP

As we wrap up this journey, let's consolidate what you've learned and chart a practical course for action. In this final chapter, we'll briefly recap the key lessons from Chapters 1-15 and then lay out a 90-day roadmap for building your brand: a flexible plan you can adapt to your own pace (whether week-by-week or month-by-month). By the end, you'll know what to expect in your first 90 days and how to keep your momentum growing beyond that.

The Journey So Far: Recap of Chapters 1-15

You've covered a lot of ground in this book. Here's a quick recap of each chapter's core insight and takeaway to remind you how far you've come:

- **Chapter 1: Find Your Spark** - You explored how finding a business idea that genuinely excites you creates the energy and motivation you need for long-term success. Your spark fuels your brand and resonates authentically with your audience.

- **Chapter 2: Pick a Problem Worth Solving** - You learned to identify meaningful problems or needs people genuinely care about. By addressing real, significant issues, you establish a solid foundation for a purposeful brand that delivers genuine value.

- **Chapter 3: Get Into a Brand Builder Mindset** - You recognized the importance of cultivating traits like resilience, confidence, and adaptability. Adopting the right mindset ensures you're well-equipped to overcome challenges and grow your brand consistently.

- **Chapter 4: Define Your Core Beliefs** - You clarified your brand's core values, vision, and the story behind your business. These beliefs serve as your compass, guiding decisions and attracting customers who share your values.

- **Chapter 5: Name and Frame Your Brand** - You discovered practical ways to choose a memorable brand name, create an engaging tagline, and clearly articulate your brand promise. This clarity makes your brand instantly recognizable and appealing.

- **Chapter 6: Give Your Brand a Look** - You learned the essentials of designing a consistent visual identity, including logo, color palette, and typography. These elements help people easily recognize your brand and reinforce your personality.

- **Chapter 7: Find Your Voice** - You focused on communicating authentically and consistently, ensuring your brand's voice resonates clearly with your audience. By staying true to yourself, your messaging becomes relatable and trustworthy.

- **Chapter 8: Make It Official** - You took essential steps to legitimize your brand, such as securing your domain, creating professional emails, and handling important legal and administrative details. This solid foundation builds credibility and trust.

- **Chapter 9: Build a Home Online** - You set up your brand's online presence with a user-friendly website and optimized social media profiles. These serve as your digital "home base," making it easy for customers to find, understand, and engage with your brand.

- **Chapter 10: Show Up in the Real World** - You expanded your branding beyond digital channels, ensuring consistency through business cards, packaging, signage, and in-person networking. By showing up consistently offline, you reinforce your credibility and create memorable experiences.

- **Chapter 11: Understand Your People** - You gained clarity on who your ideal customers are, understanding their needs, values, and behaviors. This deep customer insight allows you to tailor your offerings and messages for maximum impact.

- **Chapter 12: Share Your Story** - You embraced marketing as storytelling, using engaging, authentic content and budget-friendly strategies to promote your brand. Consistently sharing your unique story helps attract and retain customers who truly resonate with you.

- **Chapter 13: Sell Without the Sleaze** - You redefined selling as a process of helping rather than pressuring customers. By focusing on building trust and genuine relationships, selling becomes a natural, comfortable, and effective process.

- **Chapter 14: Deliver Magical Service** - You focused on delighting customers at every interaction by providing exceptional service with thoughtful touches. Consistently delivering memorable experiences helps build loyalty and turns customers into enthusiastic advocates.

- **Chapter 15: Grow Your Community** - You learned how to nurture an engaged community around your brand, turning customers into loyal fans. By encouraging referrals, rewarding loyalty, and fostering meaningful connections, you create lasting brand growth and success.

Each of these chapters is built upon the previous ones, providing you with a comprehensive toolkit for brand building. Now, armed with these insights, it's time to translate knowledge into action. The next section lays out your 90-day Brand Builder Roadmap: a step-by-step guide for the first three months of putting all this into practice.

(Note: Everyone's timeline can vary. Some might blaze through in 90 days, others might take it slower, and that's okay. Think of the following as phases or milestones to progress through, whether it takes you 12 weeks or twice as long. The focus is on sequence and consistency, not the exact speed.)

Phase 1: Laying the Foundation (Days 1-30)

Focus: Introspection, planning, and establishing the fundamentals of your brand. In this first phase, you'll clarify your brand identity and ensure that all the necessary groundwork is in place. *(If you prefer to think in weeks, consider this roughly Weeks 1-4.)*

- **Define your brand's identity:** Start by clearly defining who you are as a brand. Revisit the exercises you did in earlier chapters. Write down your brand purpose, vision, and values in a concise statement. Identify your unique selling point and what makes you *different* from others in your field. This often requires some soul-searching and honesty. One of the most common challenges new brand builders face is knowing where to start. The best way to begin is by understanding yourself: your strengths, passions, skills, and what others recognize you for. Use those insights to shape a brand identity that is authentic to you.

- **Know your audience and niche:** Clearly identify *who* you're trying to reach. Using previous exercises, define your target audience in detail: their demographics, needs, and the problems or desires your brand will address. The more specific you can be about your niche, the easier it will be to create a brand that *sticks* in people's minds.

Remember, trying to appeal to everyone often means you appeal to no one. It's better to be meaningful to a focused group that truly cares about your message.

- **Craft your brand story and message:** Take the elements from your identity and audience, and craft a compelling brand story. This is your narrative: the "about me" that conveys why you do what you do and how you can help your audience. Aim for a short elevator pitch or tagline that captures the essence of your story. Ensure your core message highlights the value or solution you provide to your audience (why it matters to *them*). Your story will be the backbone of your content and marketing, so make it genuine and memorable. The ability to communicate your story clearly is crucial. If you can't tell anything, you can't sell anything.

- **Design your basic brand visuals:** If you haven't already, pick out the visual elements that will represent your brand. Choose a color scheme and typography/font style that align with the mood of your brand (e.g., bold and modern, or warm and classic). If applicable, design a simple logo or wordmark. Even a clean type-based logo with your name or business name can work as a starting point. Ensure that these visuals are used consistently across all platforms to maintain a unified brand look. Consistency in visuals, along with your messaging and voice, is how you start building recognition and trust.

- **Set up your online presence:** Establish the key platforms for your brand. Secure your domain name (even if you just set up a simple one-page website or an "About" page for now). Create or update your social media profiles on the platforms your target audience uses. For example, LinkedIn, Instagram, Twitter/X, TikTok, YouTube, or others relevant to your niche. Ensure each profile includes a professional profile photo, your brand's tagline or bio (consistent with your story), and links to your website or contact information. Think of these profiles as digital business cards for your brand. By the end of Phase 1, you want anyone who searches for your name or brand online to find a cohesive and clear image of who you are and what you offer.

- **Plan your content strategy:** Before you start actively posting, create a simple content plan. Decide on a realistic schedule and content mix that you can stick to. For instance, maybe you'll write one blog article a week, post on social media three times a week, and send a monthly email newsletter. Identify 4-5 core topics or themes based on your niche that you'll consistently talk about (these should tie back to your expertise and what your audience cares about). Having this plan in place will make Phase 2 much easier because you won't be scrambling for what to post. You'll have a prepared roadmap for content.

By the end of Phase 1, you should have a strong foundation: a clear understanding of your brand and audience, a compelling story, cohesive visuals, and all your key online profiles ready to go. You've essentially built the "home" for your brand. Next, it's time to invite people in and start connecting.

Phase 2: Building Your Presence (Days 31-60)

Focus: Execution, creating content, engaging with your audience, and beginning to grow your visibility. In Phase 2, you move from planning to active brand building. This is where consistency and interaction become critical. *(In weekly terms, this would be roughly Weeks 5-8.)*

- **Start creating and sharing content consistently:** Put your content plan into action (drawing on your content strategy from earlier). Begin publishing content on the schedule you decided, whether that's blog posts, videos, podcasts, or social media updates. Consistency is key here. Stick to your schedule as closely as possible so your audience starts to anticipate and rely on your content. Over these 30 days, aim to produce at least a modest body of content (for example, if weekly, ~4 blog posts or videos and a dozen or more social media posts). Don't worry about being perfect. Focus on delivering helpful, authentic content regularly. As you continue to create content aligned with your brand voice and theme, you'll start to gain recognition in your niche. This consistency in content and voice will help people remember you and see you as dependable.

- **Engage with your audience and community:** Building a brand isn't a one-way broadcast. It's a conversation. As you post content, actively engage with those who respond to it. Reply to comments on your blog or social posts, answer messages or emails from followers, and thank people for sharing your content. Beyond your own channels, spend time each day engaging with your broader community: comment on others' posts, participate in discussions or forums related to your field, and offer help or insights without directly promoting your work. This genuine interaction not only increases your visibility, but also builds relationships. People start to remember you as a real person who cares, not just a brand mouthpiece.

- **Expand your network and reach out for collaborations:** By now, you should have identified some key players in your industry or niche. In Phase 2, make it a goal to connect and collaborate in at least one way. For example, you could reach out to another content creator or professional in your field to propose a small collaboration: maybe co-host an Instagram Live chat, swap guest blog posts, interview each other on a podcast, or cross-promote each other's content. Collaborations can introduce your brand to new audiences and lend mutual credibility to both parties. Even if you're just starting, don't be afraid. Many people are happy to team up if it's mutually beneficial. Networking also includes more casual relationship-building: schedule virtual coffees or attend an event (even if online) to meet people in your niche. These efforts show that who you know can amplify what you know.

- **Establish an email list or community (if fitting):** If it aligns with your brand, consider setting up an email newsletter or a community group during this phase. Even in the age of social media, email remains a powerful way to nurture your audience. You might create a simple sign-up form on your website with a free resource (e.g., a short PDF guide or checklist) as an incentive for people to join your list. Over the 90 days, aim to send out 1–2 email updates to those subscribers, sharing your latest content or exclusive tips. Alternatively (or additionally), maybe create a small Facebook or LinkedIn group for interested followers to join and discuss topics related to your brand. Building these owned channels ensures you have direct lines to your most engaged audience members.

- **Monitor feedback and tune your strategy:** As you consistently put yourself out there, pay attention to the response. Which blog posts or social posts get the most likes, comments, or shares? Which topics seem to resonate (or fall flat)? Take notes on these metrics and feedback. This is real-world data coming in during Phase 2 that you can use to adjust your approach. Set up simple analytics (such as checking your website traffic with Google Analytics or using built-in insights on platforms like Instagram or LinkedIn) to track your growth. Don't get obsessed with numbers in the short term, but do look for trends. For example, if you notice your audience really loved a how-to video you did but didn't care as much for a personal story post, that's useful to know. You can then lean a bit more into the content that brings value to your audience. Phase 2 is a learning period. You're gathering intel on what works best for *your* brand in the real world, which will inform your next steps.

By the end of Phase 2 (approximately day 60), you will have transitioned from zero to an active brand presence. You should have a routine of content creation and engagement, a small but growing audience that's aware of you, and perhaps a few new connections or collaborators. This is an exciting period where your brand starts to breathe and live publicly. Expect some trial and error. That's normal. The important thing is that you are consistently showing up and engaging. You're no longer just planning to be a brand. You are building your brand, day by day.

Phase 3: Expanding and Refining (Days 61-90)

Focus: Growth, refinement, and setting the stage for long-term success. In Phase 3, you will build on the momentum from Phase 2, make improvements, and push your brand reach a bit further. *(This roughly covers Weeks 9-12.)*

- **Evaluate your brand and make improvements:** Around the start of this phase (say, at the 60-day mark), take a step back to evaluate all aspects of your brand as it stands. Revisit your brand identity, story, and visuals. Do they still feel aligned and strong given what you've learned about your audience? It's a good time for a mini-audit: check that your bio, website "About" page, and descriptions still accurately reflect your mission and appeal to your audience's needs. You might tweak your messaging slightly if you've discovered new pain points or interests from your followers. Ensuring you have a coherent brand presentation sets you up for success and scalability. Remember, it's normal for your brand to evolve as you gain experience. The key is to keep it *purposeful* and consistent with who you are. Even big personal brands go through evolutions. Your brand isn't static; it's an extension of you, and it can be refined as you grow.

- **Double down on what works:** Use the insights gathered in Phase 2 to focus your efforts. By now, you likely have a sense of which content or engagement strategies are yielding the best results. Maybe you found that your tutorial videos get a lot of shares, or that your LinkedIn posts generate great discussions. Whatever it is, *do more of it*. Take the top-performing 20% of your efforts and see how you can amplify them. For example, if a particular blog post did really well, you could repurpose it into a short video or an infographic for social media. If Instagram has been a goldmine for engagement, consider increasing your posting frequency there or exploring new features (like Stories or Reels). Conversely, if something isn't working (perhaps you tried a platform or format that isn't gaining traction), you can dial back on it and save your energy for what clearly resonates. This refinement ensures you're putting your effort where it counts.

- **Extend your reach further:** In Phase 3, challenge yourself to take one bold step to grow your audience beyond your immediate circle. This might be the time to pitch a larger collaboration or media opportunity. For instance, consider submitting a guest article to a well-known industry blog or speaking at a local meetup or webinar. You could also invest in a small targeted ad campaign on social media to attract new followers (if budget allows and it makes sense for your brand). Another idea is to launch a free mini-project that showcases your expertise, such as a 5-day challenge, a webinar, or a valuable downloadable resource, and promote it widely. These kinds of moves can significantly boost your visibility. The aim in this phase is to go from "just getting started" to *"I'm here, and I'm serious."* Even if you still have a modest following, positioning yourself confidently through these actions can set the tone for your brand's next stage of growth.

- **Strengthen your community and credibility:** As your audience grows, keep nurturing the community you're building. Encourage more interaction. Consider starting to ask your followers questions in your posts or hosting a live Q&A session. If you set up an email list or group, engage with them more directly in this phase (e.g., send a special 90-day recap newsletter sharing what you've learned and inviting their input on what they'd like to see next). Additionally, work on further boosting credibility. By 90 days, you may have some satisfied early clients, customers, or followers. Ask for testimonials or quotes from them that you can feature on your website or LinkedIn. Social proof like this will reinforce trust in your brand. Maybe compile a few of your best content pieces or accomplishments from these 90 days and showcase them (a "portfolio" section on your site or a pinned post highlighting your journey so far). This not only celebrates your progress but also signals to newcomers that your brand delivers value and has impact.

- **Keep learning and adapting:** The end of this initial 90-day sprint is really a beginning. Take time in the latter part of Phase 3 to reflect on what *you* have learned about being a brand builder. What parts of this process did you enjoy most? Where did you excel, and where did you struggle? These insights are crucial for planning your next 90 days (and beyond). Perhaps you discovered you love making videos more than writing blogs. That's good to know as you plan future content. Maybe you realized your original niche was too broad or too narrow. You can adjust going forward. Embrace a mindset of continuous improvement. Identify any hurdles that consistently come up (like time management, or putting yourself out there) and think of ways to address them as you move forward (maybe by batching content, or seeking a mentor/accountability partner to keep you on track). Essentially, become your own coach. Congratulate yourself on milestones hit, but also be honest about what you can do better, and carry those lessons into the future.

By Day 90, if you've followed along, you will have a solid platform to build on. You've defined your brand, set up shop online, and proven that you can show up consistently with valuable content and engagement. You may have a small but real community forming around your brand. You've likely grown in confidence and learned a ton about your audience and yourself. Celebrate this! Not everyone makes it this far. Your commitment over the last three months is an achievement in itself. But remember, this is not an "end" point. It's the launch pad for even greater things ahead.

Keep the Momentum: Beyond the First 90 Days

Completing 90 days of focused brand building is a huge milestone, but it's truly just the beginning of your brand's journey. Branding is a long-term, ongoing process. Personal branding is a continuous, lifelong project with no finish line. Your brand will continue to evolve with you. The most successful brands you admire were not built in a day (or even 90 days). They grew through continuous effort, learning, and adaptation over time. Here's how to keep your momentum and continue growing:

- **Stay Consistent and Persistent:** The number one rule for long-term branding success is to keep showing up. You've developed great habits over the last three months. Don't stop now. Continue creating valuable content and engaging with your audience on a regular schedule, whether that's weekly, daily, or whatever rhythm you can maintain. Consistency over the long haul is what separates those who achieve significant goals from those who fail to reach their objectives. Remember, your brand and results will compound over time. The effort you put in now will continue to multiply. It may take another year or two (or more) of steady work to reach the significant results you want, but stick with it. You will thank yourself later.

- **Revisit and Refine Your Strategy Periodically:** Schedule regular check-ins with your brand strategy, perhaps every quarter (every 90 days) or at least twice a year. Treat it like a business would treat quarterly reviews. Look at your goals. Are they changing or expanding? Look at your audience. Are their needs the same, or do you see new opportunities to serve them? Audit your brand's messaging and design. Does anything feel outdated or off-course? It's healthy to refine your brand as you gain new experience or as the market evolves. For example, you might decide to narrow your niche further based on what you've learned, or conversely, expand into a related area. Don't be afraid to pivot or refresh aspects of your brand, as long as you remain authentic to your core values. Your brand should grow *with* you.

- **Keep Learning and Improving Your Skills:** The journey doesn't stop at branding. To deliver on your brand's promise, you'll want to keep sharpening your expertise. Invest in your own development: take courses, read books, follow other thought leaders in your field, and stay up-to-date on industry trends. The more knowledge and skill you accumulate, the more value you can provide to your audience, and the stronger your brand will become. Additionally, continue learning about marketing and branding techniques. Maybe in the next phase, you delve into advanced social media strategies, SEO, or launch a small ad campaign to boost growth. Each new skill is like another tool in your toolbox that can help elevate your brand.

- **Build Long-Term Relationships:** By now, you've started networking. Make sure to nurture those relationships for the long term. Your peers and mentors can become collaborators, referrers, or even clients (and vice versa) down the road. Continue to engage genuinely with your community. Support others' projects, celebrate their successes, and they'll likely do the same for you. As your network grows, your influence often grows with it. Some opportunities (such as speaking gigs and partnerships) will come not just from strangers discovering you, but also from people who already know and trust you. So, continue to pay it forward and cultivate a strong professional network around your brand.

- **Explore New Horizons:** After 90 days of executing the basics, you might be ready to experiment with bigger initiatives. Think about writing a longer e-book or guide, launching a podcast or YouTube channel if you haven't, creating an online course, or organizing a community challenge or event. These kinds of projects can further solidify your authority and open up new streams of audience or income. Pick one big idea that excites you and aligns with your brand's mission, and start planning how to bring it to life. Even if it's a long-term project, taking the first steps now will set things in motion.

- **Remember Your Why:** As you continue, always stay connected to the core *why* of your brand: the reason you started this journey. This sense of purpose will keep you motivated on days when progress seems slow or challenges arise. It will also shine through in your content and interactions, keeping your brand authentic and grounded. Your passion and purpose are the fuel that will carry you through the months and years ahead. If you remain passionate and focused on serving your audience, that enthusiasm becomes contagious, drawing even more people to your brand.

Finally, celebrate milestones and enjoy the process. Every new follower, every piece of positive feedback, and every small win is proof that your brand is making an impact. Take pride in how much you've grown from Day 1 to Day 90 and imagine how much further you can go in a year or two if you keep at it. Building a brand is hard work, but it's also an enriching journey of self-discovery and growth.

In conclusion, the roadmap we provided is just a starting framework: a way to launch you confidently into building your brand. Your actual journey will be uniquely yours. Stay flexible, keep learning, and adapt the advice in this book to fit your situation. There's no one-size-fits-all approach to branding, but the principles of authenticity, consistency, and value to others are universally applicable. As long as you stick to those, you will continue to rise and thrive.

Your brand is your story, and it's far from over. So, keep writing that story, one day at a time, and don't forget to enjoy each chapter. Here's to your next 90 days, and the 90 days after that, and a future full of growth and success for you and your brand! Good luck, and keep building.

ABOUT THE AUTHOR

I've spent over twenty years building thriving online communities, brands, and marketing systems across various industries. From the start, curiosity and a desire to connect people have guided me on a journey of self-education, experimentation, and constant growth. Every success and every failure has taught me invaluable lessons, shaping the insights I now share.

Throughout my career, I've had the privilege of working closely with hundreds of entrepreneurs and small business owners, helping them overcome challenges in critical areas like lead generation, marketing strategy, website design, customer service, and overall business growth. Over time, I recognized common obstacles that hinder many businesses: fear of change, unclear strategies, and self-doubt. I deeply understand the frustration and overwhelm that come with feeling stuck or unsure about the next step. That's precisely why I wrote this book.

I'm passionate about helping others navigate the pitfalls I encountered along my own path. I know what it's like to pour your heart into a business, only to lie awake at night wondering why things aren't working. My goal is to offer the guidance I wish I'd had, providing clear, practical advice born from my years of trial, error, and triumph. Above all, I aim to empower you with the confidence to move forward, wherever you may currently be in your journey.

Nothing brings me greater joy than seeing entrepreneurs I've mentored break through barriers and fully realize their potential. I firmly believe that with the proper support and mindset, anyone can achieve extraordinary results. Sharing my story and strategies is my way of helping you write your own success story.

Thank you for reading and allowing me to be part of your entrepreneurial journey. This book was written with you in mind: the entrepreneur, the dreamer, ready to take action. I'm cheering for your success and sincerely hope my experiences light your path forward.

To your success,

Dustin Sartoris

Brand and Growth Architect